AWFUL ARCHIVES

AWFUL ARCHIVES

CONSPIRACY THEORY, RHETORIC, AND ACTS OF EVIDENCE

JENNY RICE

THE OHIO STATE UNIVERSITY PRESS

COLUMBUS

Library of Congress Cataloging-in-Publication Data
Names: Rice, Jenny, author.
Title: Awful archives : conspiracy theory, rhetoric, and acts of evidence / Jenny Rice.
Description: Columbus : The Ohio State University Press, [2020] | Includes bibliographical references and index. | Summary: "An exploration of exaggerated cases of conspiracy theories, pseudo-science, and the paranormal, which helps to reveal why traditional modes of argument fail against archives of bad evidence. Looks at case studies such as conspiracy theories around the moon landing, UFO sightings, and Barack Obama's birth record"—Provided by publisher.
Identifiers: LCCN 2019046420 | ISBN 9780814214350 (cloth) | ISBN 0814214355 (cloth) | ISBN 9780814277799 (ebook) | ISBN 0814277799 (ebook)
Subjects: LCSH: Archives. | Conspiracy theories. | Persuasion (Rhetoric)—Social aspects. | Evidence—Social aspects.
Classification: LCC P301.5.P47 R63 2020 | DDC 001.9—dc23
LC record available at https://lccn.loc.gov/2019046420

Cover design by Andrew Brozyna
Text design by Juliet Williams
Type set in Adobe Minion Pro

ISBN 9780814255797

CONTENTS

ILLUSTRATIONS

ACKNOWLEDGMENTS

READING THE acknowledgments page is one of my favorite things to do when I pick up a new book. It's the place where you get to see the wider ecology from which that book emerged. *Awful Archives* was shaped by a number of ecologies, and I am grateful for the chance to acknowledge them here.

I owe so many colleagues gratitude for listening to my ideas as this project was taking shape. Many thanks to Diane Davis, Christa Olson, Meredith Johnson, Cynthia Haynes, Michelle Smith, and David Kaufer for giving me opportunities to hear feedback at many different stages of this book's development. Special thanks to the crew from the Society for the Study of Affect, and to Greg Seigworth, whose creativity and openness is a true model of intellectual generosity. I also owe huge thanks to many for their generative conversations over the years: Thomas Rickert, Nathan Stormer, Steve Katz, Byron Hawk, Caitlin Bruce, Donnie Johnson Sackey.

Two friends in particular have been on the receiving end of my daily uninvited talks. Casey Boyle and Nathaniel Rivers are my sounding boards, collaborators, as well as two of my best friends and favorite people to share awe-full things with. Casey and Nathaniel make me laugh and think in equal measure, and their friendship is a constant reminder that *joy* is central to *thought*.

Thank you to my colleagues at the University of Kentucky's Department of Writing, Rhetoric, and Digital Studies. I've been fortunate to work with some pretty amazing scholars. Special thanks to Joshua Abboud, Lauren Cagle,

Brian McNely, Sharon Yam, John Barber, Janice Fernheimer, James Ridolfo, Steven Alvarez, and Karrieann Soto Vega. Research for this book was also generously funded by the University of Kentucky College of Arts and Science. Much gratitude to Dean Mark Kornbluh for ongoing support.

I also want to thank my Couch Bat family for helping me to reconnect body, mind, and spirit. Van 1 is forever part of my family. Big sweaty love to Jodie Nicotra, Blake Scott, Nate Kreuter, Steve Wernke, and John Sloop.

Thank you to my editor, Tara Cyphers, for being so enthusiastic and supportive throughout this whole process. It's been a real pleasure to work with an editor whose guidance has led me to rethink and reshape my project in powerful ways.

Finally, my biggest thanks of all to my family. There were some tough years in the process of writing this book, but I'm lucky to have the best people in the world to walk (and write) beside. Even in the hardest times, my kids—Vered and Judah—remind me just how wonderful the universe really is. They are the brightest stars in my sky. Thank you to Jeff, who listened to my ideas and gave me support in so many ways. I am forever grateful to him.

Finally, I want to dedicate *Awful Archives* to my brother, Wes Detweiler. Our dad passed away while I was finishing my revisions, but he is very much alive in everything that I write. My brother has made it possible for me to write and mourn at the same time.

I love you. We are surviving.

What Is This Evidence Of?

The foundation of morality is to have done, once and for all, with . . . pretending to believe that for which there is no evidence.

—T. H. HUXLEY, 1886, "SCIENCE AND MORALS"

I UNDERLINED Huxley's quote on the plane as I headed to Durham, North Carolina, to visit the Rhine Research Center archives. The Rhine Research Center sits adjacent to the Duke University campus, where it was originally housed in the Department of Psychology. While it is no longer formally part of the university, Rhine is still one of the longest-running organizations devoted to paranormal investigation. I was thinking about Huxley's words as I made my way to the library, wondering if the Center's serious treatment of extrasensory perception (ESP), psychokinesis, and paranormal phenomena is an example of believing that for which there is no evidence. At the Rhine Research Center, I was greeted by one of the center's administrators. She watched me try to stamp off as much snow as possible from my shoes before entering the library, making a mess of the carpet with all the slush.

The materials archived at the Rhine Center focus primarily on the measurement, documentation, and empirical examination of extraordinary human senses and abilities. The library shelves are filled with books and manuals written by and for paranormal researchers who test things like extrasensory perception, telekinetic powers, remote viewing, and contact with the dead. Casebooks offer instruction on the proper methodologies for testing psi, or the psychic abilities that certain humans supposedly possess. In the middle of the room sat a bowl of bent metal spoons, souvenirs left behind by the telekinetic visitors who had bent the spoons using only their mental energy. I browsed documents covering topics like ESP, communication with the dead, telekinesis, and astral projection, all while wondering what to make of this evidence.

As I read and made notes that afternoon in the library, I could not ignore the heated discussion happening directly behind me. The Center's director and another administrator were engaged in an animated discussion about inviting a potential speaker to give a lecture at the Center. From what I could gather, the speaker was a specialist in past life regression through hypnosis. Whereas the administrator was in favor of letting the regression specialist speak, the head director seemed to be dead set against it. He began running down the list of problems with "past life regression" through hypnosis. "I don't have a problem with the idea of past lives or with hypnosis," he explained, "but you cannot use hypnosis to reliably establish the existence of past life." I stopped reading altogether at this point and gave the conversation my full attention.

"Hypnosis is a therapeutic tool, sure," said the director. "But it involves suggestibility. If you suggest to someone that they will experience their past life during hypnosis, they probably will come up with something. That's why it's not *scientific*." He emphasized this last word strongly. "It's just not scientific, okay?" I could tell he felt passionately about this matter. He wasn't about to let just *anyone* come speak without some regard for empiricism and the scientific process. "That's not how you establish claims," he said in an irritated tone. "It's not science at that point."

It felt strange to be overhearing this argument about science, evidence, and empiricism while surrounded by books about extrasensory perception and a huge bowl of telekinetically transformed spoons. I couldn't quite wrap my head around how the director could so vigorously defend empirical evidence while also taking remote viewing and astral projection seriously. To me, all of these things are equally implausible. Past lives, ESP, alien abductions—they all stretch the bounds of reasonability. Why worry about evidence at all once you've ventured out into the world of such extraordinary claims?

The cognitive dissonance I was experiencing might have been due to my suspicion that evidence and certain extraordinary claims—those of the paranormal, for instance—are mutually exclusive. The more "far out" your claim, the less likely it is that evidence exists to back it up. (And vice versa.) But, in actuality, the Rhine Center's long history cannot possibly be told without delving into certain empirical processes of scientific testing developed by Dr. Joseph Banks Rhine himself. Rhine began to achieve fame in the 1930s and '40s as one of the world's most esteemed parapsychologists. Beginning in the 1930s, he served as director of Duke University's Parapsychology Laboratory, which would later become the Rhine Research Center. Rhine over-saw numerous experiments with subjects, searching for any indication that some humans possess extrasensory powers. For decades, Rhine published the results of his experiments, most of which indicated that certain people can indeed read minds or affect physical objects through their thoughts. Knowing that his claims would face much opposition, Rhine repeatedly emphasized his utter devotion to putting forth evidence-based claims. As he writes in *Parapsychology: Frontier Science of the Mind,* "For the establishment of psi only the highest standards of evidence—higher than those ordinarily familiar in science—could be accepted as adequate to overcome the special skepticism encountered" (53). Although his claims were extraordinary, he went to great lengths to provide evidence that met ordinary standards of empiricism.

Meanwhile, critics pilloried the results of his empirical work. One of Rhine's most vocal critics was Martin Gardner, a mid-twentieth-century mathematician and science writer, whose 1952 book, *Fads and Fallacies in the Name of Science,* arguably helped to spawn the contemporary popular skeptic movement. In *Fads and Fallacies,* Gardner decries the trends of pseudo-scientific beliefs promoted by those operating under the thin guise of real science. He catalogs a number of popular fallacies, such as Scientology, reincarnation, ESP, and flying saucers. Gardner also devotes a significant portion of his book to Dr. Rhine. While Gardner is quick to say that Rhine is far from a shady trickster, he is adamant that Rhine's laboratory research on extrasensory perception lacks the tight verifiability of scientific methods. It is a fallacy in the name of science. Gardner argues that while Rhine reports positive results in his many empirical studies of psychic abilities, he fails to mention the problematic processes that yielded those results.

For example, writes Gardner, Rhine regularly explained away experimenters' declining success in correctly guessing hidden cards as due to the fact that psi capacities can diminish and fade over time. Likewise, when an experimenter incorrectly guessed a card, Rhine explained that the guess might actually be a case of "forward displacement" or "backward displacement," meaning that the experimenter was actually guessing a card that had either been given earlier or one that is coming up. Because Professor Rhine dabbled in claims that were unfalsifiable, therefore, Gardner concludes that Rhine's evidence is simply *bad* evidence.

Gardner further contends that bad evidence has very serious social consequences. Although some may argue that there is little harm in entertaining anecdotes of flying saucers from outer space, Gardner counters that a "regrettable effect produced by the publication of scientific rubbish is the confusion they sow in the minds of gullible readers about what is and what isn't scientific knowledge. And the more the public is confused, the easier it falls prey to doctrines of pseudoscience which may at some future date receive the backing of politically powerful groups" (7). He points to the racial quasi-science that propelled Hitler's rise to power: "If the German people had been better trained to distinguish good from bad science, would they have swallowed so easily the insane racial theories of the Nazi anthropologists?" (7). And, just like that, we hit Godwin's Law as the ultimate answer to why bad evidence matters. Bad evidence is not just poor evidence; it is Nazi-level bad.

I am not as optimistic as Gardner that millions of Jews might have been saved if Germans had been better trained to identify "bad science," just like I'm not totally convinced that knowing bad from good evidence will always save the day. Still, the very idea of "bad evidence" suggests something important about how we conceptualize evidence itself. As a rhetorician, I am interested in tracing evidence's conceptual contours across conversations inside and outside academia. After all, for rhetorical scholars, the question of evidence is always lurking over our shoulders. Many of us were introduced to rhetoric through the standard route (the Greco-Roman highway) which places a heavy emphasis on the topic of evidence. Aristotle categorized arguments according to whether evidence exists, or if the argument instead is based on probability and artistry. Down the line, in *Institutio Orataria,* Quintilian similarly outlines much about what counts as evidence and how different types of proof should be handled. And, of course, like the perfect villain of any story, Peter Ramus infamously removed argument and proof from the domain of rhetoric. But Ramus did not triumph in the end. Evidence is sort of our thing.

While contemporary rhetorical theory has been anything but unified on the theory of evidence, we mostly agree that evidence is not beholden to rules of logic. Some time ago, Richard B. Gregg argued in "The Rhetoric of Evidence" that we should stop imagining evidence as "raw material, the primordial material from which a proof is constructed," and which then leads to a logical conclusion (181). Instead, Gregg writes, we are better off examining the *rhetorics* of evidence: "We need to understand not only why arguments should or should not be accepted (the logic of an argument) but why, in fact, they are or are not accepted (the rhetoric of an argument)" (189). To this end, Gregg suggests that we should identify the rhetorical *patterns* of evidence as they interact among author/speaker, audience, and conclusion.

In the decades since Gregg made this call, scholars have indeed paid close attention to the rhetoric of evidence, including the rhetorical construction of evidence. Today we are knee-deep in questions like *Who determines what counts as acceptable evidence? How do we value different types of evidence? Can there ever be objective evidence? What is the relationship between evidence and knowledge?* These questions emerge, for example, in feminist rhetorical scholarship, which has closely examined the rhetorical construction of evidence. Because women's personal narratives and experiences are often seen as inadequate forms of evidence, scholars like Karen A. Foss and Sonja K. Foss have called for us to construct "new methods and theories that truly take women's perspectives into account" (42). These types of arguments ask us to reflect on the rhetoricalness of evidence. By calling attention to the fact that evidence is rhetorically constructed, we might begin interrogating our own concepts of "bad evidence" as equally constructed.

On the other hand, many critical rhetoric and argumentation scholars plead for us to not drop the idea of "bad evidence" altogether. For instance, Edward Schiappa vigorously advocates for a normative approach to argument evaluation, an approach that he sees lacking in contemporary rhetorical studies. He writes, "One appropriate and important function of criticism is to render judgments of the worth of individual arguments and that argument evaluation is an important part of argumentation studies" (ix). As an example of what Schiappa considers proper argument evaluation, he points to Marilyn J. Young and Michael K. Launer's essay, "The Need for Evaluative Criteria: Conspiracy Argument Revisited." Young and Launer examine conspiracy discourse, which is often filled with facts and technical details offered as evidence. Nevertheless, they write, these facts and technical details should not be considered *actual* evidence, since what is offered merely "purports to be an evidentiary process, though in fact what makes the rhetoric work is its narrativity" (21). Young and Launer suggest that conspiracy discourse is "a symbiosis of poetics and argumentation: various logical fallacies are used as artistic devices in the structure of a conspiracist tract qua rhetorical text, while consciously crafted language carries the intellectual burden of argument" (26). It is not the case, they write, that the technical details are authentic forms of evidence. Rather, what is cited by the conspiracist is simply "adduced as evidence" (21). In other words, the heavily stylized rhetoric of conspiracy discourse masks itself as evidence-based rational argument. Conspiracy discourse is thus a pretender to true evidentiary processes, a sham passing off narrative as true evidence.

Here we should pause to notice something interesting about the ways evidence is conceptualized both inside and outside rhetorical studies. In different ways, many of our discussions imbue evidence with a kind of *thingfulness*.

It is a present or absent thing, for example. It can be an authentic thing or a phony thing. It is a thing that could be potentially fabricated. It has the qualities of being good or bad. This thingfulness is no accident, according to Charles Arthur Willard, since the notion of evidence-as-thing was articulated early in rhetorical theory. "We owe to Aristotle the equation of evidence with things," writes Willard. "His 'inartistic proofs' were *things* (testimony, witnesses, objects, oaths, etc.) which 'were to be picked up and used by rhetors'" (268; emphasis added). Still today, we ask questions like whether "all the evidence is in" or if we "found the evidence," as if evidence is a parcel awaiting delivery. We critique some arguments as "lacking evidence," a shortcoming that causes teachers to instruct students on the best way of "finding evidence." The thingfulness of evidence also lends itself to the idea that there are clear demarcations between authentic and inauthentic evidence, or even between present or absent evidence.

Even T. H. Huxley's exhortation to "give up pretending to believe that for which there is no evidence" rests on the premise that evidence is a kind of thing that's either there or not. Maybe it is an irony, then, that his grandson Aldous believed that the evidence for Joseph Rhine's paranormal claims was very much *there*. In fact, Aldous Huxley was one of Rhine's biggest fans. In a lengthy 1954 essay for *Life*, Huxley extolled Rhine's discoveries of psi, praising the very tests that critics like Gardner critiqued as methodologically flawed. Huxley explained away any possible criticism of Rhine, hailing his work as a kind of breakthrough in the study of humans. In a later profile of Aldous Huxley, Clive James remarks that "Huxley was not just keen to believe that Rhine had discovered something substantial; he wanted to believe that statistical analysis had proved Rhine correct." So much did Huxley want to believe, in fact, that he managed to overlook what many saw as the poor quality of Rhine's evidence.

Perhaps Aldous Huxley was guilty of believing in things for which there is no evidence. It does not take much to see that Rhine's experimental protocols are deeply flawed. Maybe even Rhine himself was guilty of making claims based on bad evidence—or no evidence at all. Yet, when Nobel Prize–winning chemist Irving Langmuir visited Rhine's lab, he concluded that Rhine did not provide evidence that ESP exists, but, instead, he provided evidence of how well-intentioned researchers are blind to the statistical mischief they are committing (see Smith). Could it be that Huxley also saw something different when encountering Rhine's claims? Perhaps Huxley was not duped by bad evidence after all, but was simply responding to evidence of a different kind. Though psi may not actually exist, there is still plenty of evidence for it.

EVIDENCE AS PROCESS

Etymologically, *evidence* does not necessarily carry the connotation of thing-ness. As Carlo Ginzburg writes, "The word 'evidence' is a piece of historical evidence itself" ("Representing" 29). Ginzburg explains that the English word has etymological roots in the Latin word *evidentia,* which is variously translated as "obviousness," "vividness," and "distinctness." In this sense, he continues, evidentia indicated "an ability to make a topic not only evident, but palpable" (29). Palpability also marks evidentia's Greek parallel word *enargeia,* which indicates "an uncanny capacity to use words or colours to conjure up absent realities" (Ginzburg, "Representing" 29). *Enargeia* is sometimes translated as "a bringing before the eyes," another way of describing the vivid palpability contained in evidentia. According to Ginzburg, the Greek and Roman sense of how evidence relates to truth is significantly different from our current understanding:

> We can imagine a sequence of this type: historical narration—description—
> vividness—truth. The difference between our concept of history and that of
> the ancients could be summed up as follows: for the Greeks and Romans
> historical truth was based on evidentia (the Latin equivalent of enargeia pro-
> posed by Quintilian); for us, on evidence. (*Threads* 12)

As Ginzburg tells it, evidentia is all about conjuring, while evidence is all about documented data. He invites us to note that our contemporary sense of evidence did not necessarily develop or evolve linearly from evidentia. Whereas enargeia and evidentia emerged from oral cultures, evidence was born from print-based ecclesiastical culture. They are more distant cousins than parent and child.

However, while we may or may not draw a conceptual line of progression from evidentia to our contemporary notions of evidence, I want to place them into proximity. Our contemporary sense of evidence differs from evidentia's poetic conjuring, yet both are still ultimately concerned with palpability. Even in our most empirical scientific acts, we find palpability as a marker of persuasive evidence. For instance, results from an experiment must be demonstrative and repeatedly observable. They must be made visible: a bringing before the eyes. While Ginzburg's account suggests that we have historically shifted away from evidentia to enter the age of evidence, we might imagine them as orbiting satellites, with one or the other alternately emerging more strongly in certain contexts. Evidence was born from evidentia's world, and the two cannot be so easily separated out. Furthermore, there is good reason to revisit our contemporary sense of evidence by reconsidering its proximity with evidentia's uncanny conjuring.

Maybe it's due to my predisposition for the scatological, but I find *bullshit* a useful way to conceptualize a version of evidence that is in close proximity to evidentia. Although the term lacks empirical measurability and professional politeness, the advantage of a label like "bullshit" is that it bypasses such categories as present/absent or legitimate/invalid, which far too often leave a gap in the lived encounter with evidence. Evidence-as-thing limits our ability to see something about the evidentiary process itself. Even when I am faced with an outlandish claim steeped in bullshit—*a shadowy elite group of Jews secretly controls the world,* or *liberal feminists want to make euthanasia mandatory*— that bullshit evidence emerges as an encounter between me and my bullshit-prone interlocutor. James Fredal describes bullshit as an experience between bodies, where one body incapacitates the other. "If every encounter and every form of social discourse involve at least two parties, at least two perspectives," writes Fredal, "then bullshit is what results when the arrogance of one party leads the other to feel unacknowledged, taken for granted, disregarded, or unheard" (256). Bullshit is not so much a thing, therefore, as it is a happening. It is a conjuring.

While, thankfully, evidence is not all bullshit, the parallel can be useful in order to discuss the performative character of both. Like bullshit, evidence *does* something more than it *is* something. Eve Kosofsky Sedgwick echoes this sense of evidence in "Against Epistemology," where she explains her own use of performative writing: "Part of what the performativity of my essay was aimed at, in a context where the 'question of evidence' seemed all but predetermined as the question of evidential truth or credibility, was to de-emphasize the epistemology of evidence and instead stress its erotics" (136). Here again, we see evidence imagined as an emergence, a happening, an event. However, while Heather Dubrow suggests that "performance functions as an alternative to the presentation of evidence" (16), I push back against this distinction. Performance is not an alternative to evidence, but rather performative conjuring recalls evidentia's mesh of poetics and evidential truth. Framed in this way, we could almost certainly agree that the Rhine Center is dealing in evidence. After all, those paranormal manuals and testing guides perform the discourse and aesthetics of empiricism in order to vividly present the sense of science and method. Likewise, Aldous Huxley's beliefs in psi, as well as Rhine's claims of the paranormal, were very much grounded in evidence, though evidence in a different register. In order to more fully understand what evidence *does* and can potentially *do,* however, we need broader rhetorical frameworks that can (temporarily) bracket questions of legitimacy, validity, or even evaluation. But this kind of evidence is an anomaly.

REGISTERS OF EVIDENCE

If my visit to the Rhine Research Center had not shaken my notions of evidence, then my time in the Anomaly Archives certainly would have done the trick. On a very un-snowy winter day in Austin, Texas, I convinced my friend and colleague Casey Boyle to drive me to the Anomaly Archives. We pulled up to an old strip of wooden offices, but there were no signs announcing the Anomaly Archives. After looking around, we finally found a small sign on a door that read "Institute for Neuroscience and Consciousness Studies." We guessed this was the right place, so I knocked loudly. No response. I turned the doorknob and the door swung wide open to reveal two cramped rooms full of books, papers, and file folders stuffed into nearly every space.

We walked in and found the entire office completely empty. It looked like everyone had just suddenly vanished. Casey, looking nervous as hell, refused to walk past the front door. I murmured something about respectfully moseying through the materials, which I began to do before he could object. I browsed handbooks on UFO spotting, typewritten manuscripts on hollow earth and the Illuminati and free energy and water witching and any other strange claim you could imagine. I took out my phone and shot hundreds of pictures of the documents. Finally, after a couple of hours, I put a very nervous Casey at ease by telling him we could go. We laughed about how anomalous our trip to the Anomaly Archives had truly been. We came up with absurdly bizarre theories about why it was just sitting empty: *Did the aliens come? Were they busy making free energy machines? Had they time traveled and forgotten how to get back?*

Once back home, I pulled out the archival document images. I randomly began reading the manuals and self-published books that claimed to expose secrets of "hollow earth" or "inner earth." First up was Bruce A. Walton's *A Guide to the Inner Earth,* an incredibly dense annotated bibliography of historical references about a hollow core within the earth. His copious notes sent me scrambling through the other hollow earth archival materials I had copied. After spending a few hours moving from book to book, I stumbled upon a story that I would later see recounted in several popular hollow earth texts. The story is a tangled mess of details, but the gist of it is that William Morgan, accompanied by mysterious Freemasons, entered inner earth through a cave in Kentucky sometime during the late 1800s. Numerous maps of this entrance have been drawn over the past two centuries, many with incredible geological precision.

I next turned to Rodney M. Cluff's extensive research on hollow earth, where he claims the Lost Tribes of Israel now live. In one edition of Cluff's *Our Hollow Earth* newsletter, he details some of the reasons why truth about hollow earth is most likely suppressed by the government. For one thing, writes Cluff, research shows that "free energy technology has been suppressed which if given to the world would create a paradigm of abundance" (May 2012). More significantly, the hidden truth also has an even darker backstory:

> Many if not most of the flying saucers seen around the world come from the hollow interior of our own earth. . . . Those that come from our hollow earth are intimately concerned about preventing nuclear war, because they share our atmosphere through openings at the poles that lead to their inner world. Admiral Richard E. Byrd flew there several times in 1926, 1929, 1947 and 1956, but was told to keep it a secret. The Rockefellers helped fund many of his exploratory flights, so you can see why they would want to keep it a secret from we, the people, whom they have enslaved to their monetary, energy, and pharmaceutical monopolies. (May 2012)

The themes repeated by Walton and Cluff permeate much of the hollow earth archival materials I found. Research on inner earth is thick with details about Freemasonry, the Illuminati, suppressed free energy, and government cover-ups of alien life.

As I combed through all of these materials, I tried to imagine how to respond to such claims. The evidence was indeed anomalous; it was uneven, off-kilter, strange. Yet, I also found myself asking an even simpler question: *What is this evidence of?* This question paraphrases a question Cara Finnegan poses in her essay "What Is This a Picture Of?: Some Thoughts on Images and Archives," where she recounts the experience of working through archival images from the Farm Security Administration (FSA) Information file in the Library of Congress. Finnegan describes searching for the original image published in a 1936 magazine article. The image showed a white farmer in overalls standing on the porch of a rural cabin. In order to locate the original image in the archives, Finnegan searches different subject files that make the most sense for how this image might have been archived. Although she initially assumes that this image might be filed under a subject like "Farmers" or "Sharecroppers," she finally locates it under the subject heading "Shacks." This particular image's denotation gives Finnegan some pause, since it forces the question for her (as for the original archivists): *What is this a picture of?* For

Finnegan, the picture depicts a sharecropper, yet the archivist clearly saw the shack as the primary subject.

Interestingly, Finnegan's question—What is this a picture of?—goes beyond the details contained in the photograph itself. As she meditates on the practice of archival classification, Finnegan argues that this photograph also depicts a certain historical context, namely, "the FSA's liberal myth: the archive privileges the land and living conditions over individual lives and experiences" (120). In other words, this single photograph portrays a whole range of ideologies, practices, and organizations that are not literally contained in the image itself. It references an entire rhetorical and affective constellation that goes well beyond the photograph's visual contents.

I find Finnegan's question helpful as a way of approaching any kind of archive in order to dislodge the multitude of references that surround it. What might we learn, for example, by asking that seemingly banal question: *What is this evidence of?* In my encounter with the Anomaly Archive materials, this question guided me in a way that complicated how I read the documents. Specifically, I had the peculiar sensation of moving between two different registers of evidence. In one register, the hollow earth materials provided geological, cultural, and religious evidence for the claim that the earth has an inner core where something is hidden—maybe free energy, maybe aliens, maybe the lost tribes of Israel—by those in power. But, these documents also possess a second register of evidence: It is evidence of strangeness, of fringes that do not actually live at life's edges at all, of ordinariness suddenly permeated by unexpected disruption. It is evidence of our ongoing human attempts to figure out what the fuck is happening around us.

While reading these archival materials, I felt both registers of evidence emerge with equal palpability, though they were not equally persuasive by any means. Of course, I am a rhetoric scholar who makes a living by finding the polysemic and the multiple in any given text. Still, while any scholar worth her weight can read beyond what the contents contain, it is worth acknowledging that this same interpretive process can also guide how hollow earth believers read this material. Just as I had the sense that *something more* is being transmitted by these documents, the same might be the case for those who are persuaded by these claims. *Something more, something palpable,* emerges beyond the geological and historical factoids: evidence of government secrecy, occult wisdom, eternal life, a sense of purpose.

To be clear, I am no hollow earth believer. Nor am I suggesting that we should believe anything anyone offers up as evidence. Instead, I find that this double register reflects something important about evidence and argument. Rhetorical theory provides us with frameworks for describing the content-specific aspects of evidence: representation, signification, ideology, constructed meanings. Yet, these disciplinary models feel insufficient for explaining how evidence operates apart from its contents. Our familiar frameworks of evidence that emphasize validity or empirical fidelity are far too limited for understanding what is happening here. Moreover, there are serious limitations to the idea that these kinds of anomalous claims have no evidence, or that rational people should find them unpersuasive because the evidence is (for lack of a better word) bullshit.

As a rhetorician who is interested in public discourse, I find the multiple registers of evidence a productive starting point for discovering what Lloyd Bitzer calls a "fitting response." Reading evidence in this doubled register is not unique to textual scholars; it is common to everyone who experiences the evidentiary process. Consequently, I suspect that our counterarguments to extraordinary or unbelievable claims are often misdirected. What we think we are responding to when addressing problematic evidence may not be the actual referent of those claims. For instance, most of us would probably not find it difficult to refute hollow earth claims, since they are based on evidence that is unfalsifiable, largely anecdotal, and drawn from mystical and pseudoscientific texts. However, such counter-response misses the more compelling aspect of this evidence for hollow earth believers. Namely, this counter-response overlooks the rhetorical constellations of *something more* surrounding that evidence.

As I look through the maps and descriptions of Kentucky's hollow earth entry, which happens to be only an hour away from my home, affective jolts happen. *Something more* is being transmitted by these documents. *Something intense, something real. Something off. Something fucked up. Something anomalous.* While I'm sure my narrative of these jolts would sound different from those of Walton or Cluff, I'm more interested in the jolts' congruities. A two-hundred-year-old map locates the opening to earth's hollow core in Mammoth Cave, Kentucky, and we all light up with a *What the fuck is going on?* shimmer that shoots through other registers of difference.

What would it mean to call these shimmers forms of evidence? For one thing, we would need new rhetorical models that allow us to see these multiple registers, as well as how they can change our concepts of what evidence is and what it does. This multi-registered character of evidence is precisely what I explore throughout *Awful Archives*. In the chapters that follow, I use case studies of extraordinary claims in order to ask how evidence works in ways that do not mirror our expected models—either the lay models that imagine "commonsense" uses of evidence, or the various disciplinary models of persuasion. *Awful Archives* traces the lifeworld of evidence: how it operates, moves, and is sustained in ways that may not show up at first glance. I pose evidence as an *act* rather than a *thing*.

My goal in undertaking this exploration is to climb inside anomalous archives without regard for their referential fidelity. In this task, I take a cue from ethnographer Susan Lepselter, who describes her approach to studying UFO experiencers as one caught between competing senses of "the real." Lepselter recounts how her alien abductee informants share stories that defy believability while also being very real. She explains how she listens for "the real" as it has had "a chance to crystallize not as an outside referent, but inside the story itself" (*Resonance* 16). In much the same way, I strive to listen for the "the real" of weird, anomalous, or flawed evidence as it lives and moves in registers beyond validity, legitimacy, or authenticity.

Specifically, this book examines the strange world of conspiracy theories, a subject that has gained quite a bit of scholarly attention (for good reason). I find myself writing during a period where conspiracy theory and the question of evidence have gained a profound exigence. In the wake of the 2016 US presidential elections, it was impossible not to notice how discourse about life in a "post-truth era" lamented the atrophy of evidence. From a distance, it would seem as if "evidence" was an endangered, beleaguered, and withering animal. It's probably dumb luck that the face of "post-truth" happened to be named Trump. The sound bites almost write themselves. In 2018 alone, we can find books like *America's Post-Truth Phenomenon: When Feelings and Opinions Trump Facts and Evidence* and attend events such as the 2018 "What Is Evidence in a Post-Truth Society?" colloquium at the Australian National University. All around me, evidence looked in a bad way.

At the same time, it didn't seem like there were fewer claims being made in any sphere of public life. Politicians, skeptics, activists, social media trolls, friends, media personalities, neighbors, podcasters, experts, the guy who you got stuck sitting next to on the bus—they all continued to build claims from their preferred archives of evidence. I began to wonder if evidence was not, in fact, on the wane, but that perhaps we were simply at the limit of our ability to explain why evidence can be so resistant to response. I needed some way to understand this thing we call evidence, and how it acts in the most faulty, flimsy, or fallacious arguments. Therefore, my chosen archives range from the anomalous to the outrageous: images that circulate in 9/11 truther communities, top-secret archival documents revealing the government's UFO cover-up, phony Kenyan medical records that prove Barack Obama is not American. I explore these cases in order to expand our concepts of evidence as an affective process, as opposed to a static artifact.

Several rhetorical theorists have undertaken critical analyses of conspiracy discourse, focusing especially on the contents of conspiracy talk and the way these claims engage with defined social phenomenon. Taking a broad perspective on the rhetorical elements of conspiracy talk, for example, Thomas

Goodnight and John Poulakos explore the ways that conspiracy theories often allow for users to engage (albeit roughly) in a quasi-critical inquiry about rhetorical epistemology. They define conspiracy rhetoric as "a struggle to define the grounding of discourse" (301). Goodnight and Poulakos also examine how conspiracy discourse evaluates and critiques what rhetorical theorists call evidence. According to Goodnight and Poulakos, conspiracy theorists struggle to define social reality through their engagement with epistemic value of proof.

Alternatively, Shane Miller argues that conspiracy discourse is a form of critique and an attempt to speak to power. Miller writes, "By focusing on issues at the heart of the exercise of power (authority, legitimacy, credibility, grounding, etc.) conspiracy theories themselves serve as a way for non-expert citizens to critique the placement and administration of power" (53). Likewise, Marouf Hasian Jr. looks to the relationships between particular conspiracies and larger social contexts. In his analysis of the Protocols of the Elders of Zion, Hasian writes, "As critics, the challenge involves trying to balance the search for epistemic knowledge while pointing out the material conditions . . . within cultures that give rise to conspiratorial rhetorics" (209). Hasian then calls for rhetorical critics to examine "the ideological complexities of artifacts like The Protocols" in order to counteract their ongoing circulatory power (210). And, indeed, you don't have to pull too hard at the internal logics of conspiracy rhetoric to find a myriad of ideological complexities. Jodi Dean has compellingly argued that conspiracy theory "codes critical reflections on democratic society as a particular set of threats" (143). Almost any conspiracy theory can be read as an allegory for the fears, desires, and oppressions that pervade the structures of everyday life.

As many of these critical analyses suggest, conspiracy discourse can tell us a lot about how people negotiate complicated networks of power. Fredrick Jameson goes so far as to argue that "conspiracy theory (and its garish narrative manifestations) must be seen as a degraded attempt—through the figuration of advanced technology—to think the impossible totality of the contemporary world system" (38). Jameson sees conspiracy theory as an (impossible) attempt to totalize fragmentization, which is the condition of life under post-capitalism. Jameson's reading has a certain amount of explanatory power, as it works to show how conspiracy discourse is both a function of and a response to cultural conditions. Readings like this give conspiracy logic a coherence that appears to be internally lacking. However, because Jameson and other critics focus so intensely on the *contents* of conspiracy discourse, they often overlook rhetorical effects that are not necessarily coterminous with the discursive contents of those theories. Without dismissing these cultural analyses, therefore, I want to ask a different set of questions that are made visible through the lens of conspiracy theory.

In *Awful Archives*, I use the exaggerated rhetorical scenes of conspiracy theory in order to raise a question that many people (both inside and outside academic circles) are asking: *Why do traditional modes of argument often fail in the face of claims that rely on bad evidence?* This question, in turn, contains an even broader question that is simultaneously mundane and complicated: *What is evidence?* When we cite evidence in support of a claim, what is it that we are actually doing? What is the lifeworld of evidence? By probing the rhetorical functions that evidence plays in public discourse, I am also searching for a more effective way of responding to claims that we find invalid, intolerable, or just plain wrong. Put simply, how can we practice more ethical and productive forms of debate in public discourse that feels like a dead end?

This is the same question that motivated Wayne Booth's 1974 *Modern Dogma and the Rhetoric of Assent,* which addresses a different social context of deeply divided public discourse. As Booth points out in *Modern Dogma,* "We must find a common faith in modes of argument, or every institution we care about will die" (150). Four decades after Booth wrote these words, those of us who study public discourse are still asking how to find common modes of argument that can help us move past our objections in order to sustain ourselves as a healthy public. The contribution I seek to make with *Awful Archives* is to reframe the terms of what argument is and what response can be in those moments.

While the cases I examine may seem like exaggerated instances of public discourse, or even the academic equivalent of a carnival sideshow, my central questions apply to all kinds of claims that circulate in everyday life. We are constantly faced with claims we find abhorrent or off-track. Or we hear evidence that seems to be misapplied or even wholly false. By enlarging our sense of what evidence is doing—that it is affectively and auratically figuring certain meanings for its users—we can form a more ethical and public-oriented response as rhetoricians. Rather than thinking about evidence as independent from us, the "users" of evidence, we might instead begin to understand evidence as a living process that is inherently tangled up in our own movements, encounters, affects, and relationships.

SCOPE AND CONTENTS: "ARCHIVE"

Before moving ahead much further in this exploration, I want to briefly articulate a few premises I adopt throughout *Awful Archives*. Perhaps most conspicuous is my use of the term *archive,* which does not always mirror traditional disciplinary senses of that term. I frame the subject of evidence in terms of archives because our claims (ordinary and extraordinary) always draw from some kind of archive: literal documents and records, cultural memories archived through multiple retellings, family stories, preserved media files, personal archives of experience, and so forth. We retrieve evidence from an archive of some kind, whether or not it has the institutional look and smell of an archive. Long ago, Derrida pushed us past the simplistic notion that an archive refers only to a physical location or the collections of records stored there. Since then, many critical archival scholars have also pushed against the notion that archives are limited to material artifacts. In *Refiguring the Archive,* Carolyn Hamilton et al. suggest that we should widen our notions of archives "so as to engage the idea of the taken-for-granted, often implicit, 'archive' that is the foundation of the production of knowledge in the present" (9). Similarly, in *The Queen of America Goes to Washington City,* Lauren Berlant recounts the story of a colleague who objected to the way she uses the term *archive* to reference the banal, ephemeral artifacts of everyday life. Unshaken by such objection, Berlant responds that what might appear to be the "waste products of everyday communication in the national public sphere" are actually "pivotal documents in the construction, experience, and rhetoric of quotidian citizenship in the United States" (12). In other words, the term *archive* signals a range of impacted traces left in the wake of institutional-social-political structures.

My expansive sense of archive also draws from scholars who consider how the ephemeral, the nonmaterial, the temporary, and the fleeting can and must also become part of our archival sensibilities. Writing about performativity within queer and minoritarian cultures, Jose Muñoz fights the notion that archives are only composed of durability. Muñoz notes that while the ephemerality of performance often does not meet standards of evidentiary "rigor" demanded by the academy, critical archival activists nevertheless attend to "alternate modes of textuality and narrativity like memory and performance: . . . all of those things that remain after a performance, a kind of evidence of what has transpired but certainly not the thing itself" (10). What escapes more traditional categories of archival evidence are the "traces, glimmers, residues, and specks of things," he writes (10). Echoing Muñoz, Judith Halberstam declares, "We need to theorize the concept of the archive and consider new models of queer memory and queer history capable of recording and tracing subterranean scenes, fly by night clubs and fleeting trends." In these calls, there is an effort to account for (and to have counted) moments of lived experience as the stuff of archives.

Theorists like Berlant, Muñoz, and Halberstam reframe the archive in such a way that encourages us to ask not what an archive *is,* but instead what an archive *does.* In this tradition, I define archives as ordinary and extraordinary experiences in public life that leave lasting, palpable residues, which then become our sources—our resources—for public discourse. The experiences may indeed include traditional collections of documents, but they may also include ephemeral and momentary scenes that are not so easily documented. Regardless of how they leave their traces, the palpable impacts of those experiences are available to us as points of reference for all kinds of claims about the world. These are our archives.

Another premise driving my inquiry is that we can and should unlink any necessary relationship between archives and memory. Much of the scholarship on archives begins (and ends) through a memorial topos, essentially defining the archive through its relationship to memory. Jules Michelet provides the most explicit example of this link in his declaration that the historian archivist is the magistrate of the dead. "Yes," writes Michelet, "every one who dies leaves behind a little something, his memory, and demands that we care for it" (qtd. in Steedman 39). According to Michelet, the archival historian is entrusted with the dead, the forgotten, and the invisible, since the connection between memory and care is the historian's directive. Several archival scholars have echoed Michelet's conflation of archives and memory, defining archives almost exclusively through their memory function. For example, Kenneth Foote writes that for archivists, "the idea of archives as memory is more than a metaphor. The documents and artifacts they collect are important resources for extending the spatial and temporal range of human communication" (392). Archives exist for the preservation of cultural, social, and historical memory.

However, contemporary rhetorical scholars have pushed back on this notion that archives are simply the *preservation* of memory. Rhetorical archival scholarship emphasizes how archives are often deployed as tools for the *construction* of public memory. Charles Morris argues that archives "should rightly be understood not as a passive receptacle for historical documents and their 'truths,' or a benign research space, but rather as a dynamic site of rhetorical power" (115). The very existence or nonexistence of an archive already contains an element of power insofar as deliberate decisions are made about what is worthy of archiving. In the words of Davis W. Houck, "archives function as sites of preferred memory," meaning that it is only those cultural, political, and social records deemed worthy of collective memory that become identified as "archivable" (134). Like a feedback loop, the significance of those collective narratives further calcifies a wider cultural sense of what should be counted and what should not.

Feminist archival rhetoricians have been especially attentive to the effects of how archives both write and unwrite what counts in public memory. In response, Jessica Enoch argues that archives must be interrogated for how they narrate certain public memory (while leaving other narratives untended).

"Rather than using the archive to recover women," writes Enoch, "a feminist memory studies approach to the archive prompts scholars to see it as a site that creates and shapes public memories for and about women" (66). This kind of recovery work, adopting what Enoch calls "a feminist memory studies approach," accomplishes multiple goals. On one hand, it prompts us to ask how, why, and where exactly particular cultural narratives are created. At the same time, it also calls for us to recover those alternative stories that were erased or obscured from collective memory.

I am grateful for the rhetorical archival scholars who have demystified Michelet's depressing vision of archivists as simply magistrates of the dead. Furthermore, it would be ridiculous to ignore the ways that archives and memory are mutually implicated at so many turns. And yet, at the same time, I am also struck by Paul Ricoeur's reflection on how archives contain traces that give up more than their contents explicitly contain. Ricoeur finds in these traces a kind of "involuntary testimony," a witnessing to traces that fall between the said and the unsaid (Merewether 67). "The documents in archives for the most part come from witnesses in spite of themselves," writes Ricoeur (171). Although there are many good reasons why we should—we must—interrogate the public memories constructed and erased through archives, I still want to know what we overlook when archives are defined solely in terms of memory function. Archives buzz and fidget with activity that does not quite correspond to any aspect of memory. In *Awful Archives*, I look beyond archival memory functions in order to ask what *else* an archive does.

SCOPE AND CONTENTS: "THICK EVIDENCE"

It's not like we weren't warned about linking memory and archives in the first place. Plato sounded this alarm in the *Phaedrus*, where he warned that writing will inevitably "produce forgetfulness in the minds of those who learn to use it, because they will not practice their memory. Their trust in writing, produced by external characters which are no part of themselves, will discourage the use of their own memory within them" (275a). While I am no Plato apologist, I will admit that my office desk is the embodiment of Plato's nightmare, a living testament to how writing and memory often work against each other. My office is filled with giant stacks of paper and folders towering on my desk, on my shelves, and in all four corners. The piles contain lecture notes, essay drafts, conference presentations, class handouts, reading notes I took on some book I read, memos from the dean, old course rosters, notes that I've made during any number of weekly meetings. I save these things because I think that maybe I will need them or want them later. Or maybe I save them out of sheer laziness. If I stacked them up in one giant stack, they might top my own five-foot-three body. But, even if I had to, I could not tell you the specifics of anything I stuck in these piles over the years. I offloaded the memory into the stacks, and they do not give up the information very easily.

However, the fact that my paper towers serve no memory function does not mean that they are useless. Indeed, my office archives have been quite useful to me. A colleague at a different university asked if we could have a video conference about a collaborative project we were beginning. My desktop computer was experiencing problems, so I set my laptop on the desk in front of me. Maybe out of practicality, maybe out of vanity, I soon decided that the laptop's camera angle was unacceptable. My face looked weird and my neck seemed to gain unsightly folds. The machine needed to be higher. I grabbed a book to put under my laptop. Then another. In a flustered moment, I grabbed one giant stack of my archived papers, which raised the camera angle to a height that satisfied the practical need for a respectable video chat. (And, of course, a flattering angle.) In that moment, my archives were severed from their memory function and became useful as laptop support. Archives as prop. Thus, for one vain professor who wanted a decent video chat, the archive was a laptop heightener. The memories and contents housed in that particular archival mass mattered very little. Instead, they became useful in a way that is not defined through memory, but through their use.

In a much different context, Wolfgang Ernst looks to the German Weimar Republic to describe how archives function apart from memory. Ernst writes that after the First World War, records management took on a more intense role in the Weimar Republic, which required infinitesimal documentation of industrial management and all levels of social-economic life:

> Instead of fulfilling the task of antiquarian memory the archive has begun to process recorded events, moving away from a stance of reticence towards a conception of archival feedback with respect to coexistent agencies. This new aesthetics of memory is a function of Weimar political culture. The state was expected to be heedful, "for the sake of its present reputation," and to document its administrative activity, "that is, its political articulations," in a way that might enable it to justify its actions at any given moment. (18)

The Republic shifted attention away from the idea of archives as a source of memory preservation to one that used archives as a source of justification. More contemporary examples of the Weimar's archive can be found in many of our own bureaucratic archives. Take the police "evidence room," with endless shelves of artifacts and papers. Police evidence rooms are important for several different reasons, most obviously in the way that the rooms preserve artifacts that can help to solve cold cases or connect crimes that might otherwise go unsolved. Yet, the evidence room also endows the police bureaucracy with a certain kind of credibility. The preserved archives of evidence testify to a legality, or the insurance of authority.

All of these examples vividly reflect how archives boost things. They boost my laptop on a short desk. They boost the feel of legitimacy for epistemic claims. They boost bureaucracy to a state of authority. Archives wedge otherwise unstable structures into a kind of stability that allows us to keep going. Their boosting power comes not so much from the contents as from the way they consolidate and coalesce into something stable—physically and epistemically. The contents thicken into a new form altogether. They become thick evidence. Although this term may sound similar to Geertz's more familiar term "thick description," I actually am thinking of something much different than a Balinese cockfight. In fact, I am thinking of the giant stacks of paper and folders towering on my desk right now.

Another example of thick evidence caught my attention a few summers ago, when I was visiting Tel Aviv with my family. Every day, we would walk out of our apartment and onto central walkways, where large wooden poles contained hundreds of flyers and posters announcing concerts, apartments for rent, and so on. We arrived in Tel Aviv in the days leading up to the Tel Aviv Gay Pride week, and the flyers prominently announced drag shows, Tel-a-Beef events, after-hours Pride parties, and the like. Being the good academic, I decided to document the Pride ephemera that was papering the city. Being the good academic on vacation near the beach, however, I found myself promising to start that documentation "tomorrow." And somehow, tomorrow always turns into another tomorrow.

One morning, a few days after Pride week ended, I walked past one of the large posting stations and realized that the Pride flyers had been covered over with all-new announcements for concerts, plays, club events, and the usual big city happenings. I ran back to the pole to see if I could still grab pictures of any remaining Pride flyers that had not yet been covered over with upcoming events. The good academic on the beach had dropped the ball on any chance to archive Tel Aviv Pride week's street ephemera. For some reason, I touched the pole carefully, as if one of those week-old flyers would somehow appear. The feeling of the posters and flyers had a strange weight to them. Who knows how many weeks' or months' worth of flyers had been pasted and repasted? The layers had started to form a kind of solidified wall. They were a clubland palimpsest. What were in those layers? What did they announce? Because the flyers have been pasted over repeatedly, it is difficult to say for certain. It was like an archeological dig site, with sedimented layers of Pride posters, bicycles for sale, protest announcements, and any other number of things.

Weeks later, I noticed workers pulling apart the slabs of posters and dragging them to the side of the street to be picked up. Some of the slabs were almost as tall as the men who pulled and dragged them. The pasted- and matted-together slabs were exactly as I had imagined they might look. They were sturdy, like they'd been made stiff over time in the way that paper-mache hardens into a solid mass. I could tell by the way the workers dragged these little slabs that they were heavy, even though the individual flyers could have been light enough to get blown right out of someone's hand.

I thought about how wonderful it would be to drag that thick wall of layered posters back to my apartment. I pictured cutting it into smaller shapes and hanging them from my office ceiling as a kind of "found art" decoration. Or, if I could somehow hang enough of these thick rolls on my office walls, some of the sounds drifting in from the office next door might be muted a bit. In actuality, the wall of posters simply became a pile of slabs that sat in the street to serve as ad hoc shelter for Tel Aviv's outlandishly high number of feral cats. Meanwhile, for the city workers peeling them off the wooden posts, they were a heavy mass that was just another day's job.

Whatever the mass could have been or actually did become—artistic canvas, office decoration, feral cat home—those accumulated small moments of individual posters and flyers had hardened into a new formation. Whatever the slabs were or might be, they do not relate to the contents of those singular pieces. Indeed, the canvas, decoration, cat shelter would be just as possible and useful if the posters that congealed together were advertising events that actually took place, never took place, or were completely imaginary. The contents of those flyers matter less (at least for the cats seeking shelter) than the fact that they were pasted over and over again until they congealed. They took on a life apart from their contents.

This image serves as a kind of visual metaphor for my own understanding of archives. Each individual artifact within an archive testifies and speaks in any number of ways. Documents articulate a kind of memory that can help its reader to navigate particular moments of history. Preserved testimonies from archives assure that certain moments in time are not forgotten or erased from public memory. And yet, archives are also a layered amalgamation of these materials, ideas, narratives, images, and things. They take on new shapes. New weights. New uses. Whatever evidence each flyer or poster contained had now condensed and congealed into a kind of totality. This dense totality does not reference any particular element composing that whole. At the same time, this congealed mass of thick evidence still serves some kind of referential function.

While we typically think about archives vis-à-vis the archival contents, I propose that we also consider how archives congeal into contingent totalities. To be clear, there is an important distinction between the "contingent totality" of thick evidence and a naïve belief that archives can ever tell a "whole truth." While critics argue that we must acknowledge the partial, fragmented nature of archives, we can also witness how those partial and fragmented layers congeal in transformative ways.

To some extent, I am drawing upon much older theories of rhetorical density, such as accumulation, amplification, and incrementum. The incrementum, for example, operates via accumulation to achieve particular rhetorical impact. Henry Peacham's 1593 *The Garden of Eloquence* describes the incrementum like this:

> Incrementum is a form of speech, which by degrees ascendeth to the top of some thing or rather above the top, that is, when we make our saying grow, & increase by an orderly placing of wordes making the latter word alwaies exceede the former in the force of signification, contrarie to the naturall order fo thinges, for that ever putteth the worthiest, and weighiest words first, but this placeth them alwaies last, as in this example: O my Parmeno the beginnger, the enterpriser, performer and accomplisher of all my pleasures.

The incrementum is a version of the more familiar device called amplification (auxesis), which is perhaps most thoroughly outlined in Longinus's *On the Sublime*. Longinus takes issue with the ways that amplification had formerly been taught in textbooks, where amplification was reduced to "discourse which invests the subject with grandeur" (77). This is far too generic, he objects. Sublimity, pathos, and other rhetorical figures also add grandeur to a subject, after all, yet these effects are often achieved "in a single thought, while amplification is universally associated with a certain magnitude and abundance" (77). Amplification for Longinus possesses a quantitative character, which passes over into a quality. He wishes for his readers to understand amplification as "an aggregation of all the constituent parts and topics of a subject, lending strength to the argument by dwelling upon it" (77). For Longinus, amplification possesses a density that goes beyond mere adornment of pathos.

Accumulation and rhetorical density thus generate impacts that are not necessarily tied to emotional qualities. As the writer of *Rhetorica ad Heren-*

nium puts it, the impacts of accumulation are less emotional and more akin to spatialization. The writer describes accumulation as that which

> occurs when the points scattered throughout the whole cause are collected in one place so as to make the speech more impressive or sharp or accusatory, as follows: "From what vice, I ask, is this defendant free? What ground have you for wishing to acquit him of the suit? He is a betrayer of his own self-respect, and the waylayer of the self-respect of others; covetous, intemperate, irascible, arrogant; disloyal to his parents, ungrateful to his friends, troublesome to his kin; insulting to his betters, disdainful of his equals and mates, cruel to his inferiors; in short he is intolerable to every one." (qtd. in Bizzell and Herzberg 272)

This translated harangue against an unsavory defendant reveals something about rhetorical impact through accumulation and spatialization, apart from the rant's emotional contents alone. Consider the lengthy sentence detailing the knocks against this jerk:

> He is a betrayer of his own self-respect, and the waylayer of the self-respect of others; covetous, intemperate, irascible, arrogant; disloyal to his parents, ungrateful to his friends, troublesome to his kin; insulting to his betters, disdainful of his equals and mates, cruel to his inferiors; in short he is intolerable to every one.

Each of these accusations is serious enough. He is irascible, which sounds quite unpleasant. As a subordinate, he also appears to be problematic with his insults. And to those whom he is a superior, he is cruel. Not even his kin are spared, including his own parents. The picture painted by each clause reflects all sides of a man who does indeed seem to be dreadful. As the translation weaves these phrases together, however, we also see a kind of totality emerge. There is a kind of autonomous density to the passage that operates beyond or beside the individual pieces that compose it. In its own small way, the passage has the qualities of thick evidence: accumulation of small pieces that emerge as a thing.

In its English translation, this impact of accumulation and spatialization depends upon on a very small implement: the semicolon. This grammatical device marks what could be a full stop, but for some reason the writer chose to let the second part linger on. Angela Petit points out that historical linguistics renders the semicolon as "more rhetoric than rule" (68). Petit argues that the semicolon is a stylistic and rhetorical choice, as opposed to other grammatical markers that must be used in order to clearly signal meaning, such as the comma, period, or question mark. The semicolon links together ideas or phrases that would, in the writer's estimation, lose some impact from their separation. In this sense, the semicolon is best understood as creating impacts through both accumulation and spatialization. This miniature stylistic feature is one example of how rhetorical accumulation, or what I term *thick evidence,* manages to create palpable impact through an experience of densities.

SCOPE AND CONTENTS: "FIGURATION"

Thicknesses and densities are crucial for understanding an even more important feature of archives and evidence. To put it plainly: Archival densities are acts of figuration. To explain what I mean, I will briefly return to the streets of Tel Aviv where I witnessed the wall of flyers being torn down. Thanks to the all-seeing eye of Google Earth maps, I can actually take you to the very street corner where this incident took place. At the street-level view of Google Earth, I can engage with the specific details of a street corner by looking at the crosswalks, the buildings, or even the graffiti covering a nearby sign. I could move the map slightly farther along this street-level view in order to show you the spot where my daughter threw a tantrum because we refused to buy her a second scoop of ice cream.

This digital mapping technology also allows me to shift levels of sight, "zooming out" and into a wider scale beyond street level. As I change the scale, these details along Rothschild Boulevard qualitatively transfigure and refigure. I can zoom out into a view that shows a satellite view of Tel Aviv and other cities in Israel, but they now show up in their geological details of mountains, valleys, seas, and rivers. Whereas I might have used the street-level image to reference our summer apartment's location, this wider-scale map may be deployed and referenced in a wildly divergent range of discourses, including political and social. The wider-scale map certainly includes the street where I witnessed poster removal (and where my daughter demanded more ice cream), yet those details are condensed into a much different thing altogether.

The tiny details of children's tantrums and street cleaning are no longer referenced (at least not easily) in this wider-scale map. Instead, those details have been transfigured and now more easily deployed as a different type of reference: Zionist, anti-Zionist, or whatever else one might say about this thing. Zooming out even more, we could pull all the way back from this satellite view in order to condense further. The satellite image of earth, round and familiar in its bluish tint, can again be deployed and referenced in an endless number of different ways. The details that compose "earth," such as cities and territories and continents, become "thick evidence" that merges into new singularity deployable in various discourses; the details that were previously intelligible now coalesce into a new object. Rothschild Avenue becomes Tel Aviv, which becomes the Middle East region, which becomes earth. While the coalesced object is not more than the sum of its parts, it is other than the sum of its parts.

Whether we describe rhetorical density and accumulation via tropes, stylistics, or scale, the underlying operative function is one of figuration. In figuration, no details are actually gained or lost. Instead, a different kind of figure emerges from the accumulating densities. Each new congealment marks an object of thick evidence, an act of figuration. Diane Davis draws from Paul de Man, Emanuel Levinas, and Martin Heidegger in her description of figuration as "a performative gesture that gives form to formless indeterminacy" (*Inessential* 38). It is a world-giving act in which we come to know the world not through empirical data in their pure form, but instead through words-as-figures that give those empirical data a shape and form. What I am describing broadly as an "archive" is another way of describing a figuration of evidence. It is this figuration of "thick evidence" that interests me—when details become "formed" as a kind of body.

Importantly, figuration is more than a process of change or transformation. While the differences may seem slight, philosopher Owen Barfield's notes on cognition help to illuminate the distinction. Barfield explains that the conversion of unrepresentative "particles" into sensations requires something from the percipient herself. This "something" is what he comes to define as "figuration" (24). Each body must perform what Barfield calls the "work of construction" in order to coalesce sounds, bits of color and light, or movement into "the recognizable and namable objects we call 'things'" (24). For Barfield, figuration is the active work of constructing bits into objects, things, thicknesses. There is no independent transformation without a body there to figure them out. Barfield's meditation on cognition might also be described in terms of density: Particles become sensations when they accumulate enough density in order to be namable as (a) figure. In much the same way as my rescaled digital map become new "things" at each new scale, figuration is the ongoing process of naming and recognizing new objects at each new stage of density.

Likewise, an archive also involves the ongoing work of figuration. As Hamilton et al. put it, "The archive—all archives—every archive is figured" (7). My interest throughout this book is in a particular moment of figuration where evidence is concerned. I am less interested in whether arguments reference "real" evidence than I am in better understanding what we bring before

the eyes when we reference evidence at all. As I suggest throughout the following chapters, we are often not actually bringing the details or contents of
an archive into view, even when we imagine that this is what we're doing. We
are instead bringing into view a figuration, a density. Being so figured, every
archive is a coalescence that exceeds the referentiality of its contents.

GORGOYLIAN METHODS

Exploring the affective lifeworld of evidence calls for us to engage with uneven,
difficult, or anomalous claims. My method for thinking through this lifeworld
is also best described as anomalous. In the chapters that follow, I have chosen to read case studies that are themselves a bit off-kilter in order to bring
my speculative inquiry into sharp focus. Not only are the cases weird, then,
but my methodology might also seem strange. However, it's not that there is
a method to my strangeness as much as *strangeness is a method*. Imagining
new rhetorical models of evidence and response in public discourse requires
a degree of estrangement from our more familiar routes.

The chapters of *Awful Archives* unfold through stylistic mercuriality,
to borrow a phrase from Kenneth Burke (*Permanence* 69). Putting things
together in an unfamiliar proximity can be unsettling, which is precisely what
Burke advocates. This unsettling movement is part of the method I find useful. Deliberate unsettling is, Burke writes, "an attempt (or temptation?) to
think in ways to which the deliberator was not accustomed" (xlvii). Burke
also describes this method as "perspectives by incongruity," which is "the
realm of 'gargoyles" (69). If I had to give a name to the methodology I deploy
across each chapter, then, I would be tempted to simply call it *gargoylian*.
The gargoyle chimera is a previously unimagined and unseen creature who
only exists through strange incongruities: lion body with human head, cat
with bat wings, human body with bird head. Something new is made from
strange juxtaposition. Making or seeing something new is my hope, and it is
also the reason why I have chosen to work through a sometimes unsettling
methodology.

My research draws from a number of different practices, ranging from traditional fieldwork to archival research to personal narrative. When I began my
first stages of research, I dove into the world of 9/11 truthers, or those who did
not believe the government's official story of September 11, 2001. I attended
several "9/11 truth" conferences and meet-ups, where I encountered the complex world of conspiracy rhetoric. For the next two years, I interviewed nearly

one hundred conspiracy theorists, many of whom identified as "9/11 truthers," but also subscribed to a number of other conspiracy theories. I met my interviewees from online discussions I was following, as well as from in-person meetings I attended. While I had initially expected interviewees to be suspicious of an academic claiming to be writing a book on conspiracy theory, I found that a majority of them were comfortable sharing their stories with me.

I also spent considerable time "in the archives," though some of the archives resembled nothing like the hallowed and peaceful institutional special collections rooms. I was fortunate enough to conduct a significant amount of research in the archives of the Southern Poverty Law Center's Intelligence Project, housed at Duke University's Rubenstein Library. I also found myself working in strange spaces, like Christiania's archives in Copenhagen. Christiania is the longest-running anarchist community in the world, housing over 1,000 residents all living according to communal, anarchist principles. The various archival spaces I visited similarly tottered between the institutional and the bizarre.

In addition to fieldwork and archival research, *Awful Archives* is also interwoven with personal narrative. We already know that the researcher is not without a body, nor without a history, and both are certainly the case for me. Besides being a writing body, I include personal narrative here as a performative methodology. My narratives are not empirical evidence; they are the affective residue of evidence in other registers. To borrow from Sedgwick's description of her own performative methodology, I write performatively in order to "de-emphasize the epistemology of evidence" and instead stress its affectivity.

Finally, I should note that the chapters of *Awful Archives* do not necessarily progress teleologically, although the concepts in earlier chapters do help to illuminate concepts in later chapters. Each chapter examines a different dimension of evidence as an act, a living process. I employ different sets of vocabulary and concepts in each chapter in order to highlight the multiple registers of evidence. As this book's title hints, the idea of "awfulness" runs throughout each chapter, yet not always or only in a pejorative sense. The word *awful* playfully slides between more familiar definitions and a sense of awe-fullness. Therefore, resonating across all chapters is the question: *How does evidence work in awe-full ways?* The first three chapters are especially focused on this driving question, offering three different rhetorical models for expanding current concepts of evidence. While readers might note that these three different perspectives overlap, the chapters emphasize distinct features of the evidentiary process. Meanwhile, the fourth, fifth, and sixth chapters look at evidence from the perspective of counter-evidence, or moments of rhetorical response. *What can we do with awe-full evidence?*

Chapter 1, "Bits in Motion: On Archival Aura," focuses especially on the *action* of building archives. I argue that the building, making, and maintaining of archives generates "archival aura," or an affective sense that surrounds archives without necessarily being located in their contents. My case studies in this chapter range from the CIA Stargate Project to Nazi archival practices during the Holocaust. Drawing from Walter Benjamin's theory of aura as a "medium of perception," I imagine archival aura as a kind of affective glue that holds together patchworks of evidence in order to uphold particular ideologies.

Chapter 2, "Prolific Archives: Notes from Trutherworld," looks more closely at how archival aura emerges through evidentiary proliferation, or those instances where evidence borders on the excessive. My case study in this chapter examines conspiracy theories surrounding the events of 9/11. Drawing upon Aristotle's concept of *megethos,* or magnitude, I argue that the proliferation of "evidence" in conspiracy discourse refigures individual pieces of data into a qualitatively coherent whole. The huge quantity of evidence offered by 9/11 conspiracy theorists serves as an example of how quantities of data are rhetorically transformed into qualities.

Meanwhile, chapter 3, "Distal Evidence and the Power of Empty Archives," looks at the flip side of evidentiary proliferation: missing, absent, or empty evidence. The chapter begins with two archival anomalies. The first case stems from the missing original Apollo 11 tapes from the 1969 Eagle landing. For years, conspiracy theorists have pointed to these "missing" archives as evidence that Apollo 11 never landed on the moon. On a slightly different note, the second case deals with "found" archival material that purports to be top-secret military documents exposing UFO activity. Both of these cases point to instances where *something else* beyond contents is referenced in archival materials. I ask how archives such as these operate rhetorically, beyond their fidelity to facts or authenticity. In short, what is the real referent of those claims? I use these cases in order to expose evidence as an experiential and bodily phenomenon, and not merely a thing that exists "out there."

After tracing out the lifeworld of evidence in the first three chapters, I then turn to the question of a "fitting response" where troubling evidence and claims are concerned. Chapter 4, "Disfigurement: Finding the Unfitting Response," begins with the Obama "birthers," a group that claims that President Obama was actually born in Kenya. For years, birthers have circulated "evidence" that proves the official Obama birth record is a forgery. Some have even circulated copies of Obama's (supposedly) real Kenyan birth certificate.

I point to birther rhetoric as an instance of figuration. Therefore, in searching for a fitting response to these kinds of claims, I turn to the prospect of disfiguration, a term Diane Davis defines as "the spontaneous unworking of the work of the figure" (50). I argue that the rhetorical tactic of disfigurement can reorient our rhetorical responses in more ethical and productive ways.

In chapter 5, "Writing Demon Archives," I introduce another rhetorical strategy for responding to awful evidence by showing how flawed, faulty, and troubled archives can become the materials for an inventional writing practice. I use the strange case of Pizzagate in order to explore ways that we can write *with,* rather than merely *against,* evidence built from multiple registers. This chapter introduces the strategic writing practice of "demon archives" to pose an inventional question: *What can this archive do?* Building on the work of Giorgio Agamben and Hannah Arendt, I propose the *demon* as a guide for those who must wrestle with evidence that is absent, hidden, or flawed. The daimon is that which is disclosed to others, but never to us. As such, it can serve as a guide for engaging in acts of response that aim to invent new modes of public rhetorics.

My concluding outro, "The What and Where," plays us off stage to the gargoylian tunes I describe in previous chapters. This chapter imagines how all this theory might actually help us find new or different inroads to rhetorics born in a "post-truth" era. If evidence is an act, rather than a thing, then we should also imagine our responses to awful evidence in (and as) an active mode.

On one last note, I wish to offer the following chapters in the spirit of Kathleen Stewart's call for writing that cracks open questions instead of sealing them shut with answers. "Rather than rush to answer the general question—'what's going on?'—we might give pause to wedge into that question a speculative curiosity," she writes ("Atmospheric" 8). Stewart describes this kind of writing as that which aims to be not representation or critique, but "a cabinet of curiosities designed to *incite curiosity*" ("Cultural" 1029; emphasis added). I share Stewart's desire for writing that adopts speculative curiosity as a guiding ethic. Evidence is itself a cabinet of curiosities, and what follows is one attempt to pose an even more curious question: *What's going on?*

CHAPTER 1

Bits in Motion

On Archival Aura

THE CIA'S Stargate Project has all the makings of a typical conspiracy theory: a secret group inside the CIA running tests designed to harness human powers of extrasensory perceptions and telepathic projection. The ultimate goal is to use telepathy in order to retrieve sensitive intelligence information that is otherwise unobtainable. The strange thing is that it's all true. The CIA funded the Stargate Project from 1978 until 1995, and there are plenty of salacious stories to glean from those decades of secret testing. The program scooped up civilians with promising telepathic powers and honed their abilities to project themselves into buildings thousands of miles away and read sensitive documents.

Details about the Stargate Project continue to swirl with conspiracy theories, including speculation about whether this project was connected to the much darker CIA program known as MKUltra. Yet, the secrets of Stargate are not actually hidden at all. In 2017, all documents relating to Stargate were declassified and have since been made available for anyone to view on the CIA's website. I've read several accounts of this project, including Jon Ronson's popular *The Men Who Stare at Goats,* but there is something downright fascinating about looking through the documents themselves. The first time I encountered the Stargate Project archive, I sat at my computer and read documents for two straight hours. The typewritten transcripts of remote viewing sessions, the pages of hasty pencil drawings, the memos—they all held me in a fascination. They seemed to possess what Walter Benjamin calls "aura" (at least one version of it, anyway): "A strange web of space and time: the unique appearance of a distance, no matter how close it may be" ("Little" 285). Reading through the Stargate Project's mimeographed pages, I felt a kind of near-distance. Here was the real thing, yet it still somehow felt otherworldly. That archive is strange.

The transcripts of remote viewing sessions describe viewers moving through buildings that are physically located thousands of miles away. They describe what the buildings looks like, who is inside them, and what objects can be found lying around. In one transcribed session from August 28, 1980, a viewer (called #07 in the document) walks through rooms and tells the experimenter what he finds. When #07 reports seeing some kind of restricted office, a room with a "black feeling, dark, . . . threatening," the experimenter instructs him to look closely at what's on the desk. Stepping close, #07 says, "Looks like . . . giant scrapbook with all kinds of different documents taped to the big pages . . . some of the stuff looks like clippings, but there's actually some typewritten pages, photographs, jotted data . . ." (Central Intelligence Agency, "Summary Analysis D-12"). He then moves to other rooms, searching for any important detail he can report back.

These transcripts remind me of my own experiment with remote viewing. On a rainy Saturday, I found myself in a giant warehouse that was hosting a psychic fair. There were booths and tables everywhere, all advertising tarot readings, chakra realignment, and so on. I strolled through the aisles and found a woman in a makeshift tent offering to read people's "Akashic Records." I had never heard of Akashic Records before, so I signed up for a thirty-minute session. As it turns out, the Akashic Records are the ultimate archive for all living beings. They are the spiritual records of all events, words, feelings, thoughts that have existed in the past, present, and future. My reader explained that she could look into my records—sort of a celestial Google search—and tell me where I came from in past lives. Thirty-five dollars for a thirty-minute reading, local checks accepted.

After a few minutes of quiet meditation, my reader suddenly opened her eyes and began telling me about my past life in the Pleiades stellar constellation, as one of the light beings whose only desire is to love and help and spread ultimate peace. She then took my hands, looked into my eyes, and started talking softly about my aura. *My aura is warm,* she told me. *It is also hurting, which makes sense given my sensitive Pleiadian origins. Would I mind if she did some aura work to help me heal?* From a few feet away, she moved her hands up and down my body in order to pull out the negative energies she saw. Her eyes were closed and she half-whispered, half-sang, "I'm just moving the energy now. Just moving the energy." At the end of the session, she asked if I felt anything. In complete honesty, I answered yes.

As someone with a disdain for spiritualism and theosophy, Benjamin undoubtedly would have hated the way my psychic reader used the word *aura*. However, while Benjamin's concept of aura is most often familiar to us through his (later) connection to beauty, he also describes aura as an affective encounter between two bodies. In "Little History of Photography," for example, Benjamin describes aura in this kind of relational sense:

> Experience of the aura . . . arises from the transposition of a response characteristic of human society to the relationship of the inanimate or nature with human beings. The person we look at, or who feels he is being looked at, looks at us in turn. To experience the aura of a phenomenon we look at means to invest it with the ability to look back at us. (qtd. in Hansen 343)

According to Miriam Bratu Hansen, Benjamin's aura operates as a "medium of perception" (342). It belongs neither to the object nor to the seer alone, but is a medium that conducts a certain kind of seeing. She notes that his hashish experiments "pursued the paradoxical entwinement of distance and nearness as a visionary mode epitomized by the psychophysiological state of Rausch or ecstatic trance" (Hansen 354–55). Benjamin's hashish writings sometimes read very much like a strange visit to the psychic fair, filled with reflections on "automatic connections" and "loosened objects . . . lured . . . from their accustomed world" before being "inserted . . . quite quickly into a new one" (*On Hashish* 27). In one of his entries while on hash, Benjamin writes: "[Ernest] Bloch wanted to touch my knee gently. I could feel the contact long before it reached me. I felt it as a highly repugnant violation of my aura" (*On Hashish* 27). Good touch / bad touch aside, this felt contact is real.

Aura seems to be not only a mode of perception, therefore, but also a mode of conduction. To be sure, describing aura as "a medium of conduction" would likely rub Benjamin the wrong way. But this description became palpable to me as I received my auratic tune-up. It was not that my psychic actually pulled any negative energies from my body (at least, I don't think she did), yet something nevertheless showed up in that exchange between us. Perhaps it was a mutual desire to imagine energies, or the affective intensity of having hands move so close to my body as she closed her eyes and whispered words I could not hear. That moment was one of conduction, generating something between two bodies that does not reside within either one alone. I did not feel "my aura" move, but I did feel an affective impact of whatever was generated in that exchange. Something showed up.

Obsessively poring through the CIA's Stargate archives also caused something to show up. I choose my phrasing quite deliberately, as there is an important aspect of aura connected to the act of poring. Benjamin suggests something similar in "Unpacking My Library," where he reflects on his enthrallment with the act of prying open wooden crates, lifting his books from their crates, holding them in his hands. "Nothing highlights the fascination of unpacking more clearly than the difficulty of stopping," he says (66). For Benjamin, it is not the books themselves that hold fascination, but unpacking and poring over them. He reflects on the book collector's enchantment with the act of building a collection. "What I am really concerned with is giving you some insight . . . into collecting rather than a collection," he writes (59–60). Benjamin describes the very Rausch-like aura that comes from traveling to bookshops, bidding in auctions, holding books, shelving them, looking, browsing, planning, arranging. He writes, "The most profound enchantment for the collector is the locking of individual items within a magic circle in which they are fixed as the final thrill . . . passes over them" (60). This sentence could be read in a way such that the profound enchantment refers to the magic circle of acquisition, but I tend to read the collector's enchantment as found in the act of locking.

Whatever archival aura is, it is not necessarily reducible to the contents of that archive, which is why Benjamin emphasizes that he is speaking of "collecting rather than a collection." There is an entwinement between activity and aura. Likewise, my Stargate fascination cannot be described merely in terms of the documents' details (weird as they are), since I already knew about most of the particulars before ever searching the archive. Just as Benjamin found something meaning-full in the act of unpacking and collecting, I also sense a relationship between acts of archiving and the auratic modes of conductions that accompany such activity. Here we are shifting focus away from archives as fixed referents and more toward what Michael Lynch calls "archives in formation," which can be productively discussed apart from archival information (83). Rather than taking the collection and its contents as a starting place for meaning, therefore, this chapter aims to begin with archives in formation: their building, making, growing, arranging, destroying, moving, reading, poring. What are we to make of the aura that hovers around this activity? How does such archival aura generate specific orientations? And what, if anything, can archival aura tell us about the lifeworld of evidence?

USE AND PURPOSE

It probably goes without saying that archives are always performative. Even something so mundane as record-keeping is a form of rhetorical work, generating meaning beyond the contents of those records. Archival scholar Ciaran P. Trace offers a helpful distinction in order to draw out the different kinds of work done by archival contents and the act of archiving itself. She begins by differentiating the *use* of records from the *purpose* of records. Use refers to the records' ability to help organizations conduct and maintain their operations. The purpose of records, however, is different. Trace explains that records "are created in anticipation of future as well as current uses (both within and outside of the organization) and . . . these other uses are (or will be) more than the purely technical" (153). For instance, an employee might maintain records in a way that will hopefully show that she is a reliable and organized worker. As Trace argues, "records are not necessarily (or only) technical artifacts, but designed to produce an effect" (155). It's the stuff that dreams of promotion are made of.

In thinking about the uses and purposes of Stargate's archive, I am struck by how mundane those records are. When I read the transcript of #07's viewing session, my first response was disappointment. Here was a (supposedly) real out-of-body travel account, and the biggest thing #07 reported back was finding a scrapbook. Hardly the kind of scintillating detail you might expect. Then again, scrapbooks aren't exactly mundane. They are some of the most fraught of records. I learned this in the middle of researching the Stargate archive, when my father called me to say that he had been diagnosed with Stage IV bile duct cancer. He was dying. I drove fifteen hours to my parents' house to do the things you are supposed to do when your father is dying. It was like I was experiencing pre-grief, or some kind of early stage mourning before the real mourning kicks in. I rummaged through boxes that been sitting in the basement for years. I gathered up all my parents' old scrapbooks, about ten in all, stuffed with records of some great but mostly mundane aspects of our family's world.

Nine months after a terrible course of chemotherapy and surgeries, my father died. My anguish drove me to alternate between sessions of crying, writing, and reading through his biggest scrapbook. My father meticulously documented each detail of his life, from the time he was a teenager up through the earliest years of my parents' marriage. He pasted ticket stubs from ferry rides, receipts from his proud first purchase of a mobile home, his mechanic's license, and almost anything that marked a major point in his life. I could touch these artifacts for myself, hearing him tell stories that I had never heard before (and some I had). Each time I looked at the pages, I marveled at his dedication to preserving memories in this way. It felt like a gift that he had been building his whole life.

At the same time, I was suddenly struck by intense guilt about my own scrapbooking failures. When I die, it is very unlikely that my children will be able to grab piles of scrapbooks that I carefully assembled. There are none. I am a scrapbook failure. A dropout. I have walked into craft stores and carefully selected special papers and small adornments for each page, yet I have never even finished more than a couple of pages. My twelve-year-old daughter's baby book is only halfway filled, and my eight-year-old son's baby book is still in its wrapper. Maybe *guilt* is not quite the right word, since it feels like an uncanny mix of shame, sadness, or even disgrace. This hovering affect feels conductive, almost like an affective circuitry is operating. *Things show up.* While it is not novel to say that archives have an auratic quality to them, what I experience with my father's scrapbook (or in a psychic's tent, for that matter) is not locatable in the contents themselves. Rather, this aura seems to hover *around* archives, floating on the surface without ever touching the pages.

The distinction between use and purpose of archives can help to explain some of this hovering. Baby books as a technical artifact have a definite use, for instance. They first appeared in mass-marketed form around 1910 and were advertised as a way to record a baby's metrics for home records, as well as more personal details that mark events that might otherwise be forgotten over time: who attended the first birthday party, which songs a child loved the most as a toddler, what was the first full sentence a child said. When I was a new first-time mother, worried about every little strange sound or sneeze my infant had, I copied down her weight and appearance on the appropriate baby book pages. I would regularly look back at these numbers during her first few months, just to make sure she was progressing "normally." I checked the numbers from one month to another, trying to determine whether she was gaining weight along a normal schedule. When she broke out in a rash, I looked to see whether the same thing happened in prior months around the same time. Every entry was cross-checked with previous entries, all in an effort to make sure my newborn was not on the edge of death. This is an example of what Trace calls the use of records.

That first baby book also had specific purposes for me. I carried my daughter's book with me to every doctor visit for at least the first four months of her life. I knew that the doctors had all the same information I had recorded, but I thought perhaps having my own records neatly organized would make them take me more seriously when I expressed concerns. My hyperactive and exhausted new parent brain would inevitably conclude that the rash she had was a sign of some rare disease. I would show the doctor how carefully I had documented the "signs" in her baby book. *Look how carefully I observe her. Look at all this data. Look how not crazy I am.* Beyond the immediate use of these records, therefore, the baby book also served a particular purpose, designed to produce an effect for her doctors and for myself. Although I did not provide much more information than they had in their charts, I counted on the neat, orderly, detailed lists and notes to show them (and myself) that I was a competent mother, something I did not always fully believe in my daughter's first year.

This distinction between use and purpose suggests that contents of records are not the only active parts of archives. The *purpose* of archives (what goes beyond their immediate *use*) is not necessarily embedded within the contents or information of those records. Arguably, this affective hovering has been embedded within the work of scrapbooking since its popular emergence in the Victorian era. Going far beyond the useful preservation of family histories, Victorian-era scrapbooking was a means of inculcating a particular sensibility in the books' makers. As Susan Tucker et al. write, in the late nineteenth century, writers regularly proclaimed that scrapbooking had the moral benefit of eliminating idleness and unfocused attention, occupying hours that might otherwise be spent unwisely. As such, the activity of making scrapbooks was considered an act of creating moral and ethical virtue. One 1894 article, titled "Preserver of Literary Derelicts," published in the *Kansas City Star*, sounds almost biblical in the declaration: "Who so keepeth a scrapbook keepeth a good thing, and the manner in which it is kept is an indication of the presence or absence of certain qualities in the 'keeper,' as order, perseverance, continuity of purpose and fixedness of memory." Who exactly counts as "literary derelicts" is never specified, so I can only assume that those who fail to keep a scrapbook might be one of them. For the keepers, virtues like perseverance and order almost become embodied through the act of scrapbooking itself. It is not the *scrapbook* that inculcates such general virtue, therefore, but the act of *scrapbooking* that produces these effects (and affects).

Pragmatically, I have no reason to feel guilt about failing to document my kids' every stage of development. Their whole lives have practically been recorded and posted online for friends and family to share. If my children ever desire to see an archive of their life, it exists in digital form. This is the case for most parents in the twenty-first century. I have endless photos and videos of my children's most amazing and most mundane activities. We watch home videos and talk about the stories behind them, like the time my husband accidently bumped into my three-year-old son, who then angrily shouted: "*Daddy!* You *destroyed* me!" If evidence of milestones is what my kids want, they are able to call them up with a few clicks of a button. Still, there is something not quite *present* in these kinds of unpremeditated digital memory collections. Through the work of making, doing, and building an archive—even if only a scrapbook—an auratic *something* materializes. Could it be that my kids' ad hoc digital memory library gets the use right, but screws up the purpose?

_____ING UP

And there it is: I am afraid of screwing up. Like any parent (or any writer, for that matter), I really hate screwing up. At the same time, screwing up is interesting in the context of this look at archives and aura. What would it mean if I was indeed screwing up right now? What does it mean to fear screwing up my kids, or this chapter, or this book, or my choice of research areas? It's curious to see how many of the Stargate transcripts are filled with worries about screwing up. In a remote viewing session from 1980, the subject (called #10.5) attempts to "travel" psychically to a distant building, but soon finds himself frustrated: "I'm not getting anything. I'm zeroed out, something doesn't fit. Something is all screwed up. . . . It's very sparse. I'm like wandering all over the universe looking for answers and I'm not staying in one place" (Central Intelligence Agency, "Transcript"). For #10.5, feeling "all screwed up" involves a kind of disorientation. In a different session, a viewer called #10 expresses similar frustration with his lack of orientation. "I can't seem to settle in one place," #10 tells the experimenter. "And, I . . . it just keeps changing on me. Which, I'm really screwed up now" (Central Intelligence Agency, "Remote").

More than a sense of getting something wrong, screwing up encompasses a bigger sense of place in the world. Screwing up involves our relative orientations in a given moment. (Or, in the case of the Stargate remote viewers, screwing up involves a disorientation.) I find *screwing up* interesting in how its rhetorical configuration reaches out with ontological feelers. In fact, we do not necessarily have to stop with *screwing up*. Take any phrase built in the model of _____*ing up*: *gearing up, suiting up, owning up, wising up, manning up, bellying up, storing up, ramping up.* Embedded within these phrases is some kind of concrete action. Owning up, for example, is something I do when I make a mistake and finally admit it. When I say that I am ramping up for a semester's beginning, it usually involves things like finishing my syllabus and getting my course materials together. Wising up is me reconsidering some wrongheaded belief or wish.

These phrases reference a way of being, even if temporary. *Owning up* is more than me admitting a mistake; it also describes an orientation to the world and those around me. I become more deferential to those who I previously felt much differently toward. *Ramping up,* too, describes my way of being in a given moment, more focused and intense. Even a phrase like *growing up* can refer on one hand to specific physiological changes—getting taller, growing older, gaining emotional maturity—but it just as often signals a changing way of being in the world. When my tween daughter, Vered, recently complained about some drama among her friends, I offhandedly told her that growing up is hard. "Why?" she asked. I stumbled for an answer because, truthfully, I had not actually considered why. "Growing up makes you start seeing the world differently," I offered. "Like, the way you see yourself and your friends and the things you can and can't do. Growing up means your world changes." Maybe out of sheer Veredness, she smirked and asked, "Are you still growing up?" Hell yes.

I reflect on the constellation of ___*ing up* phrases because their terminological weirdness articulates a similar weirdness found in the activity that surrounds archives but is not coterminous with them. I am reaching for a descriptor that can offer a more nuanced sense of archiving. To a certain extent, I am talking about the activity of collecting, amassing, accumulating, and forming archives. However, on a connotative level, archiving (as accumulating, amassing, collecting) typically points us back to the archive. This makes sense, as we tend to do archiving in service of the archive. There is no archiving without an archive, even if it is a future archive that does not yet exist. Yet, my interest is not on the activity of archiving as it serves the archive, but rather the broader dimensions of that activity. I am interested in the *adding up* of archives.

We usually say things are adding up when fragments collect and a gestalt suddenly (or perhaps slowly) takes shape. In one of the most memorable scenes from *To Kill a Mockingbird,* Atticus Finch speaks passionately about the inevitable repercussions that have come from years of white violence against black people. "Don't fool yourselves," he says, "it's all adding up and one of these days we're going to pay the bill for it" (Lee 252). The "it" that is adding up is a pervasive constellation of moments, events, feelings, and impacts. They do not add up in a quantifiable way, but in a kind of affective density. The adding up of white racism is an ongoing making of a certain kind of world.

Finch's words point to the way that adding up involves both actions and orientations. Much like piling up, when things are adding up, they seem to accumulate on top of each other. Adding up also signals a kind of coherence emerging from that ongoing accumulation: a coherence that tells us how things really are. This is why we say that "things aren't adding up" to describe a lack of clarity, while "things aren't piling up" usually just means we are not overwhelmed with tasks. In relation to archives, adding up is a way of describing both archival accumulation, as well as the orienting coherencies that emerge from that accumulation. Adding up archives is therefore a mode of perception, to use the term we saw earlier in relation to aura.

There is a strong etymological tie between accumulation and coherence. From *cohaereo,* the word implies "sticking together." Coherence is accumulation—a sticking together until something feels whole. Coherence is a feeling. It is an experience that you've taken in something in a satisfactory way. One definition of *adding up* could be phrased like this: Adding up is the ongoing archival accumulation from which emerge new orientations among certain bodies. Or, there's the less formal definition: Adding up is what happens when all the shit being collected starts to look like *something.* Grammatically, then, *adding up* is more a gerund than a verb.

The world that Atticus Finch sees adding up is a violent one; it is a world that will break wide open at some point and demand accountability. It's a world that must be paid for. We could say that all addings up are world-making. They are a worlding, a term that we tend to attribute Heidegger's thinking on Weltlichkeit. Yet, as much as we might owe to Heidegger's worlds, theorists such as Kathleen Stewart and Lauren Berlant have expanded upon Weltlichkeit in order to more fully demonstrate worlding's affective edges. In her descriptions of worldings, for example, Stewart writes about attunements and atmospheres and "the sentience of a situation" ("Atmospheric" 449). She traces the affects and rhythms that shoot through everyday life, drawing together certain bodies, thoughts, materials, feelings, beliefs until "elements of all kinds assemble into something that feels like something ("Atmospheric" 445). Worlding, according to Stewart, is "an attunement to a singular world's texture and shine" ("Worlding" 341). That singular world shows up for us in a given moment, though it may drop away just as quickly as it came. Or it may hang around for a while.

Worlding is thus more than the experience of life's affective jolts and drags. As Berlant describes it, worlding is "the activity of sensual world-making, of finding one's sea legs in the middle of a situation and doing something to sustain it" ("Unworlding"). This phrase strikes me in the way it recalls my past attempts to "find my sea legs" on the few boats I have been aboard. Ungraceful as a newborn deer, I remember trying to transpose steadiness onto my unsteady legs. Once my body attuned to that boat's peculiar rocky rhythms, it seemed to instinctively counterbalance against the next coming shift until I was steady. This image parallels the "sea legging" that happens in worlding, where the unsteady gathering of things becomes that from which we steady ourselves into a solid state. The solidity and steadiness of sea legs are illusions, of course. Steadiness on an unsteady boat is the sense that shows up in this encounter between body, waves, boat. However, though I no longer feel my body moving in small shifts in order to maintain by balance on that boat, I am not truly steady. My sense of steadiness—that steadiness is the way things are here—is auratic.

Worldings unfold alongside aura, allowing us to get a sense of *the ways things are* within that unfolding. Thus, in worlding, in the adding up of archives, bodies are oriented in particular ways that become sensible through the aura simultaneously generated. Worlding itself is simply another way of describing our means of orienting. Reading, poring, making, collecting, packing, unpacking, constructing, deconstructing, archiving—these acts orient us in the world in particular ways, orienting our perceptions and modes of conduction.

ARCHIVING AS WORLDING

Reading through the CIA Stargate Project archives is a weird world(ing). On the surface, these documents are strange in the way they present bizarre paranormal investigations in the form of mundane bureaucratic documents. The CIA released the Stargate archives online in 2017, along with millions of other declassified documents that spanned the agency's beginning years up to 1981. The Stargate Project documents were only a tiny piece of the CIA records released to the public. Other documents include archives that, while formerly classified, were what we might expect from the CIA's vaults: Cold War intelligence, international cables, presidential briefings, and so on. In some ways, the strangeness of a program designed to test (and potentially weaponize) psychic energies melted into the flood of weirdly normal bureaucratic business.

The foggy history of Stargate also raises some other questions about modes of conduction, perception, and orientation. In her book *Phenomena: The Secret History of the US Government's Investigations into Extrasensory Perception and Psychokinesis,* journalist Annie Jacobsen argues that the US's interest in psychic abilities was kindled by the post-WWII discovery of research conducted by the Uberprüfung der Sogenannten Geheimwissenschaften, a branch of Heinrich Himmler's Nazi Institute for Research and Study of Heredity (Das Ahnenerbe). This peculiar branch was not only dedicated to finding scientific evidence of Teutonic superiority, but it also dove headfirst into mysticism and the occult. The Uberprüfung der Sogenannten Geheimwissenschaften, translated as Survey of the So-Called Occult Sciences, conducted experiments with extrasensory perception, astrology, and other paranormal phenomena. Jacobsen writes that at the end of the war, "it was from the Ahnenerbe documentation on these unusual subjects, captured separately from the United States and the Red Army, that the psychic arms race between the Soviet Union and the United States first got under way" (18). Indeed, the Stargate archives reflect just how closely the US government was measuring their own paranormal progress against the Soviets. The Cold War was literally going mental.

One fascinating detail about the Stargate archives is the way that the strange is documented so normally, with banal agency-speak and prosaic report language. The anomaly of punctuated reality flows seamlessly into business as usual. Speculating on the use and purpose of these weirdly normal artifacts of bureaucracy, we might imagine that one purpose behind these kinds of banalities was to perform normality for those government skeptics who doubted the worth of the entire Stargate program. Rather than emphasizing the bizarre and unorthodox protocols, these records are infused with a hovering sense of humdrum. Still, as unremarkable as they may seem, banality and humdrum are orienting coordinates. The humdrum is conductive, linking bodies together so that something *shows up* in particular modes of perception.

The archival humdrum of the Stargate documents echoes an important characteristic of the Third Reich's larger archival practice. The documents and records left by the Nazis are prosaic, mundane, and even dull. Yet, as many historians and critics have pointed out, this archival banality is part of what made the records so potent. "Archival principles were central to the ways in which the Nazis ruled their concentration camps and to their execution of the 'final solution,'" writes Ernst Van Alphen (369). Part of these principles included obsessive documentation as a strategy whose purpose exceeded its immediate use. Steve Katz shows a dark example in his analysis of a memo from the Nazi Party detailing how exactly extermination vans should be designed in order to maximize efficiency at killing their Jewish victims. The memo was written before the camps were operational, though exterminations were already taking place via mobile vans. The memo's language is extremely technical, almost shockingly so. In reference to the load capacity of each van, the memo states that the front axle should not be overloaded because "the merchandise aboard displays during the operation a natural tendency to rush to the rear doors, and is mainly found lying there at the end of the operation" (qtd. in Katz 255). The memo further recommends that for "easy cleaning of the vehicle," each vehicle should have a drainage hole "eight to twelve inches in diameter . . . equipped with a slanting trap, so that fluids can drain off during the operation" (qtd.

in Katz 256). Such language operates through an "ethos of expediency," writes Katz, or an ethos of organization, technicality, and precision.

In *Eichmann in Jerusalem,* Hannah Arendt likewise notes how the Holocaust unfolded through a "huge shower of regulations and directives," all designed to generate a bureaucratic buzz. "The resulting legal paraphernalia," writes Arendt, "far from being a mere symptom of German pedantry or thoroughness, served most effectively to give the whole business its outward appearance of legality" (149). Returning to Trace's distinction between the use and purpose of documents, we may read such Holocaust-related records operating along two parallel dark lines. Undoubtedly, the use of the extermination vehicle memo was to ensure that all vehicles met the specifics that would maximize each "operation." The purposes of the memo, however, have much deeper rhetorical impacts, generating an aura of technicality and even necessity around mass human extermination. Bernd Frohmann describes these rhetorical impacts as the "constitutive effects" of documents. It isn't the information that shapes a world, Frohmann argues, but, rather, the "effects . . . produced by encounters with *documents*" (82).

Concentration camps also reflect the darkly constitutive effects of Nazi documentation. As Van Alphen argues, the camps themselves "archived" their victims' bodies:

> On arrival, new detainees would have a number tattooed on their arm. They were transformed into archived objects, no longer individuals with a name, but objects with a number. Like objects in an archive or museum, the inscription classified them as traceable elements within a collection. Upon entering the camps they were also sorted into groups: men with men, women with women; children, old people and pregnant women to the gas chambers. Political prisoners, resistance fighters were not "mixed" with Jews. Artists, musicians and architects were usually sent to camps like Theresienstadt. Selecting and sorting on the basis of a fixed set of categories are basic archival activities. (369)

It almost certainly seems the case that such archiving of bodies aided the camp operators in their drive to carry out "the final solution" with as much precision as possible. After all, the operation itself was an enormous undertaking, involving millions of people and their possessions. Keeping careful records of all these "objects" was useful to the Nazi mission. More than this, however, the Nazis' archival work vividly exposes the kind of afterlife, or adjacent effects, that archives have beyond their immediate use. To drain horror of its appearance, Nazi archiving generated a sense that the "operation" was one of control, precision, technicality, scientific correctness. The horror of the Holocaust was buried beneath this affective sense, this aura, which was continually fed by the ongoing work of archiving. It was all adding up.

Of course, there is nothing really banal or bloodlessly technical about the Uberprüfung der Sogenannten Geheimwissenschaften, an S. S. branch devoted to the occult and paranormal. Hitler himself detested this piece of the Nazi machinery, disgusted by what he considered backwards superstition practiced by men such as Rudolf Hess. On June 7, 1941, Hitler launched *Aktion Hess,* which pronounced that all instances of astrology and other occult practices were to be eliminated and suppressed by the State. Tarot cards, witchcraft, astrology, fortune telling—they were all outlawed under the Führer's orders. Undeterred, men like Himmler continued to wade deeply into the occult, even as Hitler railed against Himmler's paranormal predilections. "Here we have at last reached an age that has left all mysticism behind it, and now he [Himmler] wants to start that all over again. We might just as well have stayed with the church," complained the dictator (qtd. in Jacobsen 13). He wanted nothing to do with the mystical aura hovering around divination and the paranormal.

Then again, if Hitler believed the Nazis had left mysticism behind, he certainly must have understood that the power of archival aura was still very much in effect. Such power is found, for example, in the Ahnenpass. In the wake of the Nazi regime's 1935 racial laws, Germans were expected to create and maintain an Ahnenpass, racial documentation that proved their Aryan identity. As historian Peter Fritzsche writes in *Life and Death in the Third Reich,* German citizens themselves were charged with creating their own Ahnenpass, collecting documents and materials that established their Aryan blood. This charge meant that Germans were instantly turned into both amateur genealogists and archivists. As one Aryan German described the process in 1933, "State archives and libraries have to be trawled . . . and also ranking lists, muster roles, telephone books, bills of lading, guild records. We also have to make our way to old cemeteries where tumble-down graves might reveal yet another clue" (qtd. in Fritzsche, *Life* 29). Germans could buy blank Ahnenpass books, much like the blank scrapbooks popularized in the US, which were to be filled with any kind of evidence that would make their blood purity case.

In his description of one typical Ahnenpass, Fritzsche lists the things that one average German citizen included: "an old labor pass; a four-leaf clover; a restaurant bill; a marriage license; birth announcements of children; baptismal certificates; inoculation records; divorce papers; insurance cards; Winter Relief stamps; and also a father's correspondence with his son serving on the front" (*Life* 79). These materials are not too far from what might appear in any family scrapbook, yet their purpose was quite different in the Nazi regime.

Because there was no set standard for what an Ahnenpass must include, citizens were left to seek out and add as much as possible in order to establish their Aryan heredity.

The Ahnenpass had the immediate use of allowing its holder to apply for jobs or join clubs. It was useful as a racial passport that proved its owner to be qualified, bureaucratically speaking, for certain positions. Yet, the Ahnenpass also possessed a broader purpose, creating certain effects for German society as a whole. As Fritzsche writes, the Ahnenpass "was the exemplary artifact of the extraordinary ambition of the Nazis to recast Germans into a pure racial compact. . . . The passport forced Germans to think about race" (*Life* 76). The realness of racial difference become palpable through the aura surrounding the Ahnenpass. Race and racial purity radiated like a halo around the small books, stuffed full of ephemeral scraps from everyday life.

It is no accident that the aura of racial purity was tied to domestic archives like the Ahnenpass. Archives were key to the spread of such ideology in the Nazi regime. Fritzsche quotes the director of the Bavarian archival administration, Josef Franz Knöpfler, in a remarkable 1936 statement about archives: "There is no practice of racial politics without the mobilization of source documents, which indicate the origin and development of a race and people. . . . There is no racial politics without archives, without archivists" (Fritzsche, *The Archive* 26). The Ahnenpass, therefore, is only a small model of the larger Nazi deployment of domestic archives, which tied together home life, family, documents, and national-racial identity. Nazis "racialized vernacular archives since they obligated individual Germans to maintain extensive racial archives about their bodies, lives and families," writes Fritzsche ("The Archive" 27). Archives became more than a record of genealogy; they were the conductive lines of a national mood.

The Ahnenpass—or, more precisely, the act of making, building, and curating the Ahnenpass—is yet another instance of worlding. The Nazis built a coherent and technical sense of "race" and "racial purity" among citizens through ongoing accumulations of documents, materials, categories, paperwork. The significant amounts of labor among ordinary citizens is an adding up, all in the effort to not only create a useable racial archive but also reinforce a sense of how things really are. In adding up, therefore, they encounter a world that oriented bodies according to heredity and racial identity.

The artwork of Christian Boltanski serves as a guide for understanding the ways in which archival aura generates certain orientations toward the Holocaust. For decades, Boltanski's art installations feature archives as a way of addressing the Holocaust and its afterlife, a theme he takes up across many of his works. For example, his installation *Canada, 1988* features four walls that are covered, ceiling to floor, by thousands of ordinary garments hanging limply from nails. The shirts, pants, and coats hanging from the walls are so crowded together that it is impossible to see a single part of the walls behind them. Another exhibit, *Storage Area of the Children's Museum, 1989*, similarly features wall-to-wall metal shelves stuffed full of clothing, this time folded into piles that take up every possible space on the shelves.

There is no clear reference to the Holocaust in Boltanski's works. Nevertheless, while reflecting on his artwork, Van Alphen argues that works like *Storage Area* do not directly reference the Holocaust as an event, yet "they have a Holocaust effect because they re-enact a principle that defines the Holocaust as a *method*" (369). Collecting people and property—collecting and archiving lives—was precisely the method of the Holocaust. That awful method is evoked through the effects of archival aura, existing both as part of and apart from the metal shelves and clothing. Van Alphen argues that Boltanski's work is not "Holocaust representation" but rather engages with the "Holocaust effect." We are much more used to approaching the Holocaust through the representational effect, argues Van Alphen. Films, books, and exhibits display photographs and material artifacts that seek to communicate a realism about what happened. The Holocaust effect, by comparison, "is not brought about by means of representing the Holocaust, but by means of the re-enactment of a certain principle that defines the Holocaust" (368). Boltanski's archives invent a way of speaking about the Holocaust without reliance on a representational mode.

Boltanski's artwork aims to confront us not only with the horrors of the Holocaust, therefore, but with the notion that archival aura as a powerful (and potentially horrifying) medium did not ever disappear. Indeed, writes Van Alphen quite pointedly, "if most Holocaust scholars and students privilege archival modes of research, they seem to be unaware of the fact that their privileged medium at the same time creates Holocaust effects. Their archival practices do not only have the Holocaust as object, they also uncannily re-enact the Holocaust's deadly objectifying technologies" (369–70). As good as we are at reciting the principle that archives are never neutral, this maxim does not go very far at exploring the conductive work of archival aura as a medium for perception. Boltanski's art points toward this auratical nature of archives, while also working through aura as a medium. Archival aura hovers.

ACCUMULATION ENTELECHY

Reading through the Stargate Project archives can lead to what's called "falling down the rabbit hole." It happens. Combing through some of the CIA's documents, I came across clippings from a 1977 article from *The Jewish Journal,* titled "The Israeli Secret Service: The Weird World of Psychic Espionage." The article tells of Soviet work on extrasensory perception, especially remote viewing, and boasts that Israeli special forces have actually made the most significant advances in this area. Uri Geller, the once celebrated and since debunked psychic wunderkind, is mentioned as an example of Israel's advancements in extrasensory perception. This brief mention reminded me of rumors I'd heard about Uri Geller working for the CIA as a psychic. I returned to the archives to find reports of tests and experiments that seemed to "prove" Geller's paranormal abilities. One set of reports came from Geller's time at the Stanford Research Institute (SRI) during the summer of 1977, when researchers performed numerous tests designed to evaluate his psychic power. This finding, in turn, led me to a document that summarizes a CIA interview with Dr. David Schueck, Geller's lead investigator at SRI. The summary concludes that Geller must surely either possess paranormal abilities, or else he has devised an elaborate scheme by which to fool serious researchers. If the latter is the case, according to the report writer, "the importance of the Agency's learning how this is done is even greater than the investigation of para-normal phenomena itself" ("Discussion"). And with that, I was curious if the Stargate Project ever attempted to search out and potentially weaponize fake psi. Further and further down the rabbit hole I went.

Any trip down any rabbit hole involves a strange experience of time. Unlike a focused research session, going down a rabbit hole has no true end point. One thing simply leads you to another, which leads to another, which leads to countless others until you run out of time or something snaps you back to attention. In the earliest days of the internet, hypertext theory marveled at much the same process of bouncing horizontally from one link to another to endless others. Unlike reading a book or essay, there was no real ending point. Carried along by waves of links, it really was more "surfing" than reading. Interestingly, a 2012 study suggests that people experiencing higher levels of depression tend to not only spend more time online, but they also exhibit more "flow duration entropy," switching rapidly from email to games to chat rooms to web searches (Chellappan and Kotikalapudi). I have caught myself in such flow duration entropies at times when I feel unusually blue. I typically start by checking the latest news headlines, then the weather (for the fifth time that day), moving on to email, to endless scrolls through social media, to a link that someone posted, and then on to some other site. Perhaps I keep moving for the sake of feeling forward progression, a palpable contrast to feeling emotionally stuck.

Aimless surfing or rabbit holing bears a striking similarity to the kind of endless link-making gestures that happen in conspiracy theory discourse.

Most conspiracy theories tend to sound so vast because one thread almost inevitably seems to lead to another thread and then another. As I describe in the next chapter, which focuses on rhetorical proliferation, this endless linking can create a dizzying effect for someone listening to a conspiracy theorist trying to unravel all the threads. There is no end to the accumulated links. Just as rabbit holing or aimless web surfing have no set goals that bring them to a conclusion, the aim of conspiracy linking and accumulating is precisely those actions. Accumulation is the point. In their essay "What They Don't Want You to Know About Planet X: Surviving 2012 and the Aesthetics of Conspiracy Rhetoric," Ian Reyes and Jason K. Smith define this goal as conspiracy theories' "entelechial formations." As Reyes and Smith explain:

> The perfection of a conspiracy theory does not come from achieving the status of scientific knowledge, historical fact, or religious dogma. Rather, as an adversary to these modes, the best conspiracy theory is one that most powerfully deploys conspiracism as an aesthetic end unto itself. Therefore, the entelechy of conspiracism lies not in dialectically refining its research program to match the methods of its critics but in constantly revising its arguments in the interest of maintaining the spin, oscillation, or blur that is the hallmark of conspiracist aesthetics. (412)

The work of accumulation is a way of keeping the spin going, since the spin is what conspiracy theorists are ultimately after. In short, there is something significant to acts of adding up. More gerund than verb, *adding up* is movement and activity that orients us to world in meaningful ways.

ADDING UP (AS) EVIDENCE: THE WAY THINGS ARE HERE

One reason why a concept like adding up is significant is because it suggests how the doing or making of evidentiary archives generates such powerful affects: affects that allow genocide to appear as bloodless bureaucracy, affects that give a shimmer of moral correctness to immoral acts. While we have seen how the Nazis made use of these devices, I want to note that residents in the Jewish ghettos also understood the impact of accumulation. Consider the scene from inside the Warsaw ghetto in 1941, when many Polish Jews understood that the ghetto was only a temporary pause before their destruction. Rather than quietly waiting for death, resident Emanuel Ringelblum, a historian and scholar, persuaded other residents to create an archive documenting life in the Warsaw ghetto. It was an archive devoted to the ultimate annihilation. Ringelblum's group called themselves the Oneg Shabbat (Joy of the Sabbath) Archive, since they met weekly during the end of the Sabbath day. No ordinary archive, Oneg Shabbat dared to turn residents into archivists, regardless of their age, background, ability. They recruited ghetto residents to write essays and poems. They recruited children to draw pictures. They asked for people to interview one another about life. They collected official government decrees. They asked everyone to collect everything possible.

The Oneg Shabbat archives were housed in a place that now seems ironic, given their existence as an "underground archive." In order to keep the papers and documents hidden from the Nazis, Ringelblum and his colleagues placed them all inside three large milk cans, which were buried beneath the streets of the Warsaw ghetto. In 1946, two of the large milk cans were unearthed, yielding thousands of documents. Today, one of the cans remains buried today somewhere in Warsaw.

One particular description of the archives holds my fascination more than any other. In a heartbreakingly beautiful 1947 article for the Yiddish newspaper *Arbeter Vort*, ghetto resident Rachel Aurbach describes how the underground work actually happened in the ghetto:

> The work for the Archive goes a familiar way. The general stimulus of collective activity also nourishes the energy of those who collect means. Together with contraband and food, revolvers, ammunition and bombing stuff, there are constantly small sacks in motion with "paper," packages of photographs, typewriters and all kinds of bits and pieces of the archive.

The bits in motion—the general stimulus of collective activity—is a literal image of archives in formation. Oneg Shabbat's adding up included the collection of materials, to be sure, but it also included the energies of bodies and movements. Package deliveries were diverted into textual routes. Milk canisters were transformed into safes. Bodies were rerouted into nodes of circulation. Collectively, this adding up generated different textures and rhythms to everyday life. The world-making endeavor of Oneg Shabbat was found not only in the milk cans but also in the ongoing movements that composed and sustained the archive's making. World emerged in a new way because of those bodily reorientations made possible by (and necessary for) collecting, amassing, adding up. Small sacks in motion.

To put it in slightly different terms, the activity central to Oneg Shabbat was a totality in and for itself. This is not how we usually talk about the activity of archiving. More typically, we tend to talk about archival collection and building as a work in progress, as if the "small sacks in motion" are simply a small part of a larger telos (as in the making of the Oneg Shabbat archive, for instance). Aurbach's words conjure images of all the fragments moving back and forth: the bits of paper, scraps, and pieces being added in jags of fragmented activity. The scene is almost a perfect metaphor for the critical epistemologies of archives that challenge claims to wholeness or completeness. Critical work on archives never seems to let us forget that the archive is always fragmented. "The archive is always only partially decodable," write Paul Voss and Marta L. Werner. "[It is] established in proximity to a loss—of other citations, of citations of otherness" (ii). Similarly, Richard Harvey Brown and Beth Davis-Brown write:

> It is not that archivists do not tell the whole truth about reality. It is that they cannot tell it. As soon as we accept that any process of perception and representation is a process of constructing reality from a given observer's social position and point of view, then there are more potential truths than there is possible data ultimately to confirm any of them. (22)

Whether through loss or through the impossibility of ever getting total perspective, archives bleed, leak, and trickle. Undoubtedly, the Oneg Shabbat archives can never tell the whole truth about life in the Warsaw ghetto. What could be written or shared was sharply limited by confinement and the destruction of personal property. Likewise, Ringelblum and his colleagues ultimately decided what was worthy of archiving and what was not. And then, of course, there is the missing third milk can that has yet to be discovered. The Oneg Shabbat archive is nothing if not fragmentary.

By describing the activity of Oneg Shabbat as a totality, then, I am brushing up against the fragmentary nature of archiving. After all, the materials recovered from those milk cans do not tell a complete story of ghetto life. There are only slivers or glimpses of a moment: a picture, a student's schedule of classes for school, a last will and testament, a diary. In this way, the Oneg Shabbat archives are not so different from any other archive, existing as "fragments of ethics," as historian Arlette Farge puts it: "Fragments of ethics, in the sense that the stream of words each person used to describe herself and the events reflect an ethos, an aesthetic, a style, an imagination, and the personal life that connected the individual to the community" (91). The Oneg Shabbat archives contain fragments of boredom, depression, lust, research, and desires of all kinds. The contents of the Oneg Shabbat archive are partial, though they are also traces of a people, an ethos, that is witnessed in those fragments.

It is sometimes easy to mourn the fragmented nature of archives. It would be nice to find the perfect archive, the one that does not have any leaks or missing pieces. "The perfect total archive would leave no question unanswered, no gene unsequenced, no seed unsaved, no phone call unheard, no book unread, uncatalogued or uncited," write Christopher Kelty and Boris Jardine. "But such perfections exist only in the fictions of Jorge Luis Borges." Borges does indeed give us the dreamlike image of a perfect archive in his fictional Library of Babel, which contains all possible books within its hexagonal walls. Yet, in Borges's narrative, the impossibility of working through this vast information in a useful way leaves its users depressed and angry. Outside of this dreamy and nightmarish fiction, any actual belief in a total archive seems almost childishly naïve. All archives are fragments.

I have those moments of mourning, at times. I feel the impossible desire for a total archive, though I know it can never be realized. However, this desire is not what motivates me to rethink Oneg Shabbat in terms of a totality. It is true that this archive, like any other archive, is fragmentary. And yet, something about it does not seem fragmentary at all. The "small sacks in motion" are less fragments and more of a wreckage, much like the wreckage that washes ashore after the ship has been torn apart. Fragments and wreckage exist in different registers. We do not rebuild from wreckage. Wreckage as such is a totality, existing only as itself, for itself. Benjamin describes the strangeness of wreckage as he sees it depicted in Paul Klee's painting *Angelus Novus*, which

> shows an angel looking as though he is about to move away from something he is fixedly contemplating. His eyes are staring, his mouth is open, his wings are spread. His face is turned toward the past. Where we perceive a chain of events, he sees one single catastrophe which keeps piling wreckage upon wreckage and hurls it in front of his feet. The angel would like to stay, awaken the dead, and make whole what has been smashed. But a storm is blowing from Paradise; it has got caught in his wings with such violence that the angel can no longer close them. The storm irresistibly propels him into the future to which his back is turned, while the pile of debris before him grows skyward. This storm is what we call progress. ("Theses" 257–58)

The wreckage at the angel's feet is a single catastrophe, yet it can never be made whole. Or, to put it differently, the wreckage is always whole from the moment it washes ashore. In fragments, we can only encounter the partial, but wreckage is not part of anything beyond itself. Even the way we count those nouns reflects these strange registers. Fragments of a boat are everywhere. The wreckage washes on shore. There are many fragments—infinite fragments— but only ever one wreckage.

Wreckage has no memory. What gathers at the angel's feet exists apart from mere memory. The Oneg Shabbat archive has two sides, then. As fragments from a certain hell, it tells a partial story of a smashed history. But as wreckage, it is movement that was for itself: movement of bodies, papers, things, and words. We have here two different ethics of archives: fragments and wreckages. One ethic is guided by memory. This fragmentary archival ethic is what moves us to dig up the garden and search for the missing piece. The fragmentary ethic calls for a kind of fidelity—to consider the whole that has been smashed. We need such an ethic, especially for moments of archival recovery. But another ethic—the ethic of wreckage—looks only to what is piled up at our feet. Its movement is not one of recovery, but of collective energy. Small sacks in motion as a means to survive. Archival movement in the Warsaw ghetto may look like fragments from a distance, but the collective activity (both in the sense of social activity and as actively collecting) is also ethics of wreckage.

Similarly, archival building, or archives in formation, signals work that is a whole in itself, apart from whatever archive that comes to be built (or perhaps fails to be built). This totality is not a pseudo-object of "archive building." Rather, it is the building and formation of archives, and not the archive that such work achieves, that I see as a totality. Archival adding up is not (only) work in progress, but is (also) its own *whole*. For that reason, I set aside the fragmentary sense of archives, turning instead to look more closely at the totality that is archives in formation.

THE WAY THINGS ARE HERE

Adding up is a glowing thing, orienting us in a dark room so that we know where the toe-stubbing furniture is hidden. The glow from a nightlight can help a room *show up* in certain ways; we get a sense of where we stand in relation to walls, objects, and other bodies. Of course, rooms so illuminated can sometimes show up in strange ways. One task for rhetoricians is to ask how certain orientations are produced and maintained. *What made the dark room show up like this?* When we examine certain archives in formation, therefore, it is critical that rhetoricians view accumulation and orientation as mutually constitutive acts.

Consider the ways that conspiracy theories surrounding the Stargate Project serve as an orientation device. In the years since the content of Stargate was made publicly available, plenty of people have spent time adding up. These theories are convoluted messes, at times simultaneously overlaid with both Nazi history and murky connections to "the Jews." For example, many theories point out that MKUltra, a CIA program that studied and tested methods of mind control, began under the directorship of Stanley Gottlieb. The fact that Gottlieb was Jewish strikes many conspiracy-minded people as a little too convenient, especially given that these mind-control experiments seemed to grow out of early Nazi tests. Threads are made between MKUltra and "Zionist control" in a number of theories. In the words of one such conspiracy advocate:

> When we look at the influence of The Talmudic Ashkenazi Jewish mind in Hollywood we see . . . cannibalism, zombies, vampires, chainsaw massacres, murder . . . and pedophilia in movie after movie. The net result is a form of MK-ULTRA trauma-based mind control effect to degrade and debase the morality and sensibilities and any who view . . . Jewish films. (Garrett 210)

In short, the CIA (led by a Jew) is enacting the kind of "Zionist domination" that is a familiar chorus echoed in so many conspiracy theories. MKUltra and Project Stargate are little more than yet another Jewish plot, so the story goes.

It's easy to fall down the rabbit hole when you start unraveling threads. There are the theories swirling around Columbia psychology professor Dr. Helen Schucman, for example. Together with her colleague, Dr. William Thetford, Schucman "scribed" or spiritually channeled the contents of a 1975 book eventually titled *A Course in Miracles*. However, Schucman's book falls under heavy suspicion for its connections to Thetford, who did indeed head an MKUltra project from 1971 to 1978. Due to her nominal identity as a Jew, Schucman has become the subject of many conspiracy theories. Some conspiracy theorists let her off the hook rather easily, painting her merely as Thetford's pawn: "Helen Schucman, a Jewish, atheist channeler of 'Jesus.' It has become undeniably obvious that Helen Schucman, the woman who 'channeled' or 'scribed' A Course in Miracles (ACIM) was very likely unwittingly deeply immersed in the CIA's MKULTRA activity during the years she 'scribed' ('channeled') the Course" ("The MK-Ultra Milieu"). Others see her as a scheming Zionist, who nefariously devised *A Course in Miracles* as another form of Jewish-led mind control.

Other conspiracy theories poking out from the fringes of Project Stargate and MKUltra are equally bizarre, and nearly all of them return in some way to those nefarious Jews. One popular theory surrounding the Jonestown massacre, for instance, argues that Jonestown was actually a project supported and carefully maintained by the CIA as a "testing ground" for mind-control experiments. Unsurprisingly, Lyndon Larouche attributes the Jonestown-CIA

connection to a Jew: Rabbi Maurice Davis, head of the largest Reform syna-
gogue in Indiana. According to Larouche, Rabbi Davis served as a chaplain
at one of the mental hospitals where MKUltra tests were being run, and he
helped to facilitate many of these secret operations. The rabbi then discovered
Jim Jones as the perfect pawn to create a massive mind-control cult where
experiments could take place (Larouche 34). Running with this theory, some
advocates have created elaborate videos and websites meant to expose two
of the survivors, Tim and Michael Carter, as being Jewish (possibly Mossad)
agents working undercover in Jonestown on behalf of the (Jewish-controlled)
CIA. On down the rabbit hole we go.

One of the most important studies of anti-Semitic accumulation-orientation was carried out in 1950 by Theodor Adorno, Else Frenkel-Brunswik,
Daniel Levinson, and Nevitt Sanford. Adorno himself arrived in the US after
fleeing Germany during Nazi extermination. As a Jew and an intellectual,
Adorno's life was quite literally threatened by the extremities of anti-Semitism.
Not surprisingly, then, he came to the US with a new set of very pointed questions: What drives fascism? What drives intense hatred for Jews? These questions led Adorno to join colleagues Frenkel-Brunswik, Levinson, and Sanford
to create a long study that is reported in their now-classic work, *The Authoritarian Personality*. This book reports results from their empirical study of anti-
Semitism as it exists among average citizens.

Adorno and his colleagues used surveys in order to gage respondents'
agreement or disagreement with various opinions and beliefs about Jews. Survey questions were designed to study two popular forms of anti-Semitism: one
belief that Jews are too "seclusive," meaning that they are extremely insular,
and another belief that Jews too "inclusive," meaning that are overly assimilated with non-Jews in threatening ways. Some of the questions about the
seclusive character of Jews included statements such as:

> "No matter how Americanized a Jew may seem to be, there is always something
> basically Jewish underneath, a loyalty to Jewry and a manner that is never
> totally changed."

> "Much resentment against Jews stems from their tending to keep apart and to
> exclude Gentiles from Jewish social life."

> "The Jews keep too much to themselves, instead of taking the proper interest in
> community problems and good government."

Meanwhile, respondents were also asked to rate their agreement or disagreement with statements about Jews' inclusive character. For example:

"Jews go too far in hiding their Jewishness, especially such extremes as chang-
ing their names, straightening noses, and imitating Christian manners and
customs."

"One thing that has hindered the Jews in establishing their own nation is the
fact that they really have no culture of their own; instead, they tend to copy
the things that are important to the native citizens of whatever country they
are in."

It seems reasonable to assume that people who agreed that Jews are much too
reclusive and antisocial might not also agree that Jews are much too assimilated among the wider social world. Yet, this is not what the survey results
indicate. Adorno and his colleagues instead discovered that respondents easily held both beliefs at the same time: Jews as both overly seclusive and overly
assimilated. For example, a surprising number of respondents who agreed that
"rich Jews help 'their own people' but not 'American causes'" also agreed with
the statement that "Jews donate money . . . out of desire for prestige and fame"
(76). Other correlated responses within the study hold that "anti-Semitism is
due to Jewish faults, but the Jews are unable to improve; the Jews should make
sincere efforts to change, but their 'basic Jewishness' is unchangeable" (83).
In short, the respondents who mistrusted Jews seemed to find them guilty as
charged, no matter the charge. As the authors conclude, this study "reveals a
deep contradiction in anti-Semitic ideology. As a matter of simple logic, it is
impossible for most Jews to be both extremely seclusive and aloof and at the
same time too intrusive and prying" (75). In short, there is a fundamental
"irrational quality" in anti-Semitism (57).

What keeps these contradictory beliefs from creating cognitive dissonance,
however, is a single, overarching ideological umbrella. While these beliefs may
seem to contradict one another, they are singularly unifiable within an ideology that is marked by hatred for Jews. "Imagery of Jews as personally offensive
and as socially threatening—attitudes of restriction, exclusion and the like, the
view that Jews are too assimilative and yet too clannish—these seem to be various facets of a broad ideological pattern," explains Levinson (75). The authors
go on to describe disdain for Jews as a unifying "nuclear idea" that allows all
negative beliefs to exist peacefully, even if they are contradictory (92). The
seemingly paradoxical beliefs are not mutually exclusive, therefore. Rather,
"the contradiction is . . . complete" (83). Furthermore, "once the central or
nuclear ideas are formed, they tend to 'pull in' numerous other opinions and
attitudes and thus to form a broad ideological system. This system provides a
rationale for any specific idea within it and a basis for meeting and assimilat-
ing new social conditions" (93). In short, anti-Jewish accumulation builds up

endlessly, unencumbered by contradiction. That building up, moreover, serves to solidify the larger nuclear idea that Jews are simply bad news.

What Adorno et al. call the "nuclear idea" is something like a wedge underneath a wobbly table. When a table has one uneven leg, it does not matter whether you stabilize it with a wad of paper, some napkins, or an actual wedge. Similarly, it does not matter which claims "stabilize" the nuclear idea; it is only the solidity of the overall anti-Jewish ideology that matters. Or, in a return to an early discussion about shaky legs, we might think again about the sea legs that Berlant mentions. Those respondents who scored high on the anti-Semitic scale have been gaining their sea legs for some time, pulling in any and all evidence of bad Jews into their archives. This evidentiary pull—collecting, adding up, archiving up—unfolds an aura of steadiness. It glows like a fully formed something that can be referenced and orientated to. In other words, the aura created through archiving up becomes the actual referent in anti-Semitic claims. The aura—and not the individual pieces of evidence itself—is therefore what we must also understand when hearing these claims.

Over five decades after *The Authoritarian Personality* was first published, a similar study was conducted by researchers interested in conspiracy theories. Michael Wood et al. share the results of this study in their essay "Dead and Alive: Beliefs in Contradictory Conspiracy Theories," which details results from their survey of conspiracy theory believers. Their findings reveal that conspiracy theorists often possess contradictory beliefs about a single conspiracy. Through a questionnaire method similar to the one from *The Authoritarian Personality*, Wood and colleagues found the more that participants believe that a person at the center of a death-related conspiracy theory, such as Princess Diana or Osama Bin Laden, is still alive, the more they also tend to believe that the same person was killed, so long as the alleged manner of death involves deception by officialdom (2–3). Logically, Bin Laden is either dead or alive, and a single conspiracy theory cannot somehow account for both facts at once. It is rational to eliminate one of these alternatives in order to remove a significant cognitive dissonance. Yet, both theories (Bin Laden is still secretly alive; Bin Laden was already dead when Seal Team Six arrived) bolster a larger banner of secrecy within the government. They conclude that these contradictory beliefs do not indicate a case of troubled dissonance, but rather that competing viewpoints are united in support of a "conspiracist worldview." The version of conspiracy is almost beside the larger point: Secrecy is at work, it is nefarious, and it must be revealed.

Just as Adorno and his colleagues conclude that arguing with specific anti-Semitic beliefs will not help to dismantle the larger anti-Semitic nuclear idea of intolerant people, Wood et al. argue that identifying and analyzing conspiracy theories at local levels of individual claims has only limited value. Instead, they encourage us to view these claims as extending a wider ideological (or, we might say, rhetorical) gesture. "Conceptualizing conspiracism as a coherent ideology, rather than as a cluster of beliefs in individual theories, may be a fruitful approach in the future when examining its connection to ideologically relevant variables such as social dominance orientation and right-wing authoritarianism," they write (5).

The nonsensical competing claims about Bin Laden as both dead and alive, or about Jews as both too assimilated and too withdrawn, help to sustain a much larger coherent discourse about nefarious machinations. In both cases, the contents of individual claims matter less than the accumulations themselves: the building up of an anti-Jewish or anti-government archive. It is the activity of accumulation that is coherent. The "nuclear idea" is a kind of whole, or totality, that is not so much being built up by verifiable evidence (even though the respondents may believe this to be true) as by the continual accrual of stuff that helps to support an otherwise potentially wobbly claim. Passionate anti-Semites and conspiracy theorists both collect fragments or catalogs of "evidence" showing Jews or government behaving badly, even as the archive being constructed seems not to rest upon logically coherent conclusions. Even through competing narratives, paradoxical claims, and unwarranted beliefs, conspiracy theorists arguably create something intelligible. As Wood et al. write, "the specifics of a conspiracy theory do not matter as much as the fact that it is a conspiracy theory at all" (5). They describe this kind of coherence as an ideology, or the ongoing boosterism of conspiracy thinking. It is the ongoing creation itself that serves as the real referent.

Ideology is a kind of nuclear idea, one that brings together patchy bits of belief, affect, attachments, and forms. Ideology's patchwork is held together through a glowing conductive medium—auratic glue—that generates its conductive glow through the work of building, making, doing, stoking, and feeding archives. Aura as a form of seeing (which also describes what ideology does for us) gets its mojo from adding up. Thus, it is through the act of archival building that the aura of perception is generated. As I suggested earlier, Benjamin hints at this aura in his thoughts on book collecting. In "Unpacking My Library," he meditates both on what is generated through the overall work of collecting, as well as on the much smaller act of unpacking a library. Benjamin declares that he is not interested in telling you anything about the books themselves; rather, "what I am really concerned with is giving you some insight into the relationship of a book collector to his possessions, into collecting rather than a collection" (60). The ongoing act of collecting is a way of being, in Benjamin's account. For this reason, he continues, "The phenomenon of collecting loses its meaning as it loses its personal owner. Even though public collections may be less objectionable socially and more useful academically than private collections, the objects get their due only in the latter" (67). Collecting thus serves as a body in relation to another (the "collector," in Benjamin's account). Between them is the work of conduction, a singular relation that is not simply personal.

SERIOUS EFFORTS

Admittedly, the collection I am unpacking in this chapter has been a strange one, moving from records of psychic warfare to the terrible documents of actual warfare. Yet, these cases reveal a kind of doubled referent inherent to the archive: One referent is the contents themselves in their use, but another referent is to the archive in formation. I'm interested in this double referent for what it can tell us about extraordinary claims and public discourse. This theoretical frame also calls attention to the ways that particularly vulnerable populations are impacted by acts of accumulation-orientation and their aura. Therefore, I want to end this chapter with a much different "conspiracy" example that speaks to ways in which evidence registers (or fails to register at all).

This conspiracy theory took shape in the days leading up to Supreme Court nominee Brett Kavanaugh's confirmation hearings. Dr. Christine Blasey Ford had accused Kavanaugh of sexually assaulting her years earlier, and she testified in great detail about the attack she suffered at his hands. Her testimony was moving, and women all across the country found her story resonated with much of our own experiences.

But some public responses saw a much different story unfolding. President Trump tweeted that the protesters who believed Ford and demanded that Kavanaugh be held accountable are "paid professionals only looking to make Senators look bad" (October 8, 2018). Answering the obvious question of *who* was paying, Trump stated matter-of-factly that the protests were "paid for by Soros and others." As if more proof was necessary, Trump concluded by pointing out "all of the professionally made identical signs. . . . These are not signs made in the basement from love!" Trump's mention of George Soros recalls a very familiar anti-Semitic trope whereby certain Jewish names—the Rothschilds, for example—become code words for "Jews." *Soros* is one of those coded names. Indeed, more overt white supremacist websites openly accused "the Jews" of orchestrating the accusations against Kavanaugh. *The Daily Stormer,* one of the most popular white supremacist websites, posted an essay titled "Evil Jews Transformed the Kavanaugh Confirmation Hearing into a Disgusting Circus." The essay dismisses Ford as a small pawn being controlled by a much larger force: "From start to finish, Jews have been at the very center of this smear campaign against Kavanaugh. It is very important that people understand this. Anybody who is outraged over what happened to Kavanaugh should be directing their outrage at the parasitical Jewish race" (Rogers).

This same sentiment circulated on several college campuses, thanks to a flier campaign supported by *The Daily Stormer*. The fliers featured Kavanaugh surrounded by villainous caricatures of Congress members, all with the Star of David painted on their foreheads. The large text reads: "Every time some anti-white, anti-American, anti-freedom event takes place, you look at it, and it's Jews behind it." Ford's image barely even appears on the flier, crowded out by the "evil Jews" who are clasping their hands greedily. It is almost as if, even in these conspiracy theories, Ford does not exist any more than her documentation does.

Although these anti-Semitic theories are shared by only a small faction, their circulation was arguably lubricated by a larger public response that characterized Ford's lack of documentation as suspicious. One conservative blogger bluntly stated: "She has no facts, no corroboration, no medical report, no police report. There is nothing but a claim from a woman with a bad memory and a story contradicted by all her own witnesses" (Hawkins). Although Ford did indeed release records from her older therapy sessions detailing conversations about the attack, the fact that she presented no other records made her the target of scorn and even outrageous conspiracy theories. Her accusations were not to be taken seriously. Likewise, even Ford's supporters were discussed as less than serious for their "professionally made identical signs." If they were serious, at least in Trump's eyes, the signs would have been made by hand in a basement (with love). Unfortunately, Ford and her supporters simply failed to add up.

In contrast, Kavanaugh's emotional and angry testimony literally demonstrated his commitment to adding up. His most memorable pieces of evidence were the infamous diary and calendar that he discussed in terms that were, rhetorically speaking, quite pathetic:

> I have submitted to this committee detailed calendars recording my activities in the summer of 1982. Why did I keep calendars? My dad started keeping detailed calendars of his life in 1978. He did so as both a calendar and a diary. He was a very organized guy, to put it mildly. Christmas time, we'd sit around and he'd regale us with old stories, old milestones, old weddings, old events from his calendars.

In ninth grade—in ninth grade, in 1980, I started keeping calendars of my own. For me, also, it's both a calendar and a diary. I've kept such calendar as diaries for the last 38 years; mine are not as good as my dad's in some years. And when I was a kid, the calendars are about what you would expect from a kid; some goofy parts, some embarrassing parts.

But I did have the summer of 1982 documented pretty well. The event described by Dr. Ford presumably happened on a weekend because I believed everyone worked and had jobs in the summers. And in any event, a drunken early evening event of the kind she describes, presumably happened on a weekend.

If it was a weekend, my calendars show that I was out of town almost every weekend night before football training camp started in late August. The only weekend nights that I was in D. C. were Friday, June 4, when I was with my dad at a pro golf tournament and had my high school achievement test at 8:30 the next morning.

I also was in D. C. on Saturday night, August 7th. But I was at a small gathering at Becky's house in Rockville with Matt, Denise, Laurie and Jenny. Their names are all listed on my calendar. I won't use their last names here.

And then on the weekend of August 20 to 22nd, I was staying at the Garrets' (ph) with Pat (ph) and Chris (ph) as we did final preparations for football training camp that began on Sunday, the 22nd. As the calendars confirm, the— that weekend before a brutal training camp schedule was no time for parties.

So let me emphasize this point. If the party described by Dr. Ford happened in the summer of 1982 on a weekend night, my calendar shows all but definitively that I was not there.

What is it exactly that is speaking here? In a literal sense, Kavanaugh himself is speaking. In a barely veiled sense, the calendar itself also seems to be testifying. Perhaps more than either of these witnesses, however, it is the act of documenting itself that is speaking. Kavanaugh demonstrated that he has been faithful in adding up, contributing to, building his life of witnessing (innocence). Indeed, he is a second-generation builder, which implicitly suggests that such activity is part of his genetic makeup. Never mind the question whether a teenage boy might choose not to document sexual assaults in his diary. Never mind the question whether there is actual virtue in the act of keeping diaries for thirty-eight years. Those questions are muted by the larger structure that attributes a certain virtue in adding up.

Ford was arguably erased as a subject not only because she had no physical evidence of her attack but (perhaps even more so) because she did not document, record, archive the attack. Women are quite familiar with this second part; we all too often experience the blunt end of the auratic stick. In the wake of the cultural upheavals that were sparked in 2016 by the #MeToo movement, women who managed to bring their experiences to light almost immediately faced questions about how their due diligence could be demonstrated. *Where are the records? Where are the notes? Where are the diaries? Where are the attempts to build something—even if in the lonely pages of your own diary—that you can bring forth to testify?* For many of these women, the reality of this discourse hit all too hard: If you were not capable of adding up, then perhaps your claim is worth less than the claims of those who did.

While I admit that the Kavanaugh hearings seem a world away from mid-twentieth-century anti-Semites or the Warsaw ghetto or secret ESP tests, all of these examples shine light on the ways that the act of evidence-building creates and reinforces orientations to the world. To return to a question I introduced in the introduction, this theory helps to bring our focus to different registers of evidence by asking *What is this evidence of?* There are two ways of reading this question, one more obvious than the other. The simplest way to read this question is as a question about reference: *What does this evidence refer to?* A second way of reading the question is as a question about its constitution or its makeup: *What actions compose this evidence?* I suggest that it's best to read the answers to these two questions together. That is, the accumulative, ongoing actions that compose evidence are also what that evidence references. By shifting a focus on what exactly we are encountering in particular claims, as well as what we expect to encounter, we can begin facing up to the potential (domestic) abuse of archives. The stakes are adding up.

CHAPTER 2

Prolific Archives

Notes from Trutherworld

I AM waiting to cross the street in Hong Kong. My daughter points to a piece of paper taped to a light post and asks, "What is *that*?" She's pointing to a flyer that is covered with typewritten words squeezed onto every space of the page. There are no paragraphs or breaks. One line runs into the next until, at the very bottom of the page, the font is almost miniscule. Some words leap out— "fake diseases," "sleepwalker," "anti-humankind"—but I have no clue what it's all about. Still, this frantic swarm of words communicates *something*. Something unsettling, something strange, something in motion.

The Hong Kong flyer (figure 1) reminded me of a condition called hypergraphia, a physiological disorder that causes an intense and compulsive desire to write. Hypergraphia is often described as a temporal lobe issue, usually associated with certain types of epilepsy. I first learned of the condition while reading about Reverend Robert Shields, a Protestant minister from Spokane, Washington, who achieved some notoriety as keeping the longest diary in the world. For over two decades, Shields kept a diary of his every single waking minute. Every five minutes, from 1972 until 1997, Shields wrote down each and every detail of his daily routine. Needless to say, the contents are less than thrilling. Most of his entries simply mark moments that any of us would find utterly banal: changing a lightbulb, making mac and cheese, sitting at the typewriter. The international interest in Shields's diary is not so much

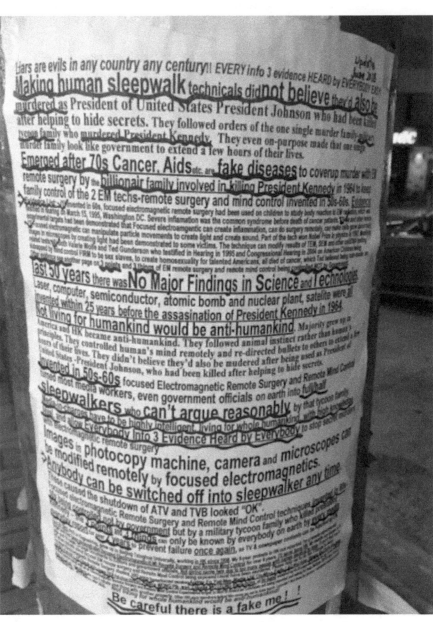

FIGURE 1. Conspiracy proliferation

in the contents of his intensive writing, but in the textual proliferation itself. By the time of his death, Shields's journal had reached 37.5 million words. I became fascinated by the strange way such proliferation communicates a sense of something.

Many of us can probably recall hypergraphic moments from our own childhood. I am only slightly embarrassed to admit that I have engaged in the particular hypergraphia often associated with young girls who have a crush. I remember being in sixth grade and writing Brad Bingham's name dozens of times in my journal, as if that repetition testified to the depths of my love. More recently, I found that my daughter's copy of *The Smart Girl's Guide to Growing Up* offers this telltale sign that you have a crush on a boy: "Even when he's not there, you . . . spend hours writing his name over and over again" (Ganeri 76). Beyond middle-school crushes, some of us are familiar with the (now passé) punishment of "writing lines," a la Bart Simpson's blackboard sentences: *I will not lie to my teachers. I will not lie to my teachers. I will not lie to my teachers. I will not lie to my teachers.*

Artifacts left by those suffering from (or perhaps blessed with) hypergraphia create a strange and sometimes disturbing effect. Stanley Kubrik made the most of its eeriness in his infamous scene from *The Shining* where the phrase "All work and no play make Jack a dull boy" fills countless typewritten pages. The terror of such frenzied mania is perfectly summed up by the look on Shelly Duval's face as she reads the hypergraphic horror. Why such repetition communicates a palpable horror (or other intense emotions) is hard to explain. Why does writing a crush's name repeatedly communicate love? Why does a 37.5-million-word diary communicate strangeness? Why does a flyer with handwritten letters squeezed into every inch of white space communicate mania?

These questions became very relevant when I started researching conspiracy theory communities, where I encountered hypergraphia in new contexts. As I walked into my first 9/11 truther conference, someone handed me what initially looked like a dollar bill. All four corners of the phony dollar featured "9-11" in large letters, while the edges were crammed with tiny words and phrases like "The Calgary Principles," "The Reichstag Fire," "Bilderburgers," "Gulf of Tonkin," "Vaccine Manufacturer," and "New World Order," among others. I must have had an intense look on my face as I stared at the dollar, trying to read the microscopic words, because the dollar-bill man grabbed my shoulder and handed me a similar dollar. "I saw you liked that," he said, "so you might like this one, too." The second phony dollar was similarly covered with tiny words squeezed on the front and back. I thanked him for both the handouts, unsure of what to say next. Confused about how to make note of this in my research notebook, I simply wrote *dollar bill = hypergraphia?*

The more time I spent with conspiracy theory communities, the more it seemed that I was not so much encountering hypergraphia, but something more like hyperevidentia. My conversations with 9/11 truthers, for example, never seemed to stand still long enough for me to locate myself on a cognitive map. Our discussions about the events of September 11 would inevitably begin with rapid-fire facts, dates, details, pictures. One piece of evidence about the World Trade Center (WTC) would quickly turn to a trove of details about the Bilderburg group, the Illuminati, Israel, reptilian aliens, the CIA, or any number of other threads. "Facts" about vaccines could easily lead to the Gulf of Tonkin, Freemasons, Jews. In many of my conversations with conspiracy theorists, I felt overwhelmed by sheer abundance, buried beneath a textual landslide.

While conspiracy theory literature is a far cry from a young girl repeatedly writing her crush's name in a diary, it's worth noting how the abundance of words produces a rhetorical effect beyond the contents themselves. There is something significant about proliferation. Just as a name repeatedly written in a diary generates the sense of deep crush, the textual and evidentiary proliferation in conspiracy discourse produces a range of intense responses. Alongside such obsessively accumulated evidence we can track rhythms of outrage, depression, disgust, attraction, or (in my own case) baffled exhaustion.

Out of sheer bewilderment, I wanted to better understand how it is that proliferation communicates. I wanted to grasp the rhetorical effects of such evidentiary magnitude. Returning to the question that I posed at the end of the last chapter, I find myself again asking: *What is this evidence of?* Is proliferation itself evidence of anything? If so, does this evidence operate in ways that surpass a more empirical sense of fidelity? Is there a way in which we can understand proliferation itself as a rhetorical tool? With these questions in mind, I want to spend a while mulling over the peculiar nature of archival proliferation.

MEGA-THINGS

Proliferation is a hallmark of conspiracy theory in general. Even the most outlandish theory offers an abundance of evidence, or something like it. As David Aaronovitch writes in *Voodoo Histories: The Role of the Conspiracy Theory in Shaping Modern History,* the approach commonly used in conspiracy texts can aptly be described as "death by footnote," with the theoretical exposition usually accompanied by "a dense mass of detailed and often undifferentiated information" (13). Richard Hofstadter likewise observes something about the "dense mass" that seems ubiquitous in conspiracy discourse. Hofstadter notes, for example, that Joseph McCarthy's "96-page pamphlet McCarthyism contains no less than 313 footnote references" (37). Hofstadter also remarks that conspiracy discourse—or the "paranoid style," in his phrasing—often contains an "elaborate concern with demonstration" that "obsessively accumulates 'evidence'" (35–36).

Similarly, E. G. Creps describes proliferation in conspiracy discourse as "an evidential mosaic," where "a huge quantity of data is assembled simply to give the impression of overwhelming proof for a specific contention" (43). According to Creps, it is typically not the case that conspiracy discourse builds a logically comprehensible whole from this evidential mosaic. Nevertheless, the evidential mosaic still manages to create a sense of something comprehensible. "The persuasive force of the conspiracy case is produced not by a single portion of testimony," Creps writes, "but by the simultaneous consideration of hundreds of pieces of evidence—much as one can be moved by the overwhelming intricacy of a great work of art" (45). The claims of any given conspiracy might actually be quite simple, he continues, yet it is "defended by a mind-boggling assortment of 'evidence'" (45). Conspiracy theories are rhizomes, to use what now has become a critical theory cliché. But, cliché or not, there they go, off on their rhizomatic lines of flight: branching, splitting, conjoining without any particular pattern.

I've frequently wondered aloud how anyone could possibly wade through all of this stuff to understand a particular conspiracy theory's claims. It sometimes feels like conspiracy theorists need a good course in argumentation, or at least they need to internalize that golden rule: *Don't overwhelm your audience with evidence.* Yet, overwhelm with evidence is the strategy I encountered time and again. Thomas Adamo writes that research into conspiracy theory is difficult because the researcher herself "becomes mired in a labyrinth of rhetoric that defies examination" (10). Mapping even a single conspiracy theory proves to be painfully complex because of the trajectories that split and grow at any particular point. When I first began fieldwork with 9/11 truthers, I had hopes of trying to understand the arguments being made among believers. Too often, though, I found myself halted by "a mind-boggling assortment of 'evidence,'" as Creps so aptly puts it.

Rhetorically speaking, proliferation cuts into the somewhat shaky alliance between epistemology and aesthetics. Aristotle explores this relationship in both the *Poetics* and the *Rhetoric*, where he discusses how size and magnitude register. He begins one such meditation by considering whether a giant thing can be beautiful:

> Again, a beautiful object, whether it be a living organism or any whole composed of parts, must not only have an orderly arrangement of parts, but must also be of a certain magnitude; for beauty depends on magnitude and order.

Hence a very small animal organism cannot be beautiful; for the view of it is confused, the object being seen in an almost imperceptible moment of time. Nor, again, can one of vast size be beautiful; for as the eye cannot take it all in at once, the unity and sense of the whole is lost for the spectator; as for instance if there were one a thousand miles long. As, therefore, in the case of animate bodies and organisms a certain magnitude is necessary, and a magnitude which may be easily embraced in one view. (*Poetics* 1.7)

So, according to Aristotle, a giant thing cannot be beautiful. Neither can a very tiny thing. These things are not beautiful, he says, because it is impossible for us to take them in. Our sense of comprehension is confounded by size. Yet, as Thomas Farrell explains, Aristotle's theory of size points to something more than measurement:

Aristotle wasn't much noted as a tropologist. But in the rhetoric, the single most frequently recurring commonplace is that of quantity, degree, largess, magnitude. It's as broad as it's long. What looks large from a distance, close up is never that big. It is interesting, by contrast, to reflect upon the poetic understanding of magnitude. The Greek word is the same: megethos. But now we find a quite different inflection placed upon meaning and function. ("Sizing" 6)

Megethos has a poetic impact to it that is not necessarily the same as its relation to precise degree or accounting. Farrell thus suggests that we should understand Aristotle's magnitude as having an aesthetic component.

To give an example of how megethos retains both a quantitative and an aesthetic dimension, Farrell points to the ubiquitous "friendly conversation" where you ask someone in passing, "Hey, how's it going?" Too much detail is unwanted. Too little detail is rude. The good response to the friendly conversation is a beautiful aesthetic of just right: "Things are going well. I'm hanging in there." Not too much to take in, but not so little as to provide nothing at all. When I am stuck waiting for an elevator in my office building (a situation I find myself in almost every day), I cringe at the occasional unpleasant interactions I have with someone who answers my friendly question (usually something like, "How's your day?") with a list of actual complaints. It is almost like my interlocutor failed to understand the beautiful *just right* of response.

Farrell also points out that Aristotle's sense of megethos pushes us to "set aside totalizing disjunctions: 'the' aesthetic vs. 'the' epistemic" ("Sizing" 7). The

NOTES FROM TRUTHERWORLD · 69

aesthetic sense of just right relates less to proper scale and more to the sense of comprehension. In Aristotle's description, the aesthetics surrounding magnitude mark a kind of coherence, or a feeling of "taking in" what is sometimes translated as a "sense of the whole." This particular translation renders Aristotelian beauty less an epistemic concept of unity and more a sense impression of unity or wholeness. As Debra Hawhee writes, Aristotle's megethos "scales magnitude to perceptive capacities" (*Rhetoric* 56). What emerges is a kind of epistemic aesthetic, where the aesthetic impact of magnitude may actually serve as part of epistemic claims.

Aristotelian megethos thus urges a broader view of how aesthetics and the epistemic relate. Megethos, writes Hawhee, "is one of the concepts that adds to rhetoric a crucial aesthetic dimension, in the ancient sense of sense perception" (*Rhetoric* 56). A tiny insect cannot be beautiful (for Aristotle) because we do not have a sense of the whole, despite the fact that we see the whole bug easily in one glance. Sense perception may be another way of thinking about as aesthetics as a way of knowing, which is not unfamiliar to certain areas of rhetorical theory. Steve Whitson and John Poulakos describe such aesthetic epistemics in their essay "Nietzsche and the Aesthetics of Rhetoric," where they draw upon the Nietzschean view that "consciousness itself is predicated on and structured by concepts whose origin is to be traced to the senses" (137). In other words, sense and sensation are the epistemic's undergirding. As Whitson and Poulakos put it, "Aesthetic rhetoric focuses on the human body as an excitable entity, an entity aroused by language" (141). Taken all together, we arrive at a view of megethos as an aesthetic inflection of quantities that gives a sense of weightiness; a sense that sustains the epistemic without relying upon epistemology to structure it. To borrow from Whitson and Poulakos, megethos operates through the human body as an excitable entity, an entity aroused by the sensation of more.

In the concept of megethos, there emerges a strange relay among magnitude, aesthetics, and the epistemic. Proliferation, then, becomes an interesting problem for rhetoric. Instances of hyperevidentia—for example, the obsessively accumulated evidence that surrounds conspiracy discourses—bounce between aesthetic and epistemic borders of comprehension. Proliferation and magnitude generate rhetorical impacts of their own, aside from the contents being prolifically communicated. Magnitude serves as what Ned O'Gorman calls "an interpretive frame," that all-important sense of comprehensibility (28). However, in order to grasp exactly what these impacts do and how the interpretive frame deploys its effects, I want to dig a little deeper into a case of conspiracy theory's evidentiary proliferation.

NOTES FROM TRUTHERWORLD

I spent a couple of years in Trutherworld, my own referential shorthand for the community of 9/11 "truthers" who do not believe we have received the real story behind the events of September 11, 2001. Truthers do not agree on every detail, but they share one unified belief: The US government had some kind of hand in the attacks that happened on 9/11. For two years, I joined Facebook groups devoted to 9/11 truth, subscribed to truther mailing lists, conducted interviews with truthers, and attended national 9/11 truth conferences.

When I first began to attend meet-ups and 9/11 truther conferences, I assumed that the participants would more or less share the same sets of assumptions about what "really happened." What I found instead was splinters and factions that argued bitterly among themselves. There are the "no-planers," for example, who believe that space beams or microwave technologies took down the Twin Towers, and images of planes hitting any buildings were simply a distraction. More common are the truthers who believe that the World Trade towers fell because of planted explosives. And then there are those who believe the government simply "allowed" the terrorist attack to take place without attempting to intervene.

I was reminded of Aaronovitch's "death by footnote" the first time I was handed a two-page 9/11 truth pamphlet that contained thirty-six footnotes with citations from different sources. I struggled to parse the dense mass of information. But proliferation was not only localized at the level of citations. The pamphlet also reflected a type of stylistic proliferation, featuring a copious amount of text squeezed on each page, not unlike the flyer my daughter found in Hong Kong. The pages were hypergraphic, pushing the limits of textual exhaustion. Such evidentiary and stylistic proliferation felt overwhelming, and I struggled to make sense out of everything I encountered. So, being the dutiful researcher, I started to take careful notes in the spiral notebooks I carried with me at all times. I began to draw a kind of map to help myself visualize the many threads of the 9/11 truther movement, hoping get a handle on how this obsessively accumulated evidence fits together.

NOTEBOOK #1—WTC 7

Sitting across from me in a coffee shop, a neatly dressed man with bright white hair handed me a glossy pamphlet about the World Trade Center and thermodynamics. His name was Dan, and I had met him at a national truther conference the previous day. "Do you know about the third tower?" he asked me with a smile. The pamphlet and its contents shared images and diagrams of WTC 7, along with a series of time-lapsed images of its eventual destruction. "You need to know about the pancake effect," Dan told me. He was referring to the infamous "third tower" that has become a central focus in contemporary 9/11 conspiracy discourse. He explained that when WTC 7 fell, the floors "pancaked" on top of one another, much like what happens in a controlled demolition. For comparison's sake, he took out another time-lapsed picture of a different building that had been purposefully demolished. Dan pointed to the two pictures, "See how the floors fall in the same way? I have so many other things like this I could show you." For the next hour, he pulled out multiple pictures, newspaper clippings, and memos he had requested through the Freedom of Information Act.

As time went on, I heard and saw these same details repeated, including countless screenshots captured from televised images on September 11. One of the most commonly circulated screenshots among truthers is a still frame taken from a BBC report made on 9/11. The image shows BBC reporter Jane Standley standing in front of a window that reveals a still-standing WTC 7. Strangely, however, the report's news caption announces that WTC 7 has collapsed, even though we can see that this has not (yet) happened. Many versions of this screenshot are annotated to help point out the "suspicious error" that suggests (to truthers, at least) a clear conspiratorial alliance playing out among the government and the media. "You've got to look closely or else you'll miss everything," Dan told me as he showed me the still frame.

Looking closely is unavoidable in this discursive realm. At times, it felt as if I were looking through the lens of a microscope, inspecting each and every granular particle. No detail is too small to ignore. No frame is insignificant. Of course, this kind of microscopic analysis is not limited to 9/11 truther discourse. The same process played out, for example, in conspiracy theories surrounding the Boston Marathon bombing. These theories primarily cast doubt on the official story behind the 2013 bombing through exhaustive (and exhausting) frame-by-frame analyses of media images. One of the most frequently shared images shows a legless bombing victim named Jeff Bauman, whose tragic injuries went viral in mainstream news coverage. In conspiracy theory circles, however, Bauman's image seemed suspicious. Soon after the attacks, conspiracy theorists began circulating Bauman's picture juxtaposed alongside an older image of a legless veteran named Nick Vogt, who somewhat resembled Bauman. Boston truthers were adamant that Bauman and Vogt are the same man, and, instead of being a victim, he is a crisis actor who merely played along with the fake bombing. Versions of this argument, always juxtaposing images of Bauman and Vogt, circulated in sites like Twitter, Facebook, and Reddit. The analyses zoom in on the microscopic details of each picture in order to arrive at the "truth."

In fact, much of the 9/11 truth movement's archival material is quite literally microscopic, dealing in the world of dust particles. Richard Gage, one of the founders of Architects and Engineers for 9/11 Truth, has become one of the loudest voices to assert claims that dust samples taken from the World Trade towers contain "nano-engineered iron oxide and aluminum particles 1000th the size of a human hair, embedded in another substance consisting of carbon, oxygen, and silicon" (Gage and Roberts). Gage and others conclude that this nano-engineered substance was actually made in US national laboratories and should not have been present anywhere near the World Trade Towers, unless these materials were deliberately used in order to cause the destruction. The numerous microscopic pictures no longer looked like the typical media images I had come to associate with September 11. They looked like something from a chemistry or biology textbook. Truthers seemed to be drilling down into the dusty archives of conspiracy, finding visible evidence emerging from the invisible. One highly circulated image collage of "nano-engineered substances" caught my attention after I began to see it reprinted, shared, and remixed in a number of different online truther spaces (an example is in figure 2). It showed four images of red thermite, a chemical that somehow signaled an inside job to believers. At times, the image was accompanied by a scientific explanation of what red thermite is. Yet, most often, I saw the image shared across various sites without much context at all.

The measurement markers at the bottom of each image suggest that these are tiny fragments, smaller than what the human eye might be able to see. In color, they appear to be glowing red and almost look meaty, as if they are a piece of organic life. My notes on Building 7 kept growing with details about nanoparticles and their role in destroying the tower that was not hit by planes. In the course of reading this evidence, I felt like I was zooming manically between the atomic and the colossal, with nothing in between. At one moment, I found myself working at the level of nanoparticles, but in the very next moment I was quickly yanked back into the macroscopic level. Even specks of dust became gigantic.

My notes on thermite theories are a chaotic mess. One page of my notes about thermite contains a confused note, scribbled in the margin, that simply reads: "Silverstein??" I made the note during an interview with a truther who was telling me about the scientific properties of nanoparticles. I was trying to understand the exact arguments about these dust particles that seem to contain multitudes, but my interviewee kept stopping to make jokes about

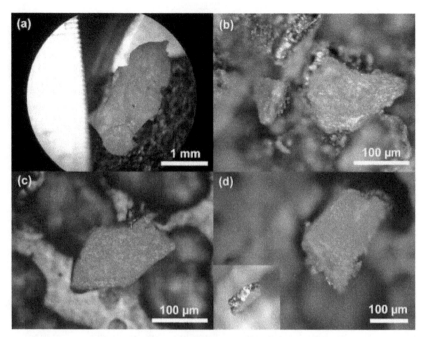

FIGURE 2. Image of nanothermite shared on 9/11 truther
website (http://investigate911.org/)

"Silverstein's arsenal of thermite." A bit annoyed at the tangents, I finally interrupted my interviewee. "I'm sorry," I said, "who is Silverstein?" My interviewee looked at me like a student who had not done her homework. "Larry Silverstein," he responded. "He took down Building 7."

NOTEBOOK #2—THE JEWS

Building 7 is a link between nanothermite and Larry Silverstein. It seemed like I could not get very far in discussions about planted explosives in the World Trade towers without hearing his name. Silverstein became a central part of 9/11 conspiracy for several reasons. First of all, he owned WTC Building 7. Most frequently cited are Silverstein's comments in the 2002 PBS documentary *America Rebuilds,* where Silverstein recalls that day where he was told that the fire ravaging his building could not be contained. Silverstein said that he was greatly troubled and finally told the fire department commander, "We've had such terrible loss of life, maybe the smartest thing to do is pull it." Silverstein's interview comments have led some truthers to specu-late that Silverstein (inadvertently) revealed that he ordered the controlled demolition of Building 7. This detail is key for many truthers. If Building 7 was brought down by controlled demolition, then it is much more likely that the similar collapses of WTC 1 and 2 were also caused by controlled demolition.

Things don't stand still for long. Almost as soon as I first heard Silver-stein's name during an interview, the target seemed to move again. James, a longtime 9/11 truther, told me that Silverstein is just one small clue in a giant evidentiary field. "Silverstein's name tells you all you need to know about who is really behind 9/11," James said offhandedly. Although he did not elaborate, I immediately understood: As a Jew, Silverstein is a reflection of the "Zionist" conspiracy. This angle has some vocal public advocates, such as Louis Far-rakhan. In 2015, Farrakhan told a congregation, "It is now becoming appar-ent that there were many Israelis and Zionist Jews in key roles in the 9/11 attacks. . . . We know that the World Trade Center was insured by its owner Larry Silverstein right before the attack. We know that an Israeli film crew dressed as Arabs were filming the Twin Towers before the first plane went in. In other words, these Israelis had full knowledge of the attacks" (Chasmar).

During another interview, a truther named Bill told me that I should look into the story behind Ptech, a software company whose clients included the Federal Aviation Administration (FAA), FBI, Department of Justice, and the US Armed Forces. Bill was especially hyped about a Ptech executive named Michael Goff. Although I tried to write down the details as quickly as I could, my notes are a jumble of phrases like "Mossad connection" and "Freema-sons" and "Israel" and "Zionist." A few days after our interview, Bill sent me link after link for websites that claimed to expose Goff's part of the conspir-acy. Many of the sites repeat the same "suspicious" details: Goff's father and grandfather were 32 degree freemasons in the Commonwealth Lodge 600 of B'nai B'rith. Ptech was partnered with an Israeli company who also did soft-ware security. And, according to conspiracy-minded folks, it was Ptech's soft-ware that allowed conspirators to override the FAA system on September 11 in order to attack the World Trade Center. From nanothermite to Building 7 to Jewish cabals—evidentiary proliferation was in full effect.

After a while, I found it difficult to not hear terms like "Illuminati," "Global Elite," or "New World Order" as code for "Zionist," which is code for "Jews." As a Jew myself, I felt more than a little unnerved by what sounded like old-fashioned anti-Semitism. But, like everything else in the truther movement, nothing fails to signify and connect. Not even anti-Semitism. I learned this firsthand during one interview I conducted with Eddie, a national 9/11 conference organizer who told me that a local newspaper had featured a small story about the upcoming conference. He was upset that the list of speakers (including speakers who have been publicly rebuked by the Anti-Defamation League) had sparked an online storm. There were over one hundred comments in the online newspaper story, many of them angry about the anti-Semitism being encouraged by the speakers. "So," Eddie continued, "we're all agreed that we're not going to allow any questions or comments about anti-Semitic anything during the conference."

Eddie continued to describe his astonishment at this turn of events. "We have been hit with major anti-Semitism," he told me in a lowered tone. "They're pushing anti-Semitism." I asked him to clarify what he meant by this, and he explained that his detractors are accusing him of being anti-Semitic in order to discredit the truth movement. "Israel and the Zionists are behind 9/11," he said, "and a Jewish person doesn't want to be associated with that." At this point, he launched into a rather confused theory about a "cabal" comprising Israel, Britain, the American Israel Public Affairs Committee (AIPAC), the US, and Saudi Arabia. In his gentle voice, Eddie spent close to thirty minutes issuing forth a stream of theories that all placed Israel (and, at times, Jews in general) at the center of 9/11 events. And yet, at the conclusion of our interview, he threw his hands up at the assertion that he is an anti-Semite. "What we're doing is scientific," he said. "What they're trying to do is kill the messenger." I stopped Eddie before he could continue down another path: "Are you saying you're being framed as anti-Semites?" He looked relieved: "Yes! That is what I'm saying." He was being framed as a malicious Jew-hater by malicious Jews.

My notes on all of these links began to take on their own hypergraphic appearance. I tried to organize them into some kind of logic pattern for easy reference, but every attempt seemed useless. When I expressed my frustration and disorientation to Jeremy, a truther whom I spent the most time talking with, he told me all of this truther talk about "Zionists" is meant to purposefully confuse people like me. When I asked him about the anti-Jewish aspects of the truther movement, he told me that these claims are part of "an intentional campaign to infiltrate the 9/11 truth movement with a variety of propaganda, disinformation, dividing points, and other nonsense. Particularly what I see as an effort to label the 9/11 truth movement as anti-Semitic." Jeremy's perspective—that anti-Semitic language is intentionally spread among the truther community in order to discredit the movement—is one shared among many other truthers. "It's a disinfo campaign," he said. On the last page of my spiral notebook, I copied down his quote and circled *disinfo*. Time to start a new notebook.

NOTEBOOK #3—DISINFO

The more time I spent in Trutherworld, the more frequently I heard accusations of "disinfo agents" across the board. I again lost track of my ability to make sense of who was spreading disinformation to whom, let alone why. I bounced between interviews that credited Alex Jones and his Infowars media empire with helping to spread the 9/11 truth, while other interviewees accused Jones of being a government plant designed to make truthers look ridiculous. The same went for Noam Chomsky, Jesse Ventura, James Fetzer, and almost any other public figure who espoused 9/11 conspiracy. While I fully expected to be accused myself at some point, things took an even stranger turn when one well-known 9/11 truther I interviewed shared a copy of my interview questions, along with his responses, on his personal blog. I was amazed at how quickly the mistrust and vitriol turned away from me and moved onto him. Because of his responses to my questions, commenters on his blog eventually accused him—and possibly even me—of being a disinformation agent.

It almost seemed like any mention of anti-Semitism in the communities I joined would immediately lead to an accusation of "disinfo." When I asked other truthers if they shared this belief that anti-Semitism is the work of disinformation agents posing as truthers in online forums, nobody disagreed. Several interviewees shared stories of having truther meet-ups and conferences picketed and protested (unfairly, in their telling) for spreading anti-Jewish messages. They blamed the bad PR on pseudo-truthers working to shut down the 9/11 truth movement by influencing the rhetorical reception of their message. Lowell, another interviewee, angrily recalled a 2007 truther conference in Phoenix, which was organized by a relatively unknown person named Eric D. Williams. The conference received local and national coverage, as did Williams himself. Curiously, said Lowell, just before the conference was set to launch, Williams came out with a host of Holocaust denial literature.

Online truther discussions leaned toward the conclusion that Williams was simply a disinformation agent trying to discredit the movement. As one writer put it: "This is shaping up to look like an intentional hit on the movement, with otherwise well intentioned people being duped by an agent who has set himself up in the movement only to publish a book about holocaust denial, just before hosting a 9/11 truth conference" ("Holocaust Denial"). Lowell recalled that the anger was so intense that Williams eventually removed his name and association from the event altogether.

This angle on "disinfo agents" added yet another layer of complexity to my already messy notes. For every far-fetched theory I heard, other truthers

would dismiss these theories as nothing more than intentional disinformation. Perhaps the most heated charges came from those who attacked a truther
named Dr. Judy Wood as a government agent working to discredit the movement. Wood, a former professor of engineering at Clemson University, is one
of the leading advocates of the "no planes" theory. According to Wood, no
planes ever hit the WTC buildings, and the damage done to the various buildings was the result of a kind of directed energy from space. When Joan, an
active participant in an online truther group, mentioned Wood in a lengthy
post, I asked her if she believed Wood was sincere. "I think she is purposefully
spreading disinformation," Joan responded. "She has done a LOT of damage to
the truth movement." Bill, another interviewee, summed up the no-planes theories even more bluntly: "They're a poison pill designed to discredit the movement as well as potential whistleblowers or Bush administration insiders."

From one point of view, the sheer amount of "disinformation agents"
seems utterly irrational. How many people would have to be on the take in
order for this to work? And, even more unlikely, how many people would have
to keep their mouths shut in order to preserve the disinfo campaign's secret?
At times, I tried to gently suggest what seemed like a more obvious explanation: Maybe they aren't disinfo agents at all. Maybe some irrational or disturbed individuals are an active part of the 9/11 truther movement. Each time
I raised this possibility, however, my words were scorned. For many truthers,
any anti-Semitic, antiscientific, or outrageous claims made in 9/11 conspiracy
communications are evidence of government malfeasance.

Looking back in my three research notebooks, I sometimes see my notes
take on a strange coherence. It is like squinting at a confusing mass of marks
until they blur together into some recognizable shape. Every claim, every piece
of evidence, every detail is part of a whole for every truther—even if the whole
looks different from different perspectives. But, more often, my notebooks
look like a mess of frantic scribbles that make no sense at all. If anything, my
own hypergraphic note-taking was working against me: The more I wrote, the
less I understood. All I really knew for sure was that truther archives are vast.

THE WEIGHT

I imagine that Aristotle would not find much beauty at a 9/11 truther conference, since beauty requires "a certain magnitude . . . which may be easily embraced in one view." It's difficult to embrace a truther's truth in one
view. Part of what makes conspiracy theorists so strange to some of us is
the gross disproportionality of their evidence. Its magnitude is not aestheti-

cally "right." Perhaps its size is too vast for the eye to take in. Or perhaps it is too tiny to perceive, its weight too insignificant to register at all. Though I spent many hours reading about the September 11 attacks as an inside job, I am not persuaded of those claims. The mountains of sprawling materials marshaled in support of those claims make them appear even less credible. The more dots that got connected, the less likely I was to give the evidence much weight.

Weighty evidence. Now *there's* a metaphor. While Aristotle tropes more about size when speaking about magnitude, weight is also useful for thinking about prolific archives. Evidence can be light, heavy, strong, solid, broad, thin, flimsy. Weight is rhetorically meaningful. However, it's not always easy to parse what weightiness means. Farrell offers helpful perspective on weight in terms of magnitude and size:

> Magnitude—in its myriad of manifestations—seems essential to the most important concerns of traditional rhetoric: namely, whether an audience may care about any topic sufficiently to attend to it, to engage it, and to act upon it; what consequences will weigh most heavily upon their prospective deliberation; what priorities will finally tip the balance in their judgment; and what appetitive attachments will need to be overcome for rational reflection to be feasible. ("Weight" 471)

What weighs on an audience is perhaps another way of describing rhetorical exigence, or a problem that calls for action. The weight of particular concerns can "tip the balance" of judgment for some audiences, while a different audience may not feel the weightiness enough to register. Similarly, there is sometimes a chasm experienced between two people who do not agree on the "weight" of a certain issue or piece of evidence.

I felt that chasm quite dramatically one day when I found an overstuffed manila envelope in my campus mailbox. I opened it to find nearly fifty pages of photocopied materials, ranging from declassified government memos to copies of reports from who knows where. A handwritten letter explained that this material proved government accountability for the September 11 attacks. The sender, a man I met at one of the truther conferences, explained that he was trusting me with the material because he felt they were important and perhaps I could use them for my research.

I sat in my office and skimmed the photocopies. As I reached the end, I felt confused. The documents were clearly quite significant to this man, yet I had a hard time understanding the significance of it all. It seemed nothing more than random pages of bureaucratic ephemera. The weight was very light to me, even though there was so much of it. To him, the sizable amount of material was damming. Eventually, I stuffed the pages back into the manila envelope and just felt the weight of it all. The heavy envelope did not tip the scale enough for me to reach the same level of concern that the sender experienced. Paradoxically, the envelope's weight made the sender's claims seem lighter than ever.

The manila envelope I held in my hands was a materialization of a common trope that connects evidence and weight. Themis, the goddess of justice, is the deity who oversees this connection. Standing tall with a scale in one hand and a sword in her other hand, Themis is a source of justice. What is being weighed on her scales, exactly? Many traditions hold that Themis is weighing the souls of those she judges, quite similar to the Egyptian deity Maat, who appears with scales in order to weigh the souls of those who have recently died. The imagery of weighing souls likewise appears throughout the Jewish bible and the Koran. In one particularly dramatic example, Job pleads in the midst of suffering, "Let God weigh me in the scales of justice, and he will know that I am innocent!" In all of these instances, the scale helps to give material form to the idea that justice has weight.

Beyond these mythological iconographies, the metaphorical concept of evidential weightiness continues to live on. In fact, scholars of both legal studies and logic have attempted to operationalize the metaphor for practical use. John Maynard Keynes, for example, describes an argument's weight as a function of quantity:

> As the relevant evidence at our disposal increases, the magnitude of the probability of the argument may either decrease or increase, according as the new knowledge strengthens the unfavourable or the favourable evidence; but something seems to have increased in either case,—we have more substantial basis upon which to rest our conclusion. I express this by saying that an accession of new evidence increases the weight of argument. (71)

However, Keynes's proposition that more evidence "increases the weight" of argument has been rebuked by other scholars who find this an insufficient explanation of evidential weightiness. The British mathematician I. J. Good snarkily notes that Keynes only considers evidence as a kind of mass without any regard for whether or not that evidence undermines a proposition. It is almost "as if he had the weight of the documents in mind" (*Good* 160). As a response, Good developed a theory of evidential weight based on mathematical probabilities and odds, which he created along with his collaborator Alan Turing. Through logarithms and equations, Good and Turing both offer a more statistically coherent sense of weight. Together, their theory has become known as the "Turing-Good Weight of Evidence."

Seeking a mathematical theory of evidence, Turing proposed something called the deciban. The ban in Turing's theory was a unit of evidence where the logarithmic base is 10. Turing then proposes the deciban, or one-tenth of a ban, as a kind of baseline for evidentiary perception. "Just as a decibel is about the smallest unit of difference of loudness that is perceptible to human hearing," Good explains, "the deciban is about the smallest unit of weight of evidence that is perceptible to human judgment" ("Weight" 253). Or, as Turing himself writes, "a piece of evidence is worth a deciban if it increases the odds of the theory in the ratio 101/10" (4). Of course, the notion of perceptibility suggests a degree of rhetoric in the Turing-Good model. To say that the deciban is the smallest unit of perceptible evidentiary weight, we must also come to understand what causes this perception. What is the nature of rhetorical perception such that a "deciban" registers at all? It's clear that weight registers. But how?

I certainly do not wish to chide Good and Turing for not being rhetoricians. Turing is working from mathematical principles, so it is not a surprise that his concept of the deciban lacks fuller rhetorical treatment. Their interests in evidence and argument are quite different from many of us in rhetorical theory. Still, the relatively underaddressed rhetorical aspect of perception in their theory exposes one of the limitations of algorithmic approaches to evidence. These units of measurement could indeed be useful to the extent that when we must make a judgment about the probabilities of competing claims, such as guilt or innocence, then such statistical probability might help in assessing the "weight" of evidence when making our judgment. Yet, we still need some way of understanding how it is that weightiness impacts us at all.

A rhetorical framework may offer some insight into this weighty question. Interestingly, Keynes's "more is better" theory of evidence echoes what Chaim Perelman and Lucie Olbrechts-Tyteca call "the locus of quantity." According to Perelman and Olbrechts-Tyteca, "most of the loci which aim at showing the effectiveness of a means will be quantitative" (87). Quantity as a rhetorical commonplace shapes arguments in terms of measurements between alternatives: Bigger is better, more is better, longevity is better than ephemerality. Keynes reinscribes this locus when he imagines that if we are presented with an argument that provides a greater degree of evidence, then our judgment is also likely to be more sound. And, indeed, the "more is better" locus informs quite a lot of our everyday reasoning. Even the endearing verses of Ecclesiastes contain quantitative loci at work:

> Two are better than one, because they have a good return for their labor: If either of them falls down, one can help the other up. But pity anyone who falls and has no one to help them up. Also, if two lie down together, they will keep warm. But how can one keep warm alone? Though one may be over-powered, two can defend themselves. A cord of three strands is not quickly broken. (Ecclesiastes 4:9–12)

Although I remember first learning these verses as a child, I still think of them whenever I hear a commercial raving about a "2-for-1" deal. Two workers can help each other through difficulties, and two hamburgers for the price of one isn't bad, either. The Ecclesiastes writer was certainly more eloquent than a burger marketing team, but the themes are notably similar: Bigger is better. The more the merrier. Two for the price of one is a great deal.

The locus of quantity is also at the heart of certain logical fallacies, such as the conjunction fallacy. This fallacy's logic leads users to erroneously con-clude that a statement with detailed conditions is more likely to be true than a statement with only a single general condition. Perhaps the most well-known empirical demonstration of this fallacy comes from a study conducted by Amos Tversky and Daniel Kahneman, who gave participants the following scenario:

> Linda is 31 years old, single, outspoken, and very bright. She majored in phi-losophy. As a student, she was deeply concerned with issues of discrimina-tion and social justice, and also participated in anti-nuclear demonstrations.

Tversky and Kahneman then asked participants which statement is more probable:

1. Linda is a bank teller.
2. Linda is a bank teller and is active in the feminist movement.

The majority of participants chose the second statement as being more prob-able, even though, statistically speaking, the first statement is logically more probable. When I posed this same question to one of my classes, students tended to repeat this same error. It is easy enough to see how such a fallacy can occur, of course. Some students drew from their own experience of people involved in issues of social justice and cultural images of "very bright" and "outspoken" women to conclude that being active in feminist movements is not outside the realm of possibility. And, while Linda could indeed be a kick-ass feminist activist, the likelihood of A will always be greater than A+B.

My students, along with Tversky and Kahneman's participants, may have been pretty good examples of what some communication scholars call the Elaboration Likelihood Model (ELM). The ELM, first proposed by Richard E. Petty and John Cacioppo, is a more empirical model that explains how prolific evidence has rhetorical impact. Petty and Cacioppo examined earlier research that hypothesized a relationship between the amount of arguments provided and the effect of persuasion on an audience or jury. Prior speculation held that an increase in the quantity of arguments would likely be more persuasive because more arguments means more information for the audience to process and base judgment upon. However, Petty and Cacioppo suggest that the quantity factor may be effective for another set of reasons. Their research was especially focused on instances of argumentative quantity upon audiences that do not pay close attention to the contents of those arguments. According to Petty and Cacioppo, "If people are unmotivated or are unable to think about the message, and no other salient cues are available, they might invoke the simple but reasonable decision rule that 'the more arguments the better'" (70). In short, the locus of quantity plays a special role in moments when we are relatively tuned out.

Consider the study that Petty and Cacioppo designed in order to study proliferation's rhetorical effects. They presented two groups of students with a scenario proposing a major change to university policies. The proposal stated that all graduating seniors must take a comprehensive examination in their major before they will be allowed to graduate. Petty and Cacioppo told one group of students that this change would take place immediately, meaning that these students would be required to take the comprehensive examination. (Hardly the kind of news college students want to hear.) The second group was told about the same plan, but they were informed that these changes would not be put into effect for at least ten years. While the specter of yet another test—another hurdle to jump—is unlikely to ever sound like a good idea to students, the proposal would have little effect on this second group. Therefore, while these students might have sympathy for the poor saps who come later, at least they will be spared the impending misery.

Petty and Cacioppo's two student groups were then further divided into additional groups. For the first group who was sweating the plan's immediate implementation, half of those students were given only strong reasons in support of the proposal. Among this strong-reason group, one half were given three strong reasons and the other half were given nine strong reasons. The other half of the "sweating" group was given only weak reasons in support. Again, one half of these were given three weak reasons and the other half were given nine weak reasons. Petty and Cacioppo then similarly divided the second group—those who believed the proposal would not affect them—along the same lines. Half of the second group were given only strong reasons why this proposal is a good idea. Again, Petty and Cacioppo gave some students three strong reasons, while other students received nine strong reasons. The remaining half of the "no sweat" group were given either three or nine weak reasons. Altogether, Petty and Cacioppo's student subjects received either a lot of arguments (whether weak or strong), or just a few arguments (again, weak or strong) for supporting the plan to add yet another test to college life.

Among the group who was sweating the possibility of having a comprehensive test imposed on them, the results were not all that surprising. For students given "weak" arguments in favor of the plan, the number of weak arguments affected how they responded. Those who were given only three weak arguments had a more favorable response to the plan over those who were given nine weak arguments. On the flip side, those who were given nine strong arguments in favor of the plan had a much more favorable response than those given only three strong arguments. Many good reasons thus appear to have a stronger impact than just a few good reasons, while multiple crummy reasons might actually intensify the group's initial feelings that, yes indeed, this is a bad idea. The more bad arguments the sweating group heard, the less they liked the plan.

The study's more interesting results come from the second group, composed of those who did not believe this plan would affect them personally. Among these students, it did not matter whether or not they were given strong or weak arguments. What did matter, however, is the number of arguments. The subgroups given three arguments (both weak and strong) had a much less favorable response to the proposal than the subgroups given nine arguments (regardless of whether those arguments were weak or strong). For this second group as a whole, then, more arguments were likely to be more persuasive, regardless of whether they were good or bad arguments.

Petty and Cacioppo explain the different results as a function of the two groups' perceived involvement. The first group had what Petty and Cacioppo call "high involvement," meaning that they were deeply invested in the subject. Since the proposed curriculum change would impact them directly, the students were more likely to pay close attention to the contents of each argument. However, the second group was dubbed "low involvement," since these students were relatively noninvested in a topic that had no consequence for them. Petty and Cacioppo argue that low-involvement groups are less likely to consider the merit of each argument as carefully as a high-involvement group. Instead, the low-involvement groups use what Petty and Cacioppo call "peripheral cues" in order to evaluate the overall argument. The peripheral cues in this study are the number of arguments provided. As Petty and Cacioppo write, "Even if the arguments are not thought about, increasing the number of arguments can still increase agreement because people may employ the simple inference, the more the better" (78). They go on to write that other peripheral cues that play a similar role include things like "the length of the arguments and the complexity of the language employed in the message" (78). When we are not deeply invested in a given subject, in other words, we can be persuaded more by the quantity than the quality of arguments. The locus of quantity is alive and well.

There is something interesting here about evidentiary proliferation. The empirical studies by Petty and Cacioppo, as well as Tversky and Kahneman, suggest that the rhetorical impact of quantity exists somewhat apart from a message's contents. Proliferation registers. We mark this registering by different names: weight, bans of perception, depth. Whatever it's called, magnitude is definitely doing some work. Moreover, proliferation's rhetorical work involves a particular kind of motion. Although motion goes relatively unaddressed in certain theories of evidentiary magnitude, it seems to hover around the edges. Something about this movement seems important for understanding exactly how proliferation generates such lasting impact. What happens, I wonder, if we rethink magnitude in terms of motion?

MAGNITUDE'S MOTION

Motion is subtly built into the rhetorical dynamic between the locus of quantity and the locus of quality. Perelman and Olbrechts-Tyteca explain that the loci of quantity and quality counterbalance each other in claims about what is preferable: "Loci of quality occur in argumentation when the strength of numbers is challenged" (89). For example, while someone may argue that a particular law will benefit a great number of citizens, an interlocutor might point out the devastatingly negative effects the new law will have for a particular, smaller group. As James Jasinski summarizes Perelman: "The locus of quality frequently is used to combat claims warranted by way of the locus of quantity. The locus of quality attempts to *shift* the basis of judgment away from factors such as magnitude and durability and onto other, more qualitative considerations" (47; emphasis added).

Yet, the dynamic between quantity and quality is more than a matter of countering one rhetorical framework with a competing one. In Perelman's formulation, "The loci of quantity and quality . . . characterize the classical and the romantic spirit [and] are attached to precisely different values" (161). Regardless of whether or not we agree with Perelman's classical/romantic parallels, he identifies something epistemically different about these loci. As Perelman and Olbrechts-Tyteca write in *The New Rhetoric*, "At a given moment, there may be a purely quantitative difference that brings about the passage to phenomena of another order" (349). The dynamic exchanges between loci of quality and quantity are not simply a matter of different values, but a movement or shift from one state of being to another. In short, "a quantitative change can bring with it a change of nature" (349). Perelman and Olbrechts-Tyteca use the example of individual sand grains that eventually build up enough to become a single heap. The same epistemic shift happens in reverse when a man loses just enough individual hairs to suddenly become bald. Such epistemic shifts—from thinking about quantities of sand grains to thinking about a wholly new thing called a *heap*—also mark a shift in rhetorical ontologies.

Heaps and baldness mark shifts in rhetorical ontologies. One memorable (if pedestrian) example of shifting rhetorical ontologies happened in the middle of a department store during my preteen years. My parents and I were shopping for school shoes in one of those discount department stores, when they held up a pair of shoes that they praised as durable and cost-efficient. The casual lace-up shoes had multiple uses, they said, since I could use them for both physical activity and everyday wear. My own tearful arguments countered that the shoes were ugly, unfashionable, and uncool. The shoes' aesthetics meant more to me than their quantitative details. Although we were all staring at the same pair of shoes, the object of our reference was not the same. The shoes existed for my parents as an object of quantity (cost, durability, uses), while they existed for me as an object of quality (unfashionable ugliness). We were referencing two different objects, from the standpoint of rhetorical ontology.

My shoe-shopping nightmare is perhaps a silly example, yet it serves as a parable for how rhetorical ontologies—they way we frame states of being—can shift in the emphasis between quantity and quality. This shift is inherent to megethos, at least as the concept has variously been theorized across many different spaces. Longinus, for example, uses the term *megethos* to indicate the sublime, which achieves "not persuasion but transport" (43). In a different sense, megethos has also been described as a kind of transportation. John Mark Balzotti and Richard Benjamin Crosby read particular ancient Roman architectural monoliths, such as Diocletian's Victory Column, as examples of how Romans used spectacular visual designs in order to disrupt prior cultural narratives. "The effects of megethos require some change from low to high, small to large," they write, "some transfixing experience that repositions the spectator in relation to his or her own cultural memory" (332). Transportation is thus central to megethos; magnitude is not so much about size as it is about the movement contained in the spectacular act of sizing up.

Size and movement work together in curious ways. Susan Stewart points to the giant, a figure we first learn through childhood stories and fairy tales, as an example. The childhood giant is a lumbering, slow-moving monolith. The *fee fi fo fum* giant from Jack and the Beanstalk moves slowly, talks slowly, and seems to even think slowly. Stewart writes that this slowly lumbering giant tells us something about *the gigantic,* which is often "represented through movement, through being in time" (86). We know the gigantic only as it pulsates through and around us. Stewart contrasts the gigantic to the miniature, which is utterly still and contained; it is a version of the finished and complete that we can (quite literally) hold in our hands. Unlike the miniature, the gigantic is not knowable through its details. Stewart writes that the gigantic involves "a severing of the synecdoche from its referent, or whole. . . . In the representation of the gigantic within public space it is therefore important that the . . . transcendent position be denied the viewer" (89). It is through the movement of ourselves caught up in a landscape that we come to know the gigantic.

Heidegger also ponders the relationship between movement and the gigantic, which he sees as something more than size. For Heidegger, the gigantic reflects a transformation between two different states. In "The Age of the World Picture," he writes:

> The gigantic is, rather, that through which the quantitative acquires its own kind of quality, becoming thereby, a remarkable form of the great. . . . As soon, however, as the gigantic, in planning, calculating, establishing, and securing, changes from the quantitative and becomes its own special quality, then the gigantic and the seemingly completely calculable become, through this shift, incalculable. (72)

The shift from "completely calculable" to incalculable is not due to the enormity of numerical calculation involved in the gigantic, but because once a thing becomes "gigantic," it takes on an essentially new state of being. As Heidegger explains elsewhere:

The gigantic was determined as that through which the "quantitative" is transformed into its own "quality," a kind of magnitude. The gigantic is thus not something quantitative that begins with a relatively high number (with number and measurement) even though it can appear superficially as "quantitative." The gigantic is grounded upon the decidedness and invariability of "calculation" and is rooted in a prolongation of subjective re-presentation unto the whole of beings. (*Contributions* 310–11)

His exemplar is the blimp, those giant airships like the Hindenburg, which fascinated the public in early days. The Hindenburg certainly had a calculable measurement, but for those who first witnessed its appearance, the gigantic blimp existed as sheer greatness. Its existence was qualitative and not quantitative, even though the Hindenburg's quantitative character was necessary to this eventual shift. The shift that happens with the gigantic thus marks a specific movement in thought, one that moves from quantity to quality. As Heidegger writes:

All calculation lets what is countable [Ziihlbare] be resolved into something counted [Geziihlten] that can then be used for subsequent counting [Ziihlung]. . . . What has been counted in each instance secures the continuation of counting. Such counting progressively consumes numbers [Zahlen], and is itself a continual self-consumption. (*Pathmarks* 235)

This process is the "consuming character of calculation," in Heidegger's terms. *Consumption* is a telling word here because it indicates that whatever came before—the calculable, the quantitative, the measurement—is swallowed up into another form. The calculable is transported into (a) quality.

Sidling up against Heidegger's gigantic is Kant's mathematical sublime. For Kant, the sublime exists in distinction to the beautiful. Whereas the beautiful is something that has comprehensible form, the sublime is marked by unboundedness, "either [as] in the object or because the object prompts us to present it while yet we add to this unboundedness the thought of its totality" (Kant and Pluhar 98). Kant's distinction between the beautiful and the sublime also includes two different forms of knowing and judgment. With the beautiful, our judgment falls under "understanding." With the sublime, our judgment falls under the concept of "reason." With the sublime, then, we see Kant reaching toward an aesthetic response to some kind of quantitative element (a very *big* mountain or a very *big* storm, for example). As he explains, "In the case of the beautiful our liking is connected with the presentation of lity, but in the case of the sublime with the presentation of quantity" (Kant and Pluhar 98).

An intense storm appears across a wide-open sky and we are shaken with awe at its magnitude. This is the sublime. We stand at the base of Mount Everest, dwarfed by the sheer awesome size. This is the gigantic. Neither the storm nor the mountains are beautiful, no matter if we are using Aristotle's or Kant's senses of that term. For Aristotle, the storm and mountains are not beautiful because they are not able to be "taken in" by the eye. They are not comprehensible as a whole. For Kant, they are not beautiful because they are not bounded objects that can be comprehended. At the heart of these various concepts is the notion that quantity can transfigure into another thing altogether, a thing that is then judged through the lens of aesthetics.

Of course, gigantic blimps and ugly shoes are not the only way of thinking about the shifting motion from quantity to quality. We might steal a more earthbound example from social science. Specifically, the qualitative methodological concept of "data saturation" is another useful description. Data saturation occurs when a qualitative researcher, working hard to gather as much data she can, finds that any additional data she gathers will not add additional information or insights. In contrast, undersaturation means that her claim is built from data that have not taken in the right quantity of all possible dimensions. We might imagine the possibility that claims made from undersaturated data are categorically different from claims made from data that have reached the saturation point. The differences might be represented like this:

Nonsaturated data sets = Claim^1
Saturated data sets = Claim^2

Let's say that I am writing about how 9/11 truthers debate skeptics hostile to the notion of a government cover-up. I interview truthers and ask about their debate tactics. With every interview, I hear something a bit different, but my funding has run out and articles are due. Although I continue to hear different pieces of information that add new dimensions to my research, I decide to write an essay that makes the following claim: *9/11 truthers often begin debates with skeptics by offering the least controversial information about 9/11 facts (as truthers see them).* By all accounts, my research did not reach a point of saturation, since additional interviews may have yielded many more types of perspectives. Perhaps I might have even found that a broader set of truthers do not begin with low-controversy information. Nevertheless, I am sticking with my claim. Maybe the deadlines are gnawing away at me, maybe I am just a lazy researcher, or maybe I just have a feeling that my claim is warranted. Whatever the reason, I'm running with it. In this example, my claim is what I would classify as a Claim[1] type of claim.

But, in reality, I am not a lazy researcher. I did interview many 9/11 truthers about this very question, conducting so many hours of interviews that I slept, breathed, and ate truther discourse. Although the individuals I interviewed have many different rhetorical characteristics—some are very confrontational and some loathe confrontation—almost all of them agreed that when talking with skeptics, you simply cannot begin with the most complex details of the conspiracy. In nearly all interviews, I kept hearing the sentiment that beginning with something mundane is best. A majority of the truthers I interviewed agreed that presenting the darkest details of 9/11 truth will only make skeptics more hostile and less likely to listen. After hearing this pattern repeated for over 150 interviews, I feel warranted in making the following claim: *9/11 truthers often begin debates with skeptics by offering the least controversial information about 9/11 facts (as truthers see them).* My claim here is built from data that have reached a saturation point. For this reason, I would classify this as a Claim[2] type of claim.

In these two instances, I end up with the same wording. Yet, I have also classified the claims as two different types of claims. The differences have to do with a murky line between quantity and quality. My Claim[1] has not reached a quantitative tipping point that we can call "saturated," which is a phenomenological concept. Saturation suggests that there is something qualitatively different about quantities, yet the quantity at work in these instances is not quantifiable. By this I mean that the data quantity that "counts" as a saturation point is never measurable. I cannot determine in advance what percentage of my overall interviewees will yield a reliable saturation point. Saturation evokes a threshold, a threshold that allows a claim to pass from one thing (an unwarranted claim) to another thing (a warranted claim). The threshold of saturation is another instance of what Heidegger calls "the gigantic," or "that through which the quantitative acquires its own kind of quality." Data saturation is thus an instance of megethos, an aesthetic inflection of quantity.

The example of saturation also suggests that magnitude, or megethos, is more than simply an instance of quantity taking on a qualitative descriptor. The threshold entails a transportation from one state of being into another. It is more than an adjective tacked onto the main noun. Consequently, instead of asking "*What* is magnitude?," a better question might be "*How* is magnitude?" *Magnitude, megethos, proliferation, the gigantic*—these are all terms that identify a transportation: the refiguration of quantity into quality. Likewise, ιypergraphic is a textual witness of such transport at work: Proliferation of words upon words upon words crosses a threshold where the number of words becomes refigured as spectacle.

These various threads—aesthetics, coherence, transportation, refiguration—bring us back to the reason why magnitude and proliferation are so important for rhetoricians. It's not just that size matters. Aristotle's megethos and Heidegger's gigantic call for different kinds of judgment than that involved in the calculable or bounded. The sublime-gigantic is not so much a category of being, therefore, but an aftereffect of judgment. What seems incalculable (or passes into incalculability) becomes gigantic in effect. What seems unbounded becomes sublime in effect. There is a refiguration that happens across a threshold: It is a rhetorical shift in states of being.

JUDGMENT AND COUNTERARGUMENT

Refiguration from quantity to quality tells us something about why and how proliferation makes such strong rhetorical impact. For one thing, while there are differences between Aristotle's megethos and the sublime-gigantic, these concepts both indicate that quantity has the potential to transform how we judge. David Hume's useful distinction between sentiment and judgment offers another perspective on the challenges presented by rhetorical magnitude. Hume writes:

> All sentiment is right; because sentiment has a reference to nothing beyond itself, and is always real. . . . But all determinations of the understanding are not right; because they have a reference to something beyond themselves, to wit, to real matters of fact; and are not always comfortable to that standard. (136)

Addressing the judgment that arises from the sentiment is one thing. We can do that in response to the content of the "archival magnitude" of evidence built up, say, around unjustifiable conspiracy theories. But, as Hume points out, it is nearly impossible to argue with the impact of sentiment, insofar as it is an aesthetic impact. The aesthetic is always true. Unfortunately, counter-strategies to troubled archives too often fall back on a mistaken faith in the essential relationship between magnitude and scale. That is, we argue against the accumulated evidence of conspiracy, false conclusions from big data, and even stereotypes by showing how the magnitude of evidence does not scale up to representational fidelity. However, this counter-strategy is likely to fail because scaling up to fidelity is not always the goal behind such accumulation.

Another way of putting all of this is to say that the presence of magnitude can shift discourse from deliberative to epideictic. O'Gorman points out how Aristotle links together megethos and epideictic. As O'Gorman writes, "Epideictic, as the aspect of discourse especially given to the invocation of magnitude, provides for the polis through lexis as phantasia images of honor and shame or virtue and vice, that can be 'sized up' and interpreted according to a logic of scale. How great was his courage? How expansive was her generosity?" (28). In the *Rhetoric*, Aristotle touches on such invocations in the case of eulogies:

> Thus, even if there is no comparison with the famous, one should compare [the person praised] with the many, since superiority [even over them] seems to denote excellence. In general, among the classes of things common to all speeches, amplification is most at home in those that are epideictic; for these take up actions that are agreed upon, so that what remains is to clothe the actions with greatness and beauty. (1.9.1368a.25–30)

Hawhee similarly explains that the very task of epideictic "is to rhetorically— through a host of images furnished by memory, by vivid comparisons, and projected into the future—produce magnitude, thereby achieving huperoche or density by calling up multiple images, and piling on excessive details" ("Looking" 145). This connection between magnitude and epideictic is important insofar as epideictic also involves different forms of judgment from deliberative or judicial discourse. Walker notes that Aristotle does not merely define epideictic speech as ornamental or ceremonial speech. The audiences to epideictic speech are expected to be theoros (one who makes observations), as distinguished from deliberative and judicial discourse audiences, who are expected to be kritai (judges). "The role of the theoros, in short, is not to make rulings but to form opinions about and in response to the discourse presented," writes Walker (9).

Moreover, epideictic discourse is not a third triangulated piece of discourse (as we sometimes teach), but actually underlies the work of deliberative and judicial rhetoric. Epideictic, continues Walker, "shapes the fundamental grounds, the 'deep' commitments and presuppositions, that will underlie and ultimately determine decision and debate in particular pragmatic forms" (9). For this reason, Walker proposes to think about epideictic discourse as foundational to public discourse, as it is also present in deliberation and in judicial discourse. As O'Gorman writes, "we can understand the epideictic function of discourse as primary, central, and primal" (33). The magnitude (and phantasia) that performs the epideictic function—or what we might call an aesthetic-epistemic—is not the same as the judicial or deliberative discourse that it energizes.

PROLIFIC RESPONSES

It's not that conspiracy theorists do not traffic in evidence. If anything, they are drowning in tidal waves of evidence all day long. Yet, those of us who disagree with their claims tend to focus on the rationality (or irrationality) of individual pieces of evidence. *Popular Mechanics* took this approach in their book *Debunking 9/11 Myths,* which aimed to respond to the most common conspiracy claims around 9/11. Using official data from reputable sources, the lengthy book explains in detail how conspiracy theorists get their science and mechanics all wrong. The *Popular Mechanics* models of argument and debate are well within bounds of idealized deliberate discourse. One claim is made using evidence, and then the responder makes a counterclaim by using evidence that has a higher degree of probable validity. But, not surprisingly, *Debunking 9/11 Myths* did not change many truthers' minds.

The limitation of this evidence/counter-evidence model of deliberation is that we are not always clear about what is being actually referenced in certain claims. When evidence of some kind is being offered, such as the presence of suspect nanoparticles, it makes perfect sense to assume that this is the evidence we should use to evaluate that claim. However, this assumption can lead us down some dead-end roads, rhetorically speaking. For conspiracy theorists, the proliferation of evidence transfigures into something else—something aesthetic. Consequently, suggestions like the ones Cass Sunstein and Adrian Vermeule make in their frequently cited essay, "Conspiracy Theories: Causes and Cures," are a bit weak. Sunstein and Vermeule argue that conspiracy theories are difficult to correct due to their "self-sealing" quality, which means that when contrary evidence is offered to conspiracy theorists, that contrary evidence is often discarded as a lie or is absorbed into the larger structure of the overall theory. Sunstein and Vermeule describe conspiracy thinking as the result of "crippled epistemology" or a "degenerating research program." They write:

> Our primary claim is that those who hold conspiracy theories of this distinctive sort typically do so not as a result of a mental illness of any kind, or of simple irrationality, but as a result of a "crippled epistemology," in the form of a sharply limited number of (relevant) informational sources. (204)

For Sunstein and Vermeule, the remedy is to increase available information sources to people who may find themselves encountering conspiracy discourse. They recommend infiltrating the online networks where conspiracy discourse happens in order to share multiple sources of information. While their suggestion is well-intentioned, it misidentifies what undergirds the conspiracy theorist's epistemology. The ground of a truther's epistemology may appear to be the (flawed) evidence they cite in abundance, yet their epistemologies are actually grounded in the aesthetic sense that crossed an important threshold long ago.

Kenneth Burke also points out the weakness of this strategy in "The Rhetoric of Hitler's Battle," which offers a look at the magnitude of Hitler's perverse archive: "If you point out the enormous amount of evidence to show that the Jewish worker is at odds with the 'international Jew stock exchange capitalist,' Hitler replies with one hundred per cent regularity: That is one more indication of the cunning with which the 'Jewish plot' is being engineered" (194–95). Any counter-evidence is simply absorbed into an ever-growing archive of anti-Semitism. Hitler's perverse magnitude of evidence scaled up to what he saw as the truth of the "International Jew." One observation that follows from Burke's analysis turns Sunstein and Vermeule's argument on its side: Perhaps unjustifiable claims are faulty not due to a lack of evidence but instead gain fuel from evidentiary abundance. Counter-evidence fails, to borrow Hume's words, because Hitler's archival magnitude references nothing beyond itself. It references only its own sentiment: its beautiful coherence of the evil International Jew.

As I discussed in the previous chapter, accumulation in action, or adding up, can often serve as its own telos. This point is vital for understanding how proliferation itself is something more than a descriptor of evidence. Proliferation is not only a *kind* of evidence but can also be a *form* of evidence. Ian Reyes and Jason K. Smith describe conspiracy theory's tendency to pursue evidence accumulation as an "entelechial formation." They argue that the "entelechy of conspiracism lies not in dialectically refining its research program to match the methods of its critics but in constantly revising its arguments in the interest of maintaining the spin, oscillation, or blur that is the hallmark of conspiracist aesthetics" (412). The work of accumulation is a way of keeping the spin going, just as what is accumulated passes over into an aesthetic sense.

And, of course, such beautiful coherence manifests in a number of ways. I discovered this during my fieldwork with 9/11 truthers when I felt the subtle shifts from the calculable to the incalculable. Many of the facts and evidence cited by truthers are far too technical for me to fully grasp. I don't know much about nanoparticles or the physics of implosion. In spite of my ignorance, I carried a strong sense that these alternative theories are *wrong*. More than that, I was convinced that these theories possess toxic rhetorical dimensions that degrade public discourse. Truthfully, though, I did not arrive at these claims based on a fine-tuned consideration of all cited evidence. Instead, the (beautiful coherence) of my claim emerges from an accumulation—the adding up—of a repulsive archive. My archive of repulsion could also be called an entelechial formation, as its accumulation feeds a spinning blur that feels like an aesthetic whole.

If I were asked to give an account of the accumulated materials in my archive of repulsion, I would offer some of the following:

Eddie's question to me, asking if I was a Jew

Instances of Jewish people associated with 9/11 labeled "Zionist" and thrown into suspicion

My memories of reading David Duke's writings about "Zionist plots," implicating all Jews

The phone conversation I had with one truther, who told me that he believed the government was listening to our call

The truther conference I attended where a Holocaust denial book was offered for sale

The articles I copied and saved (but never read) from recognized scholars who explained the faulty science behind truther claims

My notebooks that sprawled with notes about the New World Order

Memories of growing up in an evangelical church who taught that the Soviet Union was part of the New World Order and the Beast from Revelation

My discomfort with hypergraphia and forms of textual mania

The questions I received from interviewees about whether or not my institutional review board consent form was really some government ruse to spy on the truther movement

These things add up. For me, they *make sense.* My claims that 9/11 truther discourse is repulsive and wrong are infused with the kind of epistemic aesthetic that is intrinsic to megethos. As I continue adding up my archive of repulsion, I am building an archive from which I draw my claims. And while those claims may indeed sound like they are judicial ("The government most likely did not plan the 9/11 attack") or deliberative ("We should believe reputable scholarly explanations over amateur investigations"), they are grounded in a primary epideictic that is sustained by accumulation. Those rare moments when I found myself counterarguing evidence with truthers, I was referencing something more than a particular fact or piece of information. I am referencing the beautiful coherence that I have taken in. In a sense—because of sense—I move through the same process as truthers themselves.

The rhetorical impact of magnitude has a number of consequences for how we think about evidence and the way it gets deployed in public life. For one thing, it is not only conspiracy theorists who are dealing in transfiguration from quantity to quality. We already know that the proliferation of gigantic archives moves us more than the contents of those archives. A mundane example is that familiar dilemma of choosing a restaurant in a new city. Walking down the street, you see a restaurant that looks full of people and another restaurant across the street that is almost empty. In taking a risk for the best possible dinner, it's likely that many of us would choose the fuller one. Researchers identify this behavior as "social proof," which explains why we might find a business with a line out the door as more appealing than one with very few customers. Or, in the age of social media, we may find an account with many thousands of followers more worthy of attention than one with very few.

More significantly, the rhetorical impact of magnitude shapes and misshapes our sense of argument, or the ways we understand how archives of evidence are used to justify claims or beliefs. For instance, what we are responding to when we debate a conspiracy theorist may not be the same object that our interlocutor imagines. In those cases, the evidence has been transfigured, it has shifted, into something awe-full. It has become gigantic, something that emerges from an aesthetic sense. As interlocutors tasked with judgment, then, we are faced with two possibilities: responding in the role of kritai or the role of theoros. As kritai, we are called to evaluate claims as either judicial or deliberative. As theoros, however, we evaluate the claims as epideictic. Responding in the role of theoros calls for us "not to make rulings but to form opinions about and in response to the discourse presented," as Walker writes (9). The aesthetics of magnitude thus call for an aesthetic response as the most fitting.

Reading archival magnitude through the eyes of theoros instead of kritai does not mean we should abandon the responsibility of evidentiary evaluation. Rather, when we read claims that draw upon magnitudes of "evidence," we might read them rhetorically as making an aesthetic judgment. Such a reading does not make a claim less (or more) legitimate than if we were to read it as an empirical claim. An aesthetic response calls for us to listen to matters of coherence. When faced with an onslaught of evidence, our critical ears may listen to what exactly is being built from such accumulation.

> We must face proliferation on its own terms.
> We must face proliferation on its own.
> We must face proliferation.
> We must face.
> We must.

CHAPTER 3

Distal Evidence and the Power of Empty Archives

IN 1969, when the Eagle first landed on the moon and American astronauts took those infamous first human steps, the moments were filmed by a small television camera that was attached to the Eagle's door. NASA engineers had designed the camera so that when the astronauts first opened that door upon landing, the camera would immediately begin filming and transfer the live images back to earth. The camera's footage was what millions of people watched around television sets on July 20, 1969. For viewers at home, the images were astounding even if a bit blurry and fuzzy. The low quality was not the result of the Eagle's camera, however. The grainy footage was due to the fact that the televised images were actually being converted from raw footage being directly transmitted to NASA tracking stations in California and Australia. What engineers saw on their own NASA monitors at these stations was crisp and clear images of the entire moon landing and walk. NASA engineers recorded these much clearer images of the raw data on one-inch telemetry tapes and stored them in fourteen-inch canister reels. After the successfully televised moon landing took place, NASA engineers then sent the fourteen-inch canister reels to the Goddard Space Flight Center. The Goddard Space Flight Center then mailed the 13,000 reels of data to the Washington National Records Center in Maryland.

But the story becomes a bit more complicated after those reels were sent away to be archived. Decades after the Eagle landed on the moon, researchers began searching for the original raw footage that would allow them to examine the clearer images. The poor quality of the converted imagery did not provide researchers with the kind of detail that might be found on the original direct transmission. Engineers hoped to digitize the original footage into higher quality resolution video. Along with NASA researchers, several engineers with Westinghouse Electric, who had designed Apollo 11's special camera, began looking for the original footage in the Washington National Records Center (WNRC). They came up with nothing. In 2006, a team of researchers combed through over 2,000 boxes and stacks at WNRC, only to find missing records and canisters. The researchers sifted through every possible box, sometimes on hands and knees, but the original footage was still not found.

A national call went out to retired Goddard and WNRC employees, asking for any clues about what might have happened to the tapes. Although NASA and many archivists continue searching for clues as to what happened, it seems that the missing footage was not archived as carefully as it should have been. Shipped off to a government warehouse, they may have been marked incorrectly or mismanaged through sloppy record-keeping. While NASA officially remains hopeful that the data will eventually be found, the Apollo 11 tapes remain missing.

For many of us, the story of the missing Apollo 11 tapes is a lesson on the importance of proper archival and records management. Like so many other artifacts that get lost through mismanagement, the high-quality moon landing footage is a loss for the nation's historical preservation. But, for others, the missing footage tells another story about archives. Bart Sibrel is one of those who consider the Apollo 11 tapes' "missing" status as abundantly content-full. Sibrel has long been an outspoken conspiracy theorist who believes the moon landing was a hoax. Although Sibrel is far from a familiar figure, he gained notoriety as the man who got punched by none other than Buzz Aldrin. In 2002, Aldrin was leaving a Los Angeles hotel when Sibrel cornered him and demanded that the astronaut "swear on a Bible" that he had actually landed on the moon. After Sibrel repeatedly taunted Aldrin, the astronaut decided he had had enough and punched Sibrel squarely on the jaw. Video of the incident has repeatedly been circulated (and celebrated) online in the years since.

Sibrel's 2001 documentary, *A Funny Thing Happened on the Way to the Moon,* claims that the original Apollo 11 tapes were deliberately destroyed because the footage would show, in high resolution, the Hollywood production of the "moon landing" as it was actually staged in some terrestrial movie set. Other moon hoax believers have also joined in. For example, Aron Ranen's 2005 documentary, *Did We Go?,* similarly argues that the moon landing was a hoax. In a TV interview with Glenn Beck, Ranen exclaimed, "Glenn, to me it's incredible that we can keep track of Egyptian pots from 2,000 years ago, *but we lose tapes made only forty years ago?*" Like Sibrel, Ranen clearly does not buy NASA's story.

The missing Apollo 11 tapes are what we might call empty archives. They are archives that (possibly) exist, but the content is unavailable, missing, unobtainable. For people like Sibrel and Ranen, the missing content does not equate to missing meaning. On the contrary, the missing content is bursting with significance. This paradox drives my curiosity about the object of reference in moments when evidence is cited while simultaneously absent. How does evidence *work* when it is simply not there? If archives of evidence are either not available or are simply nonexistent, how is it that they still function as part of a claim? In particular instances where empty archives are cited, what *is* the referent of those claims? In this chapter, I examine archives whose contents are missing, absent, or false. Specifically, I discuss several cases of archival hoaxes, forgeries, and what we might simply call empty archives. Although the cases I discuss are vastly different, what they have in common is that the archive in each of these instances is either not *real* or else they are not available. Nevertheless, the fictional or missing archives continue to serve as reference for very serious claims.

Of course, archives can be literally or effectively empty in several different ways. While Sibrel and Ranen focus on missing documents, the inverse scenario could also be described as empty. For instance, the legal phenomenon of "document dumps" happens in a trial when one side's request for information from the other side is met with a flood of documents so extensive that no legal team or lawyer could possibly sift through them all. Tactically, dumping documents is the same as withholding information, since the relevant content is essentially buried under gigantic mountains of other information. When an ex-colleague of mine was being investigated by her university for some kind of violation, she was ordered to provide copies of emails pertaining to the case that had been sent through her university email account. Feeling that she was being unjustly accused, my friend printed out a copy of every email she had ever sent through her university account. Thousands and thousands of emails—a mind-blowing amount of papers—resulted. She wheeled in the stacks to the administration office and left them for someone to sift through. Her tactic of resistance was the document dump. In my friend's situation, much like all other document dumps, the referent is not the contents. The referent is the archive as a whole, communicating one simple message: Fuck you.

And then there are other kinds of empty archives. Consider the polarizing case of WikiLeaks. When Edward Snowden leaked thousands of National

Security Agency (NSA) documents to WikiLeaks, the document dump landed with multiple thuds across globe. It was a sensation. Yet, the sheer size of the leaked documents made it nearly impossible for anyone to fully review. Even Snowden himself admitted that he had not read each document. This point came sharply into focus in an interview with talk show host John Oliver, who asked Snowden how many of the documents he'd actually read. Snowden admitted that he had not read all of the documents, but had "evaluated" them. With darkly dry humor, Oliver responded: "When you're handing over thousands of NSA documents, the last thing you want to do is read them" (*Last Week Tonight*, April 5, 2015).

If Snowden himself had not read each document, then it is safe to assume that most people probably read much less—if any—of the NSA leaks. Nevertheless, the archive existed. One online comment is fairly illustrative of such economy:

> I have never read WikiLeaks, but God, am I thankful for it. We can't say I am proud of our boys overseas if they are raping women or children or shooting innocent civilians or torturing soldiers or deceiving other countries about our reasons for being in their lands. ("Julian")

Does it matter that this commenter "knows" facts from an archive he has not read? Perhaps. Rhetorically, however, the WikiLeaks archive here resembles something more like sharebait, which so many of us have also passed along. The term *sharebait* plays off the more familiar sense of "clickbait," or those infamous scammy headlines that draw on our curiosity for the sensational. "You won't believe this one amazing trick to lose belly fat!" shouts one clickbait story, which is right next to another link that tells me I will be "shocked by Barron Trump's IQ!" Clickbait is the digital version of a sideshow carnival barker, inviting us to enter the tent and see some freaky shit inside. And, like that sideshow, the clickbait story never fails to disappoint.

Sharebait, on the other hand, does not depend on getting individual bodies to enter the freak show tent. Instead, the digital stories that compose "sharebait" are designed in such a way that we will inevitably share with our friends and followers. I have done this. On the surface, this kind of sharing would seem to be more akin to how my mother used to clip out newspaper stories from my hometown newspaper and then mail them to me. (Pre-internet, of course.) But there is one important difference between the clippings my mother sent and what we now experience: Sharebait most frequently involves the sharing of unread articles. In one study, researchers found that the "data suggest that lots of people are tweeting out links to articles they haven't fully read" (Manjoo). One study found that 59 percent of links shared on social media have never actually been clicked. In other words, most people appear to retweet news without ever reading it (Gabielkov et al.). We share these things not because we have read all the content, but in order to say something else. Maybe we share to stay "in touch" or to signal that we are aware of a position or event. We share in order to demonstrate solidarity or distance ourselves from something. In short, the apparent referent (the article) is not the actual referent in this scenario.

For me, however, the finest visual representation of contentless archives was broadcast on January 11, 2017. It was President-Elect Trump's first press conference after the election, and questions swirled about how he would divest from his business dealings when he took office. In the rather bizarre scene, Trump stood at a podium right next to a table that was completely covered with stacks upon stacks of papers in manila folders. "These papers are just some of the many documents I've signed turning over complete and total control to my sons," Trump said. When reporters asked if they could actually see the contents of the papers, Trump refused and staffers blocked journalists from getting close to the stacks.

The spectacle of the stacks became instant fodder for critique, parody, and outright mockery in the media and in online forums. *Daily Show* host Trevor Noah lambasted what he dubbed the "manila mountain":

> Look how much work he's been doing for America! But don't look too close, because if you do, you may seem to notice things. For instance, the paper inside the folders doesn't look like weeks of contracts, it looks brand new. . . . If you had real folders of real business you were really doing, wouldn't you at least have labels on them? Come on, Donald. At this point it's not even about the lie, man, it's about the lack of respect. Just take, like, two seconds to write down a fake label. Just be like "Conflict Stuff," we don't care! (January 12, 2017)

Around the same time, a *Saturday Night Live* sketch parodied the press conference, featuring actress Cecily Strong as Sheri A. Dillon, Trump's tax lawyer, who explained divestment strategy to reporters: "This right here is all the papers that prove that Mr. Trump is really divesting. I mean, look at all these papers. If he wasn't divesting, how could there be so many dang papers?" (January 14, 2017). As Strong attempts to pick up a piece of paper to read, however, she accidently reveals that the stacks are nothing but a cardboard fake.

The accusation of empty papers in Trump's stacks went well beyond nighttime jokes, however. One reporter took a close-up photo of the stacks, which included papers that appeared to be blank. Reporters speculated that the stacks of papers were nothing more than meaningless "stage props." On social media, people zoomed in on this single photograph to analyze the seeming non-contents of Trump's documents. The British newspaper *The Independent* went even further to analyze the paper dimensions and look in order to conclude that they were most likely blank pages.

Empty archives mark a departure from the archival magnitude I discussed in the previous chapter—archives that are bursting with contents. Here, however, we are examining archives that are empty and void of contents. This raises a fair question of whether we should even call these archives at all. After all, though we may debate the proper way of defining archives, it is likely that most of us can agree on one key point: Archives have contents. Maybe it's not quite a "tree falling in the empty forest," but is an archive without contents really an archive at all? However, as the Apollo 11 tapes suggest, empty archives do not always mark an absence. Even empty archives can circulate meanings and make rhetorical impacts in public life. This was abundantly clear when watching the bizarre Trump press conference with blank pages of "evidence." Likewise, for people like Sibrel and Ranen, the empty archives become copious evidence.

Sibrel and his band of moon landing truthers open a door for new lines of inquiry. How do archives sans content manage to both not exist and still serve as evidence? In other words, if archival evidence is used to support a claim, and if that archival evidence is also nonexistent or not available for reference, then what exactly are those claims referencing? Where is the source of evidentiary power? How does evidence *act* when it is not real?

SERIOUS REFERENCE AND ARCHIVAL HOAXES

The Apollo 11 moon landing was a staged hoax. But the alien spacecraft that crashed in Roswell, New Mexico, during the summer of 1947 was real. At least, this is what Bill Moore might tell you. From a young age, Moore was fascinated by UFOs and the idea of extraterrestrial life. He worked in relative obscurity as a teacher and freelance writer until he gained notoriety in 1980, when he published *The Roswell Incident*. This book was the first major work to investigate the UFO crash in Roswell and its government cover-up. In ufologist circles, Moore became an expert on all things UFO. Maybe this explains why, in the mid-1980s, some anonymous source began mailing him typewritten postcards with strange riddles and odd references to hidden documents that would expose the government's knowledge of UFOs. The mystery of these postcards only deepened when Moore's friend and fellow ufologist Jaime Shandera received a strange envelope in the mail containing a roll of 35mm film. The envelope was plain brown with no return address, though it was postmarked Albuquerque, New Mexico. When Shandera developed the film roll, he discovered that each image contained a photograph of classified government documents that hinted at something called the MJ-12 Special Studies Project. Working with Shandera, Moore interpreted the anonymous mailings to mean that there were hidden documents in governmental archives that would expose the truth of UFOs once and for all.

Moore and Shandera headed to the National Archives and sifted through around one hundred boxes from the Air Technical Intelligence Center Archives. They did not find anything significant in those materials until they opened up Box 189 of Record Group 341. Next to file folder 4–1846 was a faded blue carbon copy of a memo addressed to General Nathan Twining by Robert Cutler, who was President Eisenhower's assistant. The memo was dated July 14, 1954, with the subject heading: "NSC/MJ-12 Special Studies Project" (see figure 3). The short memo spilled the beans on a secret group called Majestic 12 (or MJ-12), which had been organized by President Truman in 1947 (the same year as the Roswell crash) in an effort to investigate a spacecraft that landed somewhere in the US. Members of the top-secret MJ-12 included scientists, academics, government officials, and military officials. Delighted by their discovery, Moore and Shandera circulated the Cutler-Twining memo throughout the UFO researcher community. This piece of archival evidence convinced many ufologists that the government has indeed been complicit in a decades-long cover-up of alien contact on our planet.

But, almost as quickly as the MJ-12 archives came into public light, other ufologists began debating their authenticity. Could it really be the case that a highly classified memo would have been so carelessly lost in the midst of unrelated archival material in the National Archives, only to be discovered by two researchers who had been directed there through a series of enigmatic postcards? Officially, the National Archives states that the Cutler-Twining memo is most likely a fabrication. But, among the skeptical UFO researcher community, the larger question is *who* perpetrated this false document. As I read about this strange archival discovery, I found myself increasingly relying on Occam's razor to explain its origin: Moore and Shandera had made the whole thing up. And who can blame them? It makes a great story. Maybe they believed the hoax would bring more attention and activism to a cause they truly believed in. Maybe they simply wanted the fame. Whatever the motivation may have been, I saw the MJ-12 documents as signifying very little beyond two men's ability to create a good hoax.

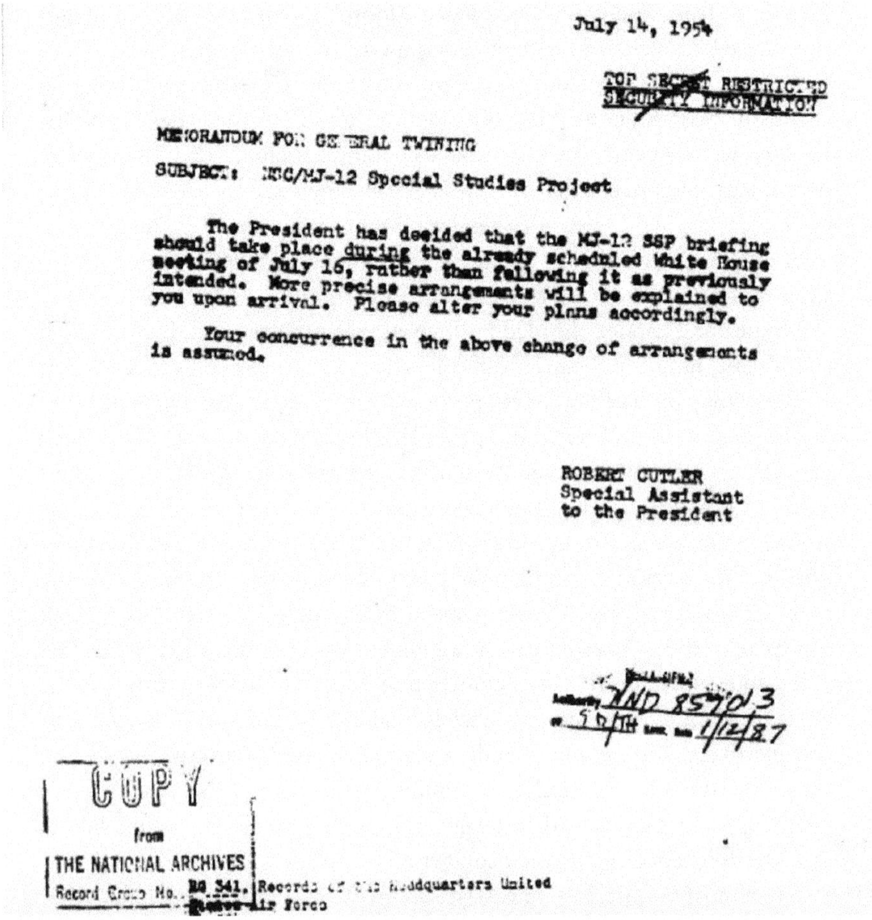

July 14, 1954

~~TOP SECRET RESTRICTED SECURITY INFORMATION~~

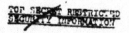

MEMORANDUM FOR GENERAL TWINING

SUBJECT: NSC/MJ-12 Special Studies Project

The President has decided that the MJ-12 SSP briefing should take place during the already scheduled White House meeting of July 16, rather than following it as previously intended. More precise arrangements will be explained to you upon arrival. Please alter your plans accordingly.

Your concurrence in the above change of arrangements is assumed.

ROBERT CUTLER
Special Assistant
to the President

Authority NND 857013
1/12/87

COPY
from
THE NATIONAL ARCHIVES
Record Group No. RG 341, Records of the Headquarters United States Air Force

FIGURE 3. The Cutler-Twining memo: "The President has decided that the MJ-12 SSP briefing should take place during the already scheduled White House meeting of July 16"

Although some skeptical UFO researchers shared my theory, I increasingly discovered that even the skeptics still find deep meaning in the fabrication. Many ufologists who doubt MJ-12's existence have concluded that documents like the Twining-Cutler memo are indeed official government materials. Yet, they also conclude that their existence in the archive is intentional and meant to be discovered by people like Moore and Shandera. Robert Hastings, a respected UFO researcher who avidly maintains that the government is covering up UFO information, is one such skeptic. Hastings argues that the MJ-12 archival discovery is the work of US Air Force counterintelligence forces, who wanted to throw legitimate UFO research off track. Any seeming authenticity of the documents, writes Hastings, "might instead be explained by the spooks who created them having done their homework." Hastings and other skeptics see the forged archives as intentional disinformation, designed to undercut and ultimately crush the work of real ufologists.

The disinformation angle only gained more traction in 1989 when Moore delivered a keynote address to the annual MUFON (Mutual UFO Network) convention in Las Vegas. Among UFO researchers, Moore's speech is still legendary. In many ways, it marked the end of Moore's status as a respected ufologist. Standing nervously at the podium, Moore told his audience that around the time of the MJ-12 document discovery, he had in fact been working with Air Force Intelligence Officer Richard Doty, a government official who had been tasked with feeding false information to UFO researchers. Moore detailed the ways that he had worked with Doty as a middleman in this disinformation campaign, but only as a kind of double agent:

> Judging by the positions of the people I knew to be directly involved in it, [the disinformation] definitely had something to do with national security. There was no way I was going to allow the opportunity to pass me by. . . . I would play the disinformation game, get my hands dirty just often enough to lead those directing the process into believing I was doing what they wanted me to do, and all the while continuing to burrow my way into the matrix so as to learn as much as possible about who was directing it and why. (qtd. in Clark 164)

After delivering his remarks, Moore abruptly left the stage without taking questions from the audience. If some ufologists were skeptical of the MJ-12 documents before this speech, many more were persuaded afterward that the archives were indeed the work of government counterintelligence.

The MJ-12 document saga has so many twists and turns that it is dizzying for most outsiders. I found myself less curious about the truth behind the mysterious archival discovery than about any general consensus in the UFO researcher community about what the documents mean. I thought perhaps talking to someone at MUFON, the largest and most active UFO research organization, might be one way to find an answer. MUFON officials pointed me to Dr. Bob Wood, an outspoken proponent of the MJ-12 documents' authenticity. When I wrote to Wood to ask if he believed the documents to be part of a disinformation campaign, he dismissed this theory immediately. He told me that he believes Moore and Shandera stumbled across the documents that were archived away by accident. "My gut feeling is that the very much most likely conclusion is that those who were trying to get any and all references to UFOs or MJ-12 deleted missed it," Wood explained. "It doesn't mention UFOs, so unless the archivist knew that MJ-12 was a possible UFO connection, they let it out for public viewing, thinking it was harmless."

After reading Wood's response, I sat on it for a few days before carefully asking a follow-up question. If the archived documents are indeed genuine, then why do so many people believe them to be a deliberate government plant? I expected him to tell me that the skeptics are ignorant or deluded. Or maybe the disbelievers have not done their homework. Instead, his response sent me down another disinformation trail:

> I think that those who favor seeing them as hoaxed documents may be strongly driven by trying to avoid considering that we figured out how they worked almost right away and started building them and dispersing the technology after the military had it under control. What they may be hiding right now in the gradual release of more MJ-12 docs is to keep us from looking at what has been done to create secret space programs that they want to still keep secret from the public.

Although I read (and reread) his response many times, I found it difficult to interpret who "we" and "they" are in Wood's world. He seemed to be saying that the archived documents had been deliberately shrouded with doubt in order to hide the existence of additional documents, no doubt hidden away (accidently or not) in some other government archives.

The more people I spoke with in the UFO community, the more I heard the waves of skepticism and belief crash together. A number of people pointed to the fact that the Twining-Cutler memo discovered by Moore and Shandera had no proper archival referencing, as you might expect from something located in the National Archives. The original story of the memo's discovery told how the two researchers found it stashed accidently in Box 189 in Record Group 341, a collection unrelated to anything MJ-12. Unlike the other materials in this collection, there was no control number. Each time I heard this fact, I was unsure of what this detail meant. My ignorance must have been obvious, since whoever I was speaking to inevitably spelled it out for me: *No reference number just shows that it's a sloppy piece of disinformation planted by that fuckwad disinfo agent Bill Moore.* Then again, maybe not. *No reference number proves that the document is real and was planted there by someone with ties to MJ-12 who wanted it to be found.* Even when archival reference numbers are absent, they aren't.

I am not sure what to make of the MJ-12 archival drama. If nothing else, it marks a contrast to the missing Apollo 11 tapes, since the documents uncovered by Moore and Shandera are not missing at all. They are very much present—perhaps even *too* present. As Carl Sagan wryly remarks, "Where the MJ-12 documents are most vulnerable and suspect is exactly on this question of provenance—the evidence miraculously dropped on a doorstep like something out of a fairy story, perhaps 'The Shoemaker and the Elves'" (Sagan and Druyan 88). At the same time, both of these cases reflect the kind of rhetorical impact artifacts can have beyond their content. If the MJ-12 documents were purposefully circulated as false information designed to be "discovered" by UFO believers, then they were put into the archives in order to distract or dis-route another narrative (maybe top-secret Air Force or military operations). It is a kind of subtraction by addition: the subtraction of one narrative by the addition of others. On the flip side, for conspiracy theorists, the missing Apollo 11 tapes form a kind of addition by subtraction: Evidence of government lies is discovered through the absence of archival material.

No matter the truth of the missing Apollo 11 tapes or the strangely present Majestic 12 documents, both cases point to the ways that *something else* is referenced by archival materials. The archives operate even beyond their fidelity to facts or authenticity. The "empty archives" (empty because they are either missing or not authentic) are not empty of referential power. In fact, the emptiness itself is what gives these archival artifacts their significance. Emptiness speaks.

SERIOUSLY EMPTY

Twenty years after a UFO crashed in Roswell and caused a massive government cover-up, a countercultural magazine called *The Realist* revealed another piece of archival material that had been previously hidden from the public. In their May 1967 issue, *The Realist* published a piece titled "The Parts That Were Left Out of the Kennedy Book," purported to expose expurgated details from William Manchester's book on the Kennedy assassination, *The Death of a President,* which had just been released. Manchester's book received early buzz after Jacqueline Kennedy, who had commissioned Manchester as author, demanded that he remove certain details from the book. That Manchester did indeed remove material from *The Death of a President* was widely known, a fact that set the context for *The Realist's* piece. A brief editorial note appeared at the beginning of the magazine's alleged excerpts:

> An executive in the publishing industry, who obviously must remain anony-
> mous, has made available to the Realist a photostatic copy of the original
> manuscript of William Manchester's book, *The Death of a President.* Those
> passages which are printed here were marked for deletion months before
> Harper & Row sold the serialization rights to Look magazine; hence they do
> not appear even in the so called "complete" version published by the German
> magazine, Stern. ("Parts" 1)

What followed read like fairly straightforward popular historical prose. The
excerpt began with details of the 1960 Democratic National Convention,
where LBJ accused Kennedy's father of being a Nazi sympathizer. From there,
the author (purported to be Manchester) shares salacious details—though
written in the evenhanded prose of a historian—of Johnson's somewhat outlandish personal habits. After several paragraphs detailing Jacqueline Kennedy's struggles as both First Lady and "First Widow," the author then turns
to a somewhat thoughtful reflection on the media's bipolar representations of
political leaders. Media "want to expose their human frailties and they don't
want to expose their human frailties" ("Parts" 18). The media cover up and
expose in equal measure.

As an example of this kind of tension, the author points to a television
interview that Gore Vidal gave in London sometime after Kennedy's death.
During the interview, Vidal explained the reason why Jacqueline Kennedy
would always have a strong resistance to Johnson: "During that tense journey
from Dallas to Washington after the assassination, she inadvertently walked in
on him as he was standing over the casket of his predecessor and chuckling.
This disclosure was the talk of London but not a word was mentioned here"
("Parts" 18). Yet, continues the author, this seemingly heartless scene is not the
most outlandish detail of that moment. Jacqueline Kennedy later confirmed
Vidal's story to Manchester and added one very important detail. Quoting
Mrs. Kennedy, the author writes:

> That man was crouching over the corpse, no longer chuckling but breath-
> ing hard and moving his body rhythmically. At first I thought he must be
> performing some mysterious symbolic rite he'd learned from Mexicans or
> Indians as a boy. And then I realized—there is only one way to say this—he
> was literally fucking my husband in the throat. The bullet wound in front
> of his throat. He reached a climax and dismounted. I froze. The next thing I
> remember, he was being sworn in as the new President. ("Parts" 18)

This shocking quote is then followed by an editor's note that shares Manchester's handwritten marginal note: "1. Check with Rankin—did secret autopsy

show semen in throat wound? 2. Is this simply necrophilia or was LBJ trying to change entry wound into exit wound by enlarging?" ("Parts" 18). And with this disturbing series of images, the outtakes from Manchester's otherwise well-respected book come to a conclusion.

Not surprisingly, the morbid outtakes from Manchester's book began to circulate with a fiery intensity. Paul Krassner, editor of *The Realist,* recalls that several media outlets and government officials actually accepted the story as true. The most infamous believer, according to Krassner, was Daniel Ellsberg, who also happens to be the notorious Pentagon Papers leaker. Even among those who did not believe in the story's authenticity, there were strong suspicions that the outtakes had been intentionally leaked. JFK assassination researcher Ray Marcus accused *The Realist* of unwittingly publishing a phony excerpt given to them by a "CIA plant in order to discredit the valid dissent on the assassination" (Krassner 143). In other words, the hoax was intentionally spread in order to make the JFK conspiracy community look foolish.

Unsurprisingly, the excerpts were indeed a hoax. Years later, Krassner himself would admit to being the author of the story and the excerpts. This admission might seem to have put to rest any further speculation about either LBJ's necrophiliac tendencies or any other unseemly actions with JFK's corpse in the hours following the assassination. Yet, the life of this strange faux-journalism did not end with Krassner's admission. Decades later, online conspiracy forums feature comments that cite "The Parts That Were Left Out of the Kennedy Book" as a legitimate source. In one thread about the Kennedy assassination, a user named "Carlosdanger" writes: "Of course, the most upsetting and disturbing account of the events immediately following JFK's assassination is highlighted in 'The Parts That Were Left Out of the Kennedy Book'—published by The Realist in 1967—the narrative is available on the Internet only here (it seems)" (Carlosdanger). He then includes a link to the online version of *The Realist's* May 1967 issue.

Many readers at the time were able to recognize the satirical nature of Krassner's hoax. Still, even those who initially believed in the outtakes' authenticity understood the larger political commentary that Krassner was attempting to put forth. Krassner himself noted that the LBJ necrophilia story was in some ways taken "seriously" because many people believed Johnson was guilty of something horrible. As Krassner explained in a 1995 interview:

> People across the country believed—if only for a moment—that an act of presidential necrophilia had taken place. It worked because Jackie Kennedy had created so much curiosity by censoring the book she authorized—William Manchester's 'The Death Of A President'—because what I wrote was a metaphorical truth about LBJ's personality presented in a literary context,

> and because the imagery was so shocking, it broke through the notion that
> the war in Vietnam was being conducted by sane men. (Simril)

Likewise, Douglas Rushkoff argues that the serious uptake of this story was
possible because it provided a kind of metaphorical truth. Although LBJ might
not have literally penetrated Kennedy's body, writes Rushkoff, it was the case
that that "Johnson was seen as 'fucking over' a president" (261). Even today,
the continued references to Krassner's phony outtakes carry a kind of truth
value for some people. Kevin Barrett, a former professor and widely published
conspiracy theorist, makes reference to *The Realist* piece in an online essay
titled "US Military Ghouls Butchered JFK's Corpse!" Barrett begins his piece
by acknowledging that Krassner's piece was a satire, yet, he continues, "little
did he know how close he was to the truth." Barrett explains, "[It] wasn't LBJ
who committed indecent acts with JFK's bullet holes. It was actually certain
members of the US military top brass—including JFK's arch-enemy Gen. Cur-
tis LeMay—who did that." In other words, the outtakes that appear in *The
Realist* were not true, but they were also not untrue. As such, they hold a kind
of value as a record that is worthy of attention.

The faux archival materials published in *The Realist* thus exist for some
readers in a strange paradox: both true and not true. Much like the phony
Cutler-Twining memo that was "discovered" by Moore and Shandera, the
account of LBJ as corpse-fucker was not empty of meaning even though it
was untrue. Archival artifacts that are both true and not true expose one of
the complexities about how evidence functions, how it takes on a vitalism,
how it makes impact. In some ways, these empty archives manage to screw
up the neat schema we have traditionally imagined about evidence and reference. The paradoxical artifacts point elsewhere, beyond themselves, in order
to sustain claims.

In 1967, the same year that *The Realist* published the pseudo-Manchester
excerpts, another instance of true and not true archival artifacts also appeared.
The Report from Iron Mountain is about as far from *The Realist* as you can get.
Written in typical bureaucratese, the report appears to be a quasi-governmen-
tal report that emerged from the secret meeting of a fifteen-member "Special
Study Group," which was asked to study the ramifications of a "lasting peace"
in the US. According to the report, the shadowy, mysterious group concludes
that a lasting peace would have devastating effects on the overall economy and
health of the country. For that reason, the government must strive to engage
in a kind of perpetual war, even if the conflicts are manufactured. The report
was never meant to be read by the public, but one rogue member of the clan-
destine group smuggled it out and handed it over to a publisher.

The Report from Iron Mountain received a lot of attention, even appearing on the *New York Times* best-seller list. It was translated into fifteen languages. However, in 1972, writer Leonard Lewin admitted that there were never any secret meetings or special study groups. Lewin himself had authored the report as a kind of hoax. However, Lewin's admission itself was seen by some as a hoax. The rightwing Liberty Lobby believed so strongly that *Iron Mountain* was a government document—and therefore in public domain—that they published their own version in 1990. (Lewin would later sue them and would settle out of court in undisclosed agreement.) Others have continued to cite the report as a legitimate piece of secret government work that was never meant for public release. In the 1990s, for example, the documentary *Report from Iron Mountain: A Blueprint for Tyranny* carefully detailed the "realities" of the document as authentic. Today, the documentary continues to circulate online among a substantial crowd of believers.

Many more conspiracy theorists accepted Lewin's admission as true: The meeting in a secret bunker never actually took place. Nevertheless, this does not stop them from reading the document as a true statement. Mark Dice, a conspiracy theorist who gained popularity online and with some media figures like Jesse Ventura, has cast doubt that the document is actually a hoax. Even so, he writes, the report's authenticity does not really matter:

> Whatever the truth is regarding *The Report from Iron Mountain,* some of its contents turned out to be chillingly accurate in regards to what the future would hold. . . . There are already plenty of authentic declassified documents, government white papers, and mainstream reports which confirm similar or even more sinister operations . . . So the authenticity of the report isn't that important. (146)

Similarly, other conspiracy-minded writers have found a central *truth* to the document that may have been written as a fiction. "The author of this book took full credit for the first book and claimed that it was a hoax," writes noted conspiracy theorist G. Edward Griffin. "The only problem with this 'hoax' is that everything in the original book has worked out to be true. So whether the original title is a hoax or not is irrelevant. The original book is a blueprint for the present and the future."

Another infamous Kennedy conspiracy theorist, L. Fletcher Prouty, similarly plays both sides of the truth/hoax debate. In *JFK: The CIA, Vietnam, and the Plot to Assassinate John F. Kennedy,* published in 1992, Prouty introduces *The Report from Iron Mountain* as "that remarkable novel by Leonard Lewin," yet he then delves deeply into the report as though it were factual (4). Prouty repeatedly points to *The Report from Iron Mountain* as a perfect account of the logic that eventually led to Kennedy's assassination by those in power who wished to maintain the endless war machine. In a footnote, Prouty admits that while Lewin does claim that the book is a novel, "its content is so close to the reality of those years that many readers insist that the 'report' must be true" (366). True and not true, it swings both ways.

In *A Rhetoric of Irony*, Wayne Booth briefly mentions *The Report from Iron Mountain* in his discussion about reading texts "against" themselves, whether that means reading the serious as ironic or vice versa. When we read a text against itself, what might otherwise seem dull suddenly becomes interesting. Booth points to *The Report from Iron Mountain* as "in some ways more interesting as a possibly true expose than as an ironic hoax" (81). Indeed, as we can see from those who read the text as a literal report of secret government conspiracies, the outcome can lead to passionate discourse (not to mention dramatic instances of extreme paranoia). Reading the text as a hoax, as Booth and I both do, is likely to generate much less passion.

Booth's serious/ironic binary is echoed in another binary that emerged during the 2016 presidential elections, when commentators struggled to make sense of Donald Trump. Trying to read the text of Trump's candidacy, some writers noted that his words could best be understood through a serious/literal distinction. This distinction first gained popularity in Salena Zito's essay "Taking Trump Seriously, Not Literally," which appeared in *The Atlantic*. Her analysis of Trump's supporters exposed two different reading strategies on the parts of Trump backers and the media. Zito argued that when the media attempted to dispute "facts" that Trump tossed around during the election, they were not operating with the same logic that Trump's supporters used. She pointed to Trump's claim that 58 percent of black youth are unemployed. In actuality, Zito notes, the Bureau of Labor statistics reports only a 20.6 percent unemployment rate for black youths between ages sixteen and twenty-four. No matter. "When he makes claims like this," writes Zito, "the press takes him literally, but not seriously; his supporters take him seriously, but not literally." In short, Trump's textual corpus has some interesting referential possibilities.

Shortly after Zito's *Atlantic* article was published, billionaire venture capitalist and PayPal founder Peter Thiel gave a speech to the National Press Club where he explicitly endorsed the serious-but-not-literal approach to Trump (October 31, 2016). When Thiel was asked about his thoughts on Trump's promise to "ban Muslims" from traveling to the US, Thiel responded:

> Media is always taking him literally. I think a lot of the voters take him
> seriously but not literally, so when they hear the Muslim comment or the

wall comment, it's not, "Are you going to build a wall like the Great Wall of China" but, "We're going to have a saner, more sensible immigration policy" and "How do we strike the right balance between costs and benefits?"

Supporters like Thiel actively deployed this reading strategy with the bulk of Trump's textual corpus. As political writer Jonah Goldberg argued in a *Los Angeles Times* essay, Trump's team has openly used the notion of serious-but-not-literal as a guiding principle. Goldberg quotes Corey Lewandowski, Trump's first campaign manager, who gave his post-election analysis as a problem of over-literalness: "This is the problem with the media. You guys took everything Donald Trump said so literally. And the problem with that is the American people didn't" (Goldberg). Goldberg concludes by warning that while "serious-but-not-literal" might be a strong communicative strategy, "it is fairly ridiculous hogwash as a prescription for how to treat an actual president, or president-elect, of the United States."

Of course, Donald Trump is hardly the only example of competing literal versus serious readings. Reflecting on Peter Thiel's National Press Club comments, writer Noah Berlatsky notes that it is not only Trump supporters who read these two modes against one another. Hillary Clinton supporters did much the same with her rhetorical and political tropes ("inclusiveness," for example), which do not necessarily come from the literal policies or proposals she shared. Beyond Trump and Clinton, nearly any political candidate could serve as an example of how literal versus serious readings work for different audiences. Berlatsky argues that while the literalness of a candidate's specific proposals is certainly of interest to special interest groups, literalness "is almost never for the public as a whole." The words, images, promises, facts that candidates offer their audiences are ones that point not so much to their actual contents, but to something *else.*

Trump's discourse, *The Report from Iron Mountain,* phony accounts of LBJ's necrophilia, secret government UFO memos: These examples relay something strange about the ways that empty archives work. The contents are "empty" of fidelity to (one kind of) reality, yet they are also filled with significance and meaning. More importantly, these texts obtain their vitality by referencing something beyond themselves. It is not their contents that have evidentiary power, but their ability to point elsewhere. For many in the UFO research community, for example, the Majestic 12 materials are crucial pieces of evidence *because* their contents are fake. Likewise, for those who are suspicious of the government, *The Report from Iron Mountain* is less important for any secret information it contains than for the fact that certain "truths" are echoed in those pages.

DISTAL EVIDENCE

As evidence, these empty archives seem prone to confirmation bias, or the habit of finding select information that confirms what one already believes. Confirmation bias is also what makes arguing with conspiracy theorists such a rhetorical clusterfuck. The same can be said about trying to "prove" that someone's claim is invalid due to faulty evidence. Political researchers Brendan Nyhan and Jason Reifler explain why simply correcting people's bad evidence does not usually end successfully. For one thing, they argue, "humans are goal-directed information processors who tend to evaluate information with a directional bias toward reinforcing their pre-existing views" (303). We perform the confirmation bias in a shockingly high percentage of our daily lives. Yet, when contradictory information suggests that our beliefs are wrong, there can be a "backfire effect," whereby people "counterargue incongruent information and bolster their preexisting views" (305). In other words, we double down on our mistake by seeking out even more information that confirms our original belief.

Beyond confirmation bias, however, empty archives involve another interesting rhetorical maneuver worth exploring. In those instances where empty archives serve to support a claim (e.g., Apollo 11 did not land on the moon, the government is hiding information about UFOs, there are secret government agencies conspiring to oppress citizens), the actual referent is not the materials themselves (missing footage, found documents). The source of evidentiary and rhetorical power lies somewhere else besides the archive. This is why any attempt to debunk artifacts like *The Report from Iron Mountain* is not necessarily the most effective response or counterargument. Not only do texts like *Iron Mountain* reconfirm prior frameworks of belief and feeling, but the "truth" and "fact" of the texts point beyond themselves.

Maybe diagramming the argument will help illustrate this strange rhetorical structure. Being a good rhetoric student, I still find the Toulmin "T" one of the most satisfying diagram aesthetics I've ever encountered. It is an artificial arrangement, but the balance is hardly without beauty. The T links together a logic and design. To use Toulmin's own example: *Claim→ Harry is a British subject. Evidence→ Harry was born in Bermuda. Warrant→ A man born in Bermuda will generally be a British subject.* If we diagrammed some of the claims made in our cases above, we might end up with something like what is shown in figure 4.

I've always liked the Toulmin model for the way it diagrams claims. More than that, though, there is something about that T's spatialization that

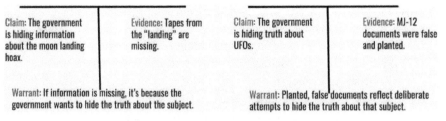

Claim: The government is hiding information about the moon landing hoax.

Evidence: Tapes from the "landing" are missing.

Warrant: If information is missing, it's because the government wants to hide the truth about the subject.

Claim: The government is hiding truth about UFOs.

Evidence: MJ-12 documents were false and planted.

Warrant: Planted, false documents reflect deliberate attempts to hide the truth about that subject.

FIGURE 4. Toulmin diagrams of conspiracy claims

reminds me of the probe that Michael Polanyi describes in his discussion of tacit knowledge. Polanyi writes, "In an act of tactic knowing we attend from something for attending to something else; namely, from the first term to the second term of the tacit relation. . . . It is the proximal term, then, of which we have a knowledge that we may not be able to tell" (10). His example is someone lacking sight who uses a probe as a way to feel their way around a room. A probe applies pressure against my hand, yet I interpret the "meaning" of that pressure to be at the probe's end, away from me. Polanyi writes, "When we make a thing function as the proximal term of tacit knowing, we incorporate it in our body—or extend our body to include it—so that we come to dwell in it" (16). In the act of deploying tacit knowledge, we bring that proximal term "inside," so to speak, by dwelling within it. Polanyi calls this a kind of "interiorization" (17). The particulars are "interiorized" and "dwelled within," rather than explicitly stated. A focus too much on particulars renders an entity somewhat meaningless, like repeating a word over and over again.

The probe comes to mind when I think of the Toulmin T, especially because I consider the ways in which we treat evidence as a proximal object that is outside of us, helping us to feel our way around, but which we imagine and feel as part of us. Evidence that seems to exist "out there" in the world may, in some cases, be our own feelings we identify as being "out there." Once that evidence is made manifest, those feelings (which already existed) "become" a judgment. To get spacey for a minute, we might imagine the top line of the T as a probe extending out from an invisible hand. The hand uses the probe to poke, sweep, bump against things.

I am probing my way around these ideas with examples of archives. The above cases I just described are like Polanyi's stick, helping me find the edges and open spaces. I'm trying to remember how I came to discover these archives in the first place. To the best of my recollection, I was online one afternoon, searching for stories about hoaxes and fake archives. I wanted to write about archival materials that had fooled people. Somehow, I found mentions about *The Report from Iron Mountain* and began frantically making notes. The rhythm and intensities of my read, write, read, write process were fast as I moved back and forth from essay to my own keyboard. I was probing *with* the evidence, as a proximal term that is also an extension of my body. I dwell with it. As a probe, the top line of the T is a connection between the point where we "find" something outside and the points where something registers. It registers because we are holding the probe that made contact.

Empty evidence is therefore distal in that there is *always content,* just like there is always something that comes to our attention when we are the ones holding the probe. The term *distal attribution* is commonly used in both media studies and cognitive psychology. As psychologists Malika Auvray et al. note, "Distal attribution can be defined as the ability to attribute the cause of our proximal sensory stimulation to an exterior and distinct object" (506). Similarly, cognitive scientists Joshua H. Siegle and William H. Warren describe distal attribution as the "perceptual experience of objects in external space" (208). Jessica Hartcher-O'Brien and Malika Auvray give the example of the wind rushing in our ears, when "changes in air pressure or vibrations arriving at our cochlea are perceived as arising from an object in the environment (such as a moving car) rather than from the cochlea itself" (Hartcher-O'Brien and Auvray 422). Distal attribution is pervasive enough that we do not even notice it happening, which is why the subject has been so fascinating for those studying everything from physiology to phenomenology.

Mapping distal attribution on top of Toulmin's argument model produces interesting results. We usually lodge things like personal belief, desires, experience at the very bottom of the T. The warrants are where the "gut level" explanation of argument often lives. Warrants make an argument fail or succeed, dictating how we see the claim and evidence working together. The Toulmin model of argument is useful for explaining how human weirdness affects the ways that claims and evidence are read by different audiences. Warrants can make or break the persuasiveness of a given claim, no matter how good or bad the evidence is. Yet, the model also reflects an unfortunate tendency to externalize evidence as somewhat separate from the human weirdness found in warrants. Evidence is just *out there,* ready for us to use, see, ignore, hide, trample over, massage, or miss. Of course, the Toulmin model does not preclude the fact that we *feel* certain ways about that evidence: We consider it, doubt it, believe it, question it, debate it, and so on. Nevertheless, this framework fundamentally poses evidence as something separate from us.

If we instead imagine evidence as distal in nature, the embodied aspect of evidence becomes clearer. Evidence is not necessarily out there, just waiting to be found, but is more like the registering of a connection made when a hand feels the probe hit something solid. Evidence registers *as* something because our body is there to feel it. The case of the missing Apollo 11 tapes is a good example of how distal evidence registers in this way. Bart Sibrel and other moon landing hoax conspiracy theorists feel the missing tapes as a buzzing connection. Something registers. It becomes evidence for all kinds of claims: NASA is lying, Buzz Aldrin is a phony, the government is hiding something. For me, the missing tapes fail to register much of anything. Then again, I am not holding much of a probe. Maybe some other time, I might find myself probing the dark corners of bureaucratic inefficiency or incompetence. With that probe in hand, I may find those missing tapes registering strongly. I feel its pressure against my own body. *Did you feel that? Evidence of government fuckup.*

What I'm describing here has strong correspondence to two familiar concepts: pareidolia and confirmation bias. The latter term is quite familiar: We seek out evidence that supports what we already believe. The former term is less familiar as a term, but is a common experience for most of us. Pareidolia is what happens when you see a face in something inanimate, such as a light socket that appears to have two eyes and a mouth. The face is not literally there, yet it *feels* to be the case. There is the buzz of something registering: a face, a drunk octopus, and so on. The *distal* of distal evidence is similar to both of these things in that what is not there on its self-obvious way registers as important, recognizable, real. Missing archives or phony secret documents can look like a recognizable case of government conspiracy, just as long as you know what *that* looks like.

But the rhetorical power of distal evidence goes beyond this buzzing register found in confirmation bias and pareidolia. Distal evidence also relies upon an explicit sense of distance. It involves a sleight of hand with the rhetorical element of presence. Presence is often theorized as a primary rhetorical strategy. As Perelman and Olbrechts-Tyteca write, "Things present, things near to us in space and time, act directly on our sensibility" (17). As illustration, they recount a Chinese fable about a king who was observing an ox being led to slaughter. He saw the ox, big and innocent, and the king was moved to pity. He demanded that a sheep be sent to slaughter in place of the ox. And with that decree, the ox was spared a terrible death. The sheep, however, was slaughtered with the same cruel stroke that the ox had just been spared. When asked why he pitied the ox but not the sheep, the king replied that he could see the ox, but not the sheep. The ox was present. Making things feel present is the task of a rhetorician, since "it is not enough indeed that a thing should exist for a person to feel its presence" (Perelman and Olbrechts-Tyteca 116–17).

In the case of distal evidence, however, presence is upended. Rather than making things feel close, distal evidence is made to feel remote. Evidence is "out there," away from ourselves. Presence thus turns into a kind of ventriloquist act, where the sound seems to be coming from somewhere else. When evidence of government conspiracy shows up as evidence, as it does for some in the *Report from Iron Mountain,* there is a simultaneous recognition of something familiar. It *looks like* conspiracy, just like two dots and a line can look like a face. That recognition happens, of course, because I know the patterns. They are an embodied sense. Yet, at the same time, that familiarity must also be accompanied by a sense that the evidence exists apart from me. It possesses a distance that makes such evidence available to and graspable by not only me, but everyone.

If I listen for evidence as that which is truly outside—on that far end of the T, outside of our bodies altogether—then I would say that claims about secret government bunker meetings and moon landing hoaxes are empty. Yet, if I listen for evidence as the real that is within the story itself, then I hear something different. Not something that has an empirical measurement of fidelity, at least not in the same way, but something that still speaks about what we recognize as publics. When we begin to see argument less as a model T and more of a moving process of proximities and felt connections, then we are also freed up to respond to more than a single element of an argument (the claim, the evidence, the warrant). Instead, we can turn to the ways such felt connections happen, as well as to the effects and aftershocks of those connections. Evidence is always real in its reference, which is to a felt experience of proximities.

FUTURE PERFECT ARCHIVES

The concept of distal evidence upturns a number of commonplaces about distance and presence. Consider one of the most infamous cases of an archive that is simultaneously distant and present, missing and found, real and false. Few cases signify these intertwinements more than the *Protocols of the Elders of Zion,* which have a complex history that is still not completely clear. The overall context of the *Protocols* begins with a mix of unhappy European post-WWI environments and a frightful Russian revolution. A general sense of fear had spread across continents. Questions naturally emerged. Why is this happening? Why is this happening to us? The answer, for many Europeans and Russians, was clear: All of the misery must be caused by Jews. This was the scene that gave birth to the *Protocols.*

The *Protocols* were purported to be a kind of secret playbook by Jews who had plans to dominate all sectors of life for goyim everywhere. Each of the twenty-four protocols appeared to instruct Jews on how to manipulate banking systems, governments, and even cultural entertainment so that non-Jews would be lulled into submission and, ultimately, controlled by a worldwide Jewish cabal. The *Protocols* also boast that this process is already happening around the world. Poverty, misery, and despair: They are all part of the Jews' carefully orchestrated plans. Around the same time in the US, the *Protocols* gained popularity after Henry Ford funded its publication under the title *The International Jew*. Pieces of the *Protocols* appeared between 1920 and 1922 in *The Dearborn Independent,* which was also owned by Ford.

By the time I was old enough to learn of the *Protocols,* they were almost always contextualized as anti-Semitic forgeries. A quick dip into the history behind the forgery yields all kinds of dramatic characters and nefarious plotting. There is Matvei Golovinski, born into Russian aristocracy, who is said to have composed them in the early twentieth century at the request of the Russian secret police. In the account of Russian-born Polish Princess Catherine Radziwill, Golovinski visited the princess in the winter of 1905 and showed her a manuscript of the *Protocols,* which he had claimed to have written. However, Radziwill's account has been repeatedly discredited as anachronistic and faulty, since the *Protocols* were likely published years earlier than 1905.

Then there is Sergei Nilus, an almost cinematic figure who was a self-described mystic and a contemporary rival to Rasputin. Between holding séances and other mystical practices, Nilus printed a full copy of the *Protocols* as a chapter of his 1905 autobiography, *The Great within the Small and Antichrist, an Imminent Political Possibility. Notes of an Orthodox Believer.* Nilus claimed to have been given the *Protocols* in 1901 by a trusted source who had obtained them from their original context, a secret meeting of Jewish Freemason leaders that was held somewhere in France. Later, however, Nilus would change his story to say that the *Protocols* were actually notes taken by those attending the first Zionist Congress held in Basel, Switzerland, in 1897.

Although it is not easy to untangle the conflicting stories of Russian secret police, Polish princesses, and Orthodox mystics, one thing about the *Protocols* does seem relatively clear: They were not only forgeries, but they were plagiarisms. Even within the earliest days of the *Protocols'* circulation, researchers discovered that major portions of the *Protocols* resemble an earlier fictional work, titled *The Dialogue in Hell between Machiavelli and Montesquieu,* written by Maurice Joly in 1864. Unsurprisingly, the fictional piece shows the two historical figures meeting in Hell, locked in a debate about politics. *The Dialogue in Hell* was intended as a political satire and critique of Louis-Napoléon Bonaparte's rule. Throughout the dialogue, both Machiavelli and Montesquieu dream up manipulative and conniving tactics for rulers who desired worldwide domination. With a simple twist of attribution, Joly's fictional dialogue was turned into anti-Semitic propaganda. The author of the *Protocols* simply put Machiavelli's fiendish words into the mouths of very much nonfictional Jews.

Having heard this history, tangled as it is, I had always imagined that a trove of archival evidence undergirded every part of the story. Yet, the archives themselves are surprisingly empty. In 1933, the Swiss Federation of Jewish Communities and the Jewish Congregation of Bern sued the Swiss Nazi Party for distributing the *Protocols,* which the plaintiffs maintained were an anti-Semitic forgery. The defendants included Silvio Schnell, who maintained that the *Protocols* were an authentic document that emerged from the first Zionist Congress in 1897. Ultimately, the judge determined that the *Protocols* were indeed a ridiculous forgery, and Schnell and his right-wing codefendants lost their case. However, the pieces of evidence provided at the trial—mainly the testimonies of witnesses and counter-witnesses—were some of the only materials actually produced. The larger archive was absent.

According to historian Michael Hagemeister, the stories given as evidence for the "true story" behind the *Protocols'* forgeries are lacking in substance. Hagemeister argues that the plaintiffs'

> detailed and coherent narrative was created and later authorized by a legal court. This narrative is, in itself, a conspiracy story, a dubious construction based on equally dubious witnesses. Thus the response to the myth of the Jewish conspiracy has been a counter-myth, which is no less mysterious than the one it aims to oppose. (94)

In fact, it was not until 1999 when a historian named Mikhail Lepekhine discovered a *Protocols* manuscript buried in the archives of a French agent who was also working as a Russian agent. The manuscript and other archival documents supported the narrative that Golovinski did indeed have a hand in turning Joly's political satire into an anti-Semitic pseudo-historical document. Yet, Hagemeister points out, even this discovery fails to tell us "by whom, when, and for what purpose the Protocols was fabricated" (94). To put it bluntly, any archival materials that reveal the whole story of the *Protocols* simply are not available.

At the same time, the *Protocols'* murky history was never much of an issue either for those who celebrate it or for those who loathe it. "Perhaps we will never discover the origins of the Protocols," writes Hagemeister. "But that should be frustrating only for a handful of historians. Everyone else already knows all too well what they want to believe" (95). That certainly seems to be the case for historical figures who helped to promote the *Protocols*. Once the revelation of Joly's manuscript came to light, *Protocol* apologists used several different tactics to salvage them. One tactic was to flatly deny that the forgery was actually a forgery at all. None other than Lord Alfred Douglas, best known for being Oscar Wilde's lover, advanced such a theory. Douglas proclaimed that Maurice Joly was actually Moses Joel, a Jew who was masking the truth of Jewish conspiracies behind the guise of a fictional dialogue. The truth of the *Protocols* was right there, hidden in plain site. Therefore, the revised versions were little more than a direct reading of Joly/Joel's revelations.

Lord Alfred Douglas's narrative was popular enough to legitimate the *Protocols* for many of his contemporaries, though another narrative emerged that gave the *Protocols* an airtight defense. This second defense is perhaps best summed up in the words of two men who, taken together, distinctly shaped the course of the twentieth century: Adolf Hitler and Henry Ford. In *Mein Kampf,* Hitler directly addresses the accusation that the *Protocols* are a forgery:

> *The Frankfurter Zeitung* is forever moaning to the people that they are supposed to be a forgery; which is the surest proof that they are genuine. . . . What matters is that they uncover, with really horrifying reliability, the nature and activity of the Jewish people, and expose them in their inner logic and their final aims. But reality provides the best commentary. (228)

Hitler readily admits that the *Protocols* may indeed be a forgery. Maurice Joly may or may not have actually been the cunning Jew Maurice Joel. These details mattered very little to Hitler, however, since he found the truth of the *Protocols* to be in the "nature and activities of the Jewish people" who were all around him.

Hitler's words are eerily echoed in Ford's comments about the *Protocols*, which he published and circulated with great zeal. In 1921, Ford responded to the same forgery claims that had prompted Hitler's statement, although Ford's conclusion was much more direct: "The only statement I care to make about the Protocols is that they fit in with what is going on now. They have fitted the world situation up to this time. They fit it now" (qtd. in Glock and Quinley 168). Once again, what legitimates the *Protocols* as evidence is not their authenticity but the way they appear to mirror what people like Ford already assume about Jews. Tellingly, Joseph Goebbels shared Ford's exact sentiments, as his diary entry dated April 10, 1924, reflects:

> I believe that The Protocols of the Elders of Zion is a forgery. That is not because the worldview of Jewish aspirations expressed therein are too utopian or fantastic—one sees today how one point after the other of The Protocols is being realized—but rather because I do not think the Jews are so completely stupid as not to keep such important protocols secret. I believe in the inner, but not the factual, truth of The Protocols. (qtd. in Bytwerk 212–13)

Hitler, Ford, and Goebbels maintained that the "inner truth" of the *Protocols* surpassed whatever archival documents might show about their authorship, whether forgery or not.

This second line of defense for the *Protocols* is what we might call a "future perfect archive." The grammatical future perfect tense points to action that will have been completed (finished or "perfected") at some point in the future. *In a year from now, I will have traveled to all fifty states. By this time tomorrow, I will have completed my first marathon.* Future perfect tense is noteworthy for the way it indicates a finished action that does not yet exist. The defenses of Hitler and Ford frame the *Protocols* as a future perfect archive in the way the contents are imagined as simultaneously not true and true. The contents may be forged or plagiarized, yet they are made true by their future fulfillment.

David Duke, the infamous white nationalist, renewed interest in the *Protocols* when he announced in 2014 that he was publishing an updated version, titled *The Illustrated Protocols of Zion.* In his original announcement, Duke explained that his version "takes the basic assertions of the protocols and proves them in the present time. It is a brand new edition of the classic work which takes the 'old' Protocols of Zion and shows, using present-day practical examples, its prescience and astonishing accuracy—despite being more than century old!" While Duke admits that the *Protocols* may indeed have been a forgery, he also asserts that "they are in reality a highly predictive work of 'fiction.'" Predictive fictions allow the *Protocols* to exist as an archival anomaly: true and not true, all at once.

The *Protocols* as future perfect archives remain an ongoing line of discourse for anti-Semites of all stripes. Polish defense minister Antoni Macierewicz echoed the likes of David Duke in a 2002 Radio Maryja interview, when he argued that while the documents may not be authentic, "experience shows that there are such groups in Jewish circles" (Syal). Likewise, an article on the white supremacist website *Jew Watch* adopts this same language:

> When the Protocols were first published, they were the typescript of a drama which had not yet been performed. But today it has been running for over eighty years, and its title is "The Twentieth Century." . . . So even if you don't believe in the authenticity of this remarkable document, one thing you can't

deny is their fulfillment. . . . This is the greatest proof of their authenticity: That they are now fulfilled.

In comments like these, we find a strange relationship between archival evidence and reference. The claim that Jews are diabolical is supported by the evidence of the *Protocols* on one hand, although the specific evidence contained in the *Protocols* is fabricated. Of course, the *Protocols'* "evidence" is not the contents themselves. There is a simultaneity of archival evidence and something else that the archives *will have contained.*

Interestingly enough, while we may never have full archival evidence of the *Protocols'* origins, that fact does not seem to bother either those who promote its hateful content or those who refute it. "Everyone else already knows all too well what they want to believe," remarks Hagemeister. I suppose I am one of those people who already knows what I want to believe. For years, whenever I would see someone citing the *Protocols* as a legitimate source, I felt an uncontainable rage. I *knew* that they were a forgery, designed to make Jews look evil, conniving, and utterly lacking morals. I also knew that the documents had been used in a very real way to kill, attack, and oppress Jews for over one hundred years. I knew that there was a trove of archival sources I could surely point to that would bear out this point. I had not done that archival work, since it was a bit outside my own scholarly focus. But they were out there. I just knew it.

Or, I thought I knew it.

In actuality, as Lepekhine's celebrated 1999 discovery of the Golovinski artifacts shows, there is very little archival evidence to fill in the gaps. Even Lepekhine's archival find does not tell the whole story in a reliable way. Still, I was persuaded that the *Protocols* were anti-Semitic forgeries. The belief that the archives exist was enough for me to dwell within, though my evidence is distal. I am a Jew with Jewish-Israeli children, and I am holding a probe. The probe I hold points to many things, including the entire history of anti-Semitism that follows the same pattern as the *Protocols.* I am referencing something that does not yet appear with full contents. I am dwelling in the evidence.

EVIDENCE AS DWELLING

Dwelling in the archives might seem a strange way of speaking. How do we dwell in archives or evidence? We likely find it easy to take note of the ways we think and feel *about* evidence. Or we might see ourselves dwelling *alongside* evidence, though the evidence does necessarily appear to house us. It's hardly novel to observe that we "embody" or "narrate" evidence, which is another way of saying that archives do not speak on their own, nor are they self-evident. That claim will cause very few eyebrows to raise. But by asking how we *dwell* in archives, I am reaching toward something quite different. To put it plainly: I wonder how we (as interlocutors/audience) might begin seeing "empty archives" as actually having content. Rather than saying that there is no evidence for a particularly outlandish claim, is it possible or even productive to rethink that position? I argue that the answer is yes. Evidence is always there, though it is always distal evidence.

In all of the claims we have seen in this chapter, the primary referent is not the archival contents, but the dwelling afforded by those empty archives. Feeling-full sense needs a dwelling, a house, to live within—sort of like how a ghost without a material body needs to "jump on" electronic frequencies to be heard, or how a spirit needs to take on a human body in order to be seen. The archive becomes a dwelling—an ethos, an *oikos*—for the real point of reference, which is feeling or affect. As a dwelling for sense, the archive does not need the literal contents in order to exist. We can create the idea of an archive—even if it is missing, invisible, not accessible—and it then becomes an economy of sorts. Rather than investing in the contents themselves, we re-reroute our affective energies to the dwelling of what might be, what will be, what will have been.

Still, from a counterargument perspective, it is not ridiculous to critique someone for citing archival evidence to support a claim while also admitting they have not read that evidence. And yet, from a rhetorical perspective, we should also find compelling the ways that this critique does not always diminish that claim. Why is that? I argue that it is because the archival contents are only a secondary reference in these kinds of claims. The primary reference is that new dwelling.

Dwellings and distances intertwine in powerful ways, creating a referent that glows with an aura of evidentiary power. The dwelling is an *oikos* where we can house our shared disgusts, loves, repulsions, attractions, desires. It is that shared *oikos,* then, that we must focus on when dealing with discourse that seems to be grounded in evidence that, for one reason or another, is not truly there. All of this matters in terms of how we consider response to that evidence. Counter-responses must consider the spatial aspects involved in such claims. Once again, these cases suggest that we should be more earnest in our responses, asking not just *how* to respond but also *where* we are responding.

CHAPTER 4

Disfigurement

Finding the (Un)Fitting Response

BARACK OBAMA *is an alien.* If you don't believe me, you can ask the birthers, those who believe that Obama was not born in the US and illegally faked his own American birth certificate. The birther narrative gained steam in 2004 when a little-known political wannabe named Andy Martin issued a press release that accused Obama of hiding his true identity as a radical, fervently anti-American Muslim. Soon after Martin's accusations received media attention, a parade of eccentric personalities began to float the claim that Obama had actually been born in Kenya, not Hawaii. Being an alien resident, therefore, he is ineligible to sit as president of the United States.

There is also a much different group of people who could tip you off about Obama's alien secrets. This group cares little about birth certificates, since they believe that Obama is not an alien in terms of American citizenship, but rather is (more importantly) a shape-shifting reptilian alien who possesses nonhuman DNA. The larger theory of reptilians was made popular by David Icke, a British soccer star turned politician, who gained notoriety with his claims that aliens (reptilian in their natural bodily form) long ago came to earth to enslave humanity and gain endless power from us. According to Icke, reptilians exist in human form among us, and they operate at the highest levels of political, economic, and cultural power centers. A quick dip into Icke's theories will whisk you through claims about the Illuminati, New World Order, the Rothschilds, mind-control technologies, and secret government plots to poison the atmosphere, just to name a few.

Obama is one of those shape-shifting reptilians, masking pretty convincingly as human most of the time. Yet, as Icke teaches his followers, it is possible to detect reptilians in brief moments when they temporarily lose the ability to maintain human form. Usually, a reptilian's shape-shifting happens too quickly for human eyes to process, but video technology can be used in order to expose the truth. True believers have built a cottage industry around sharing online videos of television feeds where a politician or celebrity appears to shape-shift ever so briefly into their true reptilian form. The videos show an otherwise normal face temporarily disfiguring into a blur. It might be the eyes, looking unnaturally black and lizard-like for a split second. It might be the tongue, slipping into a forked shape ever so briefly before returning to its humanoid appearance. But whatever it is, it certainly does not look human. Going one step further than birthers, therefore, reptilian theorists have used visual evidence of Obama's shape-shifting in order to reveal his alien nature. Videos and images of Obama's reptilian body circulate widely online. They show his face blurring into nonhuman forms, or his skin temporarily taking on a strange pattern (see figure 5).

Claims about Obama-as-alien (both in the terrestrial and extraterrestrial sense) call for some kind of response. After birthers first lobbed accusations of fake birth records, Obama himself released a short-form version of his birth certificate online in June 2008. Ideally, this kind of evidence would have served to quell birther theories, but this move seemed to only intensify their claims. Conspiracy monger Jerome Corsi, author of *The Obama Nation: Leftist Politics and the Cult of Personality,* told Fox News on August 14, 2008, that "the campaign has a false, fake birth certificate posted on their website . . . it's been shown to have watermarks from Photoshop. It's a fake document that's on the Web site right now, and the original birth certificate the campaign refuses to produce."

In a second attempt to counter birther claims, President Obama released his official long-form birth certificate in 2011, publishing it on the White House website for anyone to inspect. However, this response again appeared only to add more fuel to the conspiracy fire. Maricopa County Sheriff Joe Arpaio, one of the most outspoken birthers, held a press conference in 2012 to announce that a "forensic analysis" of the long-form birth certificate proved it to be a forgery. According to Arpaio, Obama's birth certificate had been forged from the real records of Johanna Ah'Nee, who was born in a Hawaiian hospital only nineteen days after Obama's birth in 1961. During Arpaio's press conference, he and his supporters spent nearly an hour showing extremely

FIGURE 5. Evidence of shape-shifting

close images of paper, ink marks, typing—all in an effort to demonstrate that Obama's birth certificate could not possibly be authentic. They concluded that the long form released online was simply a photoshopped fraud stolen from Johanna Ah'Nee.

Or maybe it was stolen from one of the Nordyke twins, who were born a day after Obama at the same Hawaiian hospital. After years of watching the birther uproar gain popularity, Eleanor Nordyke, the twins' mother, contacted a journalist to share her own memories of being in labor at the same time that Obama's mother was delivering the future president. Nordyke told journalists that the birthers were nothing short of racist fearmongers. As proof of her own story, Nordyke shared images of her twin daughters' birth certificates. Yet, almost as soon as the Nordyke documents appeared online, birthers determined that even *these* birth records were forgeries. In a convoluted series of steps, several vocal birthers attempted to demonstrate that Obama's birth certificate was actually a forgery of the Nordyke documents, which were themselves forgeries.

Perhaps because so much birther discourse hinged upon claims of digital manipulation, representatives from the politically neutral website *FactCheck. org* physically inspected the actual Obama birth certificate. Their conclusion was that the document is absolutely authentic: "We can assure readers that the certificate does bear a raised seal, and that it's stamped on the back by Hawaii state registrar Alvin T. Onaka" (Henig). Not surprisingly, the testimony from those who physically touched the birth certificate did nothing to quell birther claims, which have continued years even after Obama left office. One national poll taken in 2010 revealed that only 25 percent of respondents who were registered as Republicans "agreed" with the statement "Barack Obama was born in the United States" (Travis). Somehow, somewhere, the counter-evidence of Obama's actual birth failed to connect.

Responses to the other Obama-as-alien claim follow a similar trajectory as the counter-birther response. While reptilian believers see Obama's blurred or pixelated images as a sign of alien emergence, most skeptics answer back with details about compression rates and technological glitches. For example, filmmaker and skeptic Alan Melikdjanian produced a short video showing exactly what causes such glitches to happen. Melikdjanian breaks down the technological details of online video compression in order to explain exactly how and why such glitches happen. After his short explanation of the technology, he then encourages viewers to try creating such glitches for themselves— a creative form of glitch hacking. "Maybe, just maybe," he concludes, "if the effect keeps being popularized through creative work, there will be no one left to take the conspiracy mongers seriously" (CaptainDisillusion).

However, while the rest of us might simply look past a digital glitch or distortion as meaningless, Icke's followers fixate upon the glitch itself as content. Casey Boyle argues that technology glitches disclose the bi-stable literacy that Richard Lanham dubbed *looking at* and *looking through* (93–110). We tend to look through styles and genres that do not call attention to themselves; they do not show up as having any particular style at all. When we look through a text or image, the discourse itself seems to be transparent, leaving only the content for us to consume. Yet, when a style or genre somehow calls attention to itself, they lose their transparency and become the source of spectacle. In the case of reptilian shape-shifting videos and their believers, the moment of glitch becomes a source of meaning that cannot simply be looked through. The skeptical counter-response to Icke's crowd argues that the content being looked at does not, in fact, exist.

But, just as birthers did not respond to the counter-evidence of Obama's American citizenship, not too many Icke acolytes were persuaded by evidence that suggests alien shape-shifting is nothing more than compression artifacts. In a discussion thread on David Icke's website, one contributor offered a lengthy explanation of why "compression artifacts" is simply disinformation nonsense. According to the writer, disinformation agents "love to call it all off as compression artifacts. Do[es] not matter if they cannot provide a single shred of evidence why they are compression artifacts—but that's the way they work. . . . If you want to debunk any video, post your proof of how these morphs take place due to compression" ("Some Of"). The almost two hundred responses to this original post debate the likelihood that shape-shifting videos are caused by normal compression glitches, with most commenters in agreement that glitches are not the main culprit.

In short, counter-evidence does not always persuade those who make extraordinary claims that exist along the anomalous fringes of public discourse. And yet, the rhetorical critic in me persists in asking what the fitting response is in these situations. Lloyd Bitzer writes that "discourse is rhetorical insofar as it functions (or seeks to function) as a fitting response to a situation which needs and invites it" (6). The question of a fitting response pervades every extraordinary claim that seems to stretch the acceptable bounds of credibility: pictures of Area 51's alien bunkers, claims of children becoming autistic after receiving immunization shots, UFO abductions, Jewish cabals secretly running the world's financial sectors, government programs that spray poisons into the air or unleash it into our water through fluoride. In the case of Obama birthers, what exactly is a fitting response? Ideally, we would simply provide sound, credible evidence that presents a persuasive challenge to the rather unsound, noncredible evidence that birthers cite. But, as it so happens, that move does not seem to change many birther minds. If there is indeed a fitting response to any of these claims, what would it look like?

Fitting or not, responses to such claims tend to be one of mocking disgust. *They're crazy, naïve, stupid people. They're misguided and sad.* Most of us have had the strange experience of getting locked into a conversation with someone who rattles off a bizarre string of evidence. Maybe we debate the evidence with our interlocutor, or maybe we try to get the hell out of the conversation as quickly as possible. I have done both. Yet, these reactions never seem to be a satisfying response, let alone a fitting one. To find some way into a more productive response, therefore, we might need to return to the very question of what it means to fit.

FITTING FIGURES

Fit and figure have a pretty tight relationship. Part of me wants to add something about trying on jeans in a dressing room, but that would be a little too flip. Then again, there is something suggestive about the idea of comportment. My body has expanded and contracted many times, especially after giving birth twice. Each altered figure requires a new kind of fitting—new clothes, new senses of how to move, new ways of responding to the different figure that appears before me in the mirror. Perhaps this metaphor is stretching its elastic, but there's something to be gleaned in all this. What is fitting depends upon the figuration. Throughout my previous chapters, I have argued that evidence and archives are figurations. I've argued that evidence can have a thickness that is used differently than its individual contents; that adding up is an object in itself; that lots of evidence transfigures into an aesthetic something else; that evidence is distal and actively embodied while being "seen" as distant/separate; that searching for evidence can become valuable as its own thing.

The figure of Obama-as-alien is revealing for what is actually happening in the act of figuration. As Diane Davis describes, figuration is "a performative gesture that gives form to formless indeterminacy" (*Inessential* 38). If the existence of Obama's Kenyan birth certificate is a formless indeterminacy, then birthers are most certainly the ones performing the gestures giving it shape and form. In some cases, the real fake (or the fake real) birth certificate has literally been shaped through manipulations, forgeries, and a well-massaged framing. Paul de Man writes that figuration is "the element in language that allows for the reiteration of meaning by substitution" (114–15). He goes on to write that "the particular seduction of the figure is not necessarily that it creates an illusion of sensory pleasure, but that it creates an illusion of meaning" (115). De Man thus recalls Nietzsche's earlier declarations about the metaphorical nature of language and meaning: "What is truth? A mobile army of metaphors . . . which were poetically and rhetorically heightened, transferred, and adorned, and after long use, seemed solid, canonical, and binding to a nation" (250). Everything is everything else.

We might say that birthers have substituted the figure—the face—of Kenyan/Foreigner/ Other in an otherwise unruly indeterminacy. In the case of Obama, that indeterminacy is a stubbornly cosmopolitan amalgam of multiple races, regional histories, and a marker of difference from what has otherwise been uninterrupted in the highest executive office. It does not take an overly degreed humanities professor to read the mobile army of metaphors being deployed in birther figuration. Similarly, the reptilian narrative also attempts to tame epistemic knottiness by figuring Obama as something comprehensible (alien as it is). As Travis L. Gosa and Danielle Portner Sanchez write, "Framing Obama as an alien, Illuminati operative in a larger New World Order scheme undermines the symbolic significance of a Black president. . . . As an alien, he fulfills the xenophobic and racist tropes of being an 'other'" (113). In both cases, the figurations produce meanings that erase any epistemic uncertainty.

The act of figuration possesses a certain kinship with pareidolia, which is the tendency for humans to see patterns in things that are actually random. The most familiar instances of pareidolia are when we see faces in things that are not actually faces at all. During a recent visit to Denmark, I was delighted

FIGURE 6. Pareidolia

by Danish electrical outlets whose three plug holes always looked like a very happy, smiling face. When someone discovers the face of Jesus in toast, or sees the "drunk octopus who wants to fight" in the bathroom stall coat hanger, they are experiencing pareidolia. In pareidolia, we perform the kind of figuration that de Man describes, creating an illusion of meaning that is not actually there (see figure 6).

Pareidolia can also emerge in cases of auditory figuration. Electronic voice phenomenon (EVP) is a rather sexy example of sonic figures. EVP is the process by which dedicated ghost hunters capture the voices of spirits on tape. Typically, the researcher asks a question or invites the ghost to speak, and the voice is then recorded. Recording spirit voices on tape is necessary, since the spirit world often speaks in a register that cannot be heard by the live human ear. For this reason, paranormal investigators must listen back to the recordings in order to "hear" the spirits as they spoke. Excluding obvious hoax recordings, EVP recordings can be genuinely chilling. Listening to the tapes, it is quite possible to hear what sounds like words or phrases.

In one EVP recording made in 2007, paranormal investigators captured the voices of spirits present in a century-old New York hotel. The investigators, members of the Central New York Ghost Hunters, provide a transcript of the almost eleven-minute recording. While listening to the recording and reading the transcript, I could make out the phrases that the researchers identified. Some phrases are short: "I lost you." Some are strangely complex: "This swallowed up my money, the old bitch." But, like almost all EVP recordings, the phrases just as easily melt into pure noise. What sounded like a word becomes nothing more than an auditory scratch or glitch caught on tape. As I listen without the aid of a transcription's prompts, I must admit that all I hear is the muffled sounds of wind and clicks. The voices become less of a solid figure as they melt apart.

Instances of pareidolia—whether visual or auditory—are a form of recognition where we perceive the outline of something sensible. Yet, unseeing or unhearing those sensible forms is a bit trickier. We might jokingly say that we can "never un-see" some objectionable image once it is pointed out, but the sentiment holds water. Cognitive researchers have long been interested in the act of unseeing, especially in the case of ambiguous images. Ambiguous images offer the capability of more than one possible meaning, though we initially tend to see only one meaning. The most famous example of ambiguous images is the duck-rabbit drawing, where we tend to see either the duck or rabbit first and then, sometimes with great effort, we see the other possibility. Psychologists refer to our ability to double-see the duck *and* the rabbit as a perception of reversible figures. The question for researchers is how reversible perception takes through a disruption: How does the duck's image (or the rabbit's) become disrupted in order to allow us to see the other?

One important 1977 study of figure reversibility examined the effects of knowledge on the rate of reversal. Specifically, researchers sought to determine whether a viewer's knowledge that the image was reversible would affect the rate at which they saw both images. Two groups of subjects were shown the same sets of reversible images. One group was told that the images were reversible, while the other group was only instructed to tell researchers what they saw in the image. The results indicated that while the "informed" group all managed to reverse the images, approximately half of the "uninformed" group failed to reverse the images whatsoever. The researchers conclude by stating that "the present experiments indicate that reversals do not normally occur easily or rapidly. They do so only in certain conditions, such as when the subject is informed as to the alternatives" (Girgus et al. 556). In other words, seeing ambiguous images is not easy, but it certainly helps to know that ambiguity is there.

Unseeing recognizable forms is a kind of disfigurement: a dissolve of the figure's solid borders. Maybe we are told (by our friendly experimenter) that the image of a duck is actually *two* different figures. Or maybe, after your tenth listen to a ghost saying "I lost you," the words start to sound like nothing more than wind. If figuration is an epistemic making, then disfigurement is an epistemic unmaking. As Diane Davis writes, "Disfiguration is the spontaneous unworking of the work of the figure, which . . . describes a depropriative instant in which a figure is suddenly divested of the meaning it is charged with transporting" (*Inessential* 50). What once seemed solid dissolves at the borders. In cases of EVP, this kind of dissolve happens quite easily. Slowing down a tape has the (admittedly disappointing) effect of unworking what previously sounded like a spirit trying to make contact. Similarly, once you see *both* the duck and the rabbit, it is difficult to see only one or the other. What is disrupted in such disfigurement is the ongoing work of figuration: the thickness of a thing, the transfiguration of something into an aesthetic whole.

Yet, figuration and disfiguration operate in an ongoing mutuality. Figures are unworked, depropriated of their meaning, and then reworked into a different figure with new borders. Claims about Obama-as-reptilian traffic in this kind of complex interchange between figuration and disfiguration. In this discourse, the figure of a human unravels. Obama is disfigured as human in a kind of epistemic unmaking, which is at the heart of every rhetorical disfigurement. Obama's smooth figuration as human is grotesquely disrupted, and he is stripped of the vested meanings of humanity. At the same time, while Obama's humanness is disfigured, a new kind of figuration goes to work. For reptilian theorists, there is a newly transfigured sense of a whole: the reptilian. The nonhuman. Likewise, birther discourse unmakes the figure of "American" and remakes the figure of "Foreigner." Figurations of similarity dissolve and become replaced with the Other.

In figuration, there is a process of fitting, just as disfiguration involves a process of unfitting or refitting. What fits into our epistemic categories also fails to fit into other categories. Of course, this is hardly unique to conspiracy theorists and their often repugnant discourse. The interplay between figuration and defiguration is central to rhetorical meaning-making. They are unavoidable and mutual modes of worlding. In thinking about fitting responses, therefore, we might as well begin with the unfitting response. If figuration is what drives those anomalous claims that call for response, then it is perhaps time for us to consider the operating drive of disfiguration.

DISFIGUREMENT: UNFITTING RESPONSES

Although his terminology exists in a slightly different register, Gilles Deleuze
has quite a lot to say on behalf of disfiguration. Far from reproach, however,
he declares that disfigurement is necessary to thinking, to liberating thought
from the forces that would suppress it. In his account, Deleuze distinguishes
between the figurative and the figure (6). The figurative is what he calls the
representation of image to object, whereas the figure is the object itself as it
exists outside of (or prior to) representation. Here we should make a conceptual distinction between what others call figuration, which is akin to Deleuze's
figurative, and the figure as he describes it. For Deleuze, the figure is that
which exists prior to all form of narration or assigned meaning-making. This
Deleuzian figure is prior to figuration, our face-giving significations.

The figure is almost never available to us in its non-narrativized state, but
is already appropriated with meaning. We do not first encounter the figure
and then load it with signification, like a painter adding meaning to a previously blank canvas. In fact, for Deleuze, the painter's canvas is not blank at all,
but is already filled with commonplaces that invest the blank canvas with a
world of meaning. "On the contrary," he writes, "modern painting is invaded
and besieged by photographs and clichés that are already lodged on the canvas
before the painter even begins to work" (12). We do not encounter the figure
temporally prior to meaning, but (if at all) only after we unmake those meanings through a disfiguration.

Because the figure exists prior to—or outside of—its manifest figurations, Deleuze writes that the figure itself has no face. It does, however, have
a head (19). "For the space is a structured, spatial organization that conceals
the head," he explains, "whereas the head is dependent on the body" (19). Of
course, Deleuze is not referencing literal heads, faces, or bodies; the head in
this sense is simply a shorthand way of describing pure corporality, a primary
materiality as it exists outside of our classifications: human or animal, man or
woman, good or evil. It is corporeal life as it exists outside of the assignments
of significations and identities. Meanwhile, the face is exactly where those
assignments emerge. The face is shorthand for how such significations are
structured and organized.

Our task, according to Deleuze, is "to dismantle the face, to rediscover
the head or make it emerge from beneath the face" (19). We must "extract
the figure from the figurative" in order to break with predetermined modes
of thinking, living, being. Dismantling the face—a process we might also call
disfiguration—leaves us with a "zone of indiscernibility more profound than
any sentimental identification" (22). Rather than seeing meaning as a process

of relationships between resemblances, we instead proceed through different types of relations: "an intensive reality, which no longer determines within itself representative elements, but allotropic variations" (39). In short, what emerges after dismantling the face is sensation, or those forces that sweep through zones that exceed individual bodies (whether people, organizations, concepts, and so forth). Sensation is, for Deleuze, the key to such dismantling. It is "the master of deformations, the agent of bodily deformations," he writes (43). Sensation precedes individual bodies and the personal, and it is the force to which we return when we disfigure the figurative.

Deleuze's words strike me in just the right way, including his discourse on sensation and disfigurement. Something about the poetics of it all helps me to better understand what we are dealing with in the realm of rhetorical meaning-making and unmaking. Yet, as a pragmatist, I also find myself wondering if "Dismantle the face!" is really the best slogan when trying to find a fitting response to troubling public discourse. At the same time, I am not one to dismiss theory simply because it does not have an easy translation from one discursive register to another. And in this regard, where figuration and disfiguration do indeed play out in a very pragmatic way, I see his words as a promising starting point for fitting responses. This is especially the case when thinking about how the disruption of representations happens at an affective or felt level.

In a somewhat less poetic discourse, I translate Deleuze's words like this: Dismantling the face is a moment where the sense of recognition is broken and something else floods out. Something else hits, jolts, jostles before we have a chance to "re-face" it with an interpretation. Evidence does indeed have a face, as we have seen throughout the previous chapters. Evidence is a process of figuration, where we assign a fixed form to buzzing and unruly sensations. When the figuration of evidence is broken, the recognizable features of that figure momentarily lose their ability to keep their shit together (so to speak).

The image of figures losing their shit is unfitting in all kinds of ways. Dropping the S-bomb into the middle of a scholarly passage could be seen as unfitting for the way it disrupts whatever flow academic prose is expected to have, for example. But the moment of disfiguration also invites unfitting responses. Stopped in our tracks, we lose sight of what was once clear. We lose our own shit. Unfitting responses surge from moments of unmaking, when once perfectly comprehensible figurations no longer maintain their vested meanings.

I experienced an unfitting response a few years ago while working in the archives of the Yad Vashem Holocaust museum in Jerusalem. For lack of a better phrase, it was a moment when I simply lost my shit. The whole ordeal began with me losing my shit (almost) literally. One hot summer day in Jerusalem, I had planned to take the light rail to Yad Vashem while my husband and children toured the city. We were spending the day in Jerusalem, but our rented apartment was hours away, in Tel Aviv. I said good-bye to my family as they headed toward the market and I headed to the light rail station. We agreed to meet back at the hotel that evening. After about thirty minutes, the train came into view and I reached in my backpack for my wallet. It was then that I realized I had left my wallet in our hotel room, along with my phone. Panic set in: no money, no phone, no train pass. All I had was an iPad and a notebook. I decided to sneak onto the light rail, where nobody ever really checks your ticket anyway. If someone stopped me, I would play dumb American tourist who spoke no Hebrew. (An easy role, because I was a dumb American who spoke no Hebrew.) While stowing away on the train, I frantically tried to think of how I would talk my way into the archives without identification.

By the time I arrived at Yad Vashem, I must have looked every bit of the frenzied mess that I was. The archivists took pity on me and led me into the air-conditioned collection room. I was there to look at photographs taken from the Warsaw ghetto, specifically from the underground archives that the Oneg Shabbat group collected in years leading up to their own slaughter. I was interested in learning more about the resistance efforts bravely led by ordinary Jews who refused to go quietly into the camps. Those stories of Jewish resistance felt—and still feel—erased from public memory of the Holocaust. I yearned to connect with the faces of those who fought their violent oppression. There in the archives were images of unsung revolutionaries. One picture stood out to me of a woman, young and defiant looking. Her picture was exactly the kind of image I had hoped to find: a resistance fighter who looked like she was about to give a giant "fuck you" to those who were planning her death.

In the midst of this bittersweet archival experience, I came across a different photograph that caught me off guard. It was a black-and-white photo of a brick wall with a white turtle painted on it. The English words above it said, "Work slowly." The picture looks different from any other photograph collected from the Warsaw ghetto. This photograph is different in too many ways. The image too crisp. The words too, well, too English. The paint on the bricks too untextured. It looks photoshopped or created after the fact. I called over the archivist to ask her about the photograph (figure 7), but she was busy and overworked. My question seemed to be a slight annoyance, so I opened my iPad and furiously wrote notes to myself.

FIGURE 7. Graffiti from the Yad Vashem's
Holocaust archive. Photo courtesy of Yad Vashem
Photo Archive, Jerusalem. FA159/B497.

When I returned to our apartment in Tel Aviv, I wrote to Yad Vashem to ask once again about the photograph's origins. Where did the image come from? Who took it? What's the story? After a few days, I received a short email response:

Most of the graffiti made in Warsaw during the Second World War was in Polish so that it can be understood by the local population and to bolster civilian morale. It seems like the photograph in question might depict graffiti made by Americans residing in the Wawer district of Warsaw. The photograph in question is a part of a bigger collection Yad Vashem received from a donor. We don't certify the authenticity of every photograph in the collection.

The last sentence of the email struck me hard. *We don't certify the authenticity of every photograph in the collection.* I read it multiple times, ever so slowly losing my shit each time.

The possibility of an inauthentic photograph in the Holocaust archive set me adrift. I could not quite wrap my head around the melting borders of authenticity, especially where Holocaust resistance archives are concerned. If this graffiti photograph is not authentic, then what about the faces of those I had invested with so much revolutionary significance? Unwilling to let this figure melt, I spent months performing my own archival detective work: searching online images for similar graffiti in the Warsaw ghetto, asking Photoshop experts if they could analyze the image, reading about English speakers in Warsaw. No answers came; only more questions.

At some point in this wild chase, I started referring to the photo as "the graffiti turtle" in my notes. After writing this phrase several times, I suddenly remembered a different set of notes I had written years earlier about a "graffiti turtle." The previous turtle came from my time visiting Detroit during the summers and breaks I spent with my boyfriend who was living there. While walking and driving through the city center, we found scores of spray-painted turtles covering buildings, overpasses, and anything else that stood still. Sometimes it would be a single, giant turtle and other times it would be a line of turtles, tumbling head over tail (figure 8). They were usually accompanied by the tag *TRTL,* presumably the graffiti artist (or artists) who were covering all of Detroit with these simple turtles. Fascinated by their omnipresence, I read anything I could about TRTL and the turtles. What were they for, if anything at all? Why were they covering the city? Why turtles?

As I was deep in my obsession over the "Work slowly" turtle, I searched for those other turtle notes. I checked all my old files and online spaces where I sometimes remembered to back up my notes. Nothing. Did I leave the notes on one of my discarded old laptops? Did I make all those notes in some kind of actual journal? Where are those boxes, anyway? Had I only imagined that I had made notes from my Detroit visits? Hours of searching computers and boxes turned up nothing, and I felt the tremendous guilt and self-loathing that every disorganized scholar surely feels in these moments. I had pulled a work stoppage on myself. *Work slowly.*

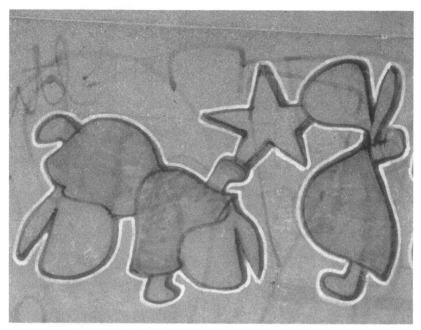

FIGURE 8. Graffiti from Detroit's TRTL. Photo credit Jeff Rice.

A strange constellation emerged around the turtles and their manifold slowness. Turtles are not a completely unreasonable symbol for Detroit's late-twentieth-century state. It was a place that dragged in comparison to the lightning-speed progression of other cities. Detroit had been infamously slowed by the weight of economic clusterfuck that resulted from Ford Motor Company's desire to move somewhere whiter. The Detroit turtles were ultimately not preserved, much like my notes were not preserved. At the same time, while the Yad Vashem turtle is carefully preserved in an archive, what exactly is being preserved by that photograph is not entirely clear. The turtles, me, Detroit, the Wawer district: We are all tangled up in a constellation of preservation precarity. There is a zone of indiscernabilty between Warsaw and Detroit, between Jerusalem and my fieldwork notes. The turtles are evidence of an emergent *something*—the inchoate sensation triggered by proximities of things that do not belong together. Except when they do.

In that momentary constellation, evidence as such was disrupted and disfigured. I had gone to the archives with a figure in mind: the Holocaust archive and its documentary testament to small acts of rebellion, protest, or the like. What I ended up with was defacements. Literal defacement, in the case of spray-painted walls, but also the defacement that comes from losing a sense of what the archive itself holds. The evidence I encountered at Yad

Vashem refused to face me as a recognizable form of fidelity. Instead, there was what Davis describes as a "a depropriative instant in which a figure is suddenly divested of the meaning it is charged with transporting" (*Inessential* 50).

My response to the "Work slowly" turtle is unfitting, in many ways. I am not quite sure that anyone else will agree that Warsaw ghettos fit with late-twentieth-century Detroit. More than that, I risk appearing indecorous by threading together lost journal notes and Holocaust archives, though both have so much to say about preservation's tenuousness. However, my response is also unfitting in the sense that a set figuration came undone through this process. Put differently, my response was a kind of unfitting. Against my own wishes, meanings were disrupted and unmade. What was left was indeed a defacement. In an unfitting response, we are not prone to saving face, but to dismantling it.

UNFITTING RESPONSES: QUALITY CONTROL

As my turtle encounter suggests, things fall apart when evidence disfigures. Things that seemed to be coherently stuck together as a qualitative whole tend to de-aggregate into so many pieces. To be honest, I am not comfortable with things falling apart. I tend to prefer qualitative wholes. My professional choices reflect this preference, which is why I gravitate to rhetoric (studying the quality of discourse as a whole) rather than linguistics (where discourse is broken into the small pieces of sounds, usage, phonemes, etc.). I do not traffic in numbers or decimals or math. My professional field tends to be a "big picture" kind of discipline.

Yet, while humanities folks tend to think of ourselves as the ones who primarily deal with qualitative evidence, Bruno Latour suggests otherwise. Latour considers the tensions between qualitative wholes and quantitative pieces in his discussion of the methodological rift between social sciences and natural sciences. Although we presume that social sciences have a predilection for qualitative methods and the natural sciences are invested in quantitative approaches, Latour draws upon the work of Gabriel Tarde to argue that the inverse is actually true. Social sciences traffic in quantitatives, argues Latour, while natural sciences are actually dealing in qualitative realms. At first glance, this sounds wrong. Surely someone who studies communities is steeped in much more qualitative thinking than the scientist who studies rocks. However, Latour explains, "For Tarde . . . the more we get into the intimacy of the individual, the more discrete quantities we'll find; and if we move away from the individual toward the aggregate we might begin to lose quantities, more and more, along the way because we lack the instruments to collect enough of their quantitative evaluations" ("Tarde's" 149). In other words, when dealing with magnitude, we fall back upon the qualitative. Natural scientists are grappling with infinitely greater "societies" than those who practice social science, and the level of detailed information is not equally available to the scientist who studies stars and to the social scientist who studies a social group.

What Tarde-cum-Latour suggest, then, is that quantification is not in opposition to the individual, the local, the situated. Likewise, qualification is not necessarily the best instrument to investigate the local and individual. Yet, Tarde's sense of quantification is markedly different from a rationalistic model. As Latour puts it, "For human societies, there is no reason to limit quantification to only some of the ways of doing statistics" ("Tarde's" 150). Latour points to the notion of variation as an instance in which Tarde's view on quantification and statistics looks a bit different from how these are often practiced: "What we observe either in individual variations or aggregates are just two detectable moments along a trajectory drawn by the observer. . . . To follow those rays . . . is to encounter, depending on the moment, individual innovations and then aggregates, followed afterwards by more individual innovations" (151).

The example Latour uses is familiar to those of us in academic fields. In journals, conferences, and academic spaces, we produce individual arguments that slowly gain consensus and become a kind of paradigm for the field. This marks a kind of aggregate in disciplinary thought, yet the individual pieces are not erased in the aggregation. Latour remarks on the traces that are aggregated: "There exists—thanks to footnotes, references, citations—an almost uninterrupted set of traces, that allow us to move from each individual innovation, up to the aggregate, and then back to the individual resistance that can develop in response to the given paradigm" ("Tarde's" 151). Both an individual trace and an aggregate are moments, in Latour's language. We might take a concept like the *linguistic turn* as an example. I can use this phrase with confidence in my disciplinary spaces, knowing that my audience will more or less understand the aggregated ideas it signifies. The concept is an aggregate of many individual traces—collections of essays, journal essays on this, lectures, and so on. But I may also follow one particular trace that is part of the aggregation.

The trace—that which gets absorbed and occluded in aggregation—remains discoverable through a return to quantity. As Latour points out, of course, the individual trajectories begin to mess with that particular transfiguration. The threads unravel the narrative of wholeness or coherence. But when we do not unravel or follow those trajectories, instead opting for the aggregation of thick evidence, the claim is built from the thing that the aggregation is. Compare that with a claim built from individual trajectories possible from within that aggregation. De-aggregation, then, is a kind of tactical disfigurement through a process of following traces. A tactical de-aggregation can be deliberately practiced in moments where figuration has taken hold on all sides, and the (un)fitting response must be found.

As an (unfitting) example, we might return to David Icke's reptilian conspiracy theory. What kind of response is possible to claims that national leaders, such as Barack Obama, are actually reptilian hybrids who are oppressing and enslaving humans in order to gain power? One thoughtful mode of response has been offered by critics who see Icke as *figuring* quite serious issues in the form of the lizard. David G. Robertson offers one such analysis in an essay that attributes Icke's theories as emerging from the broader realm of "New Age" hopes of a coming worldwide peace and environmental harmony. According to Robertson, by placing agency for nearly all problems squarely on the presence of reptilians, "the Reptilian Thesis thus allows Icke to address the problem of evil within a pantheistic, globally humanistic worldview" (42). In another vein, other critics call out Icke's reptilians as figurations of thinly veiled anti-Semitism. Other responses simply hail Icke and his followers as more mundane figures themselves: the lost, the angry, the sad, the crazy.

All of these various responses seem fitting insofar as they are practicing epistemic comportment. The response fits a face to the words, so to speak. But an unfitting response does not aim at saving face. The unfitting unravels a figure's wholeness by pulling the threads of individual variations. I experienced one moment of defacement when viewing some of the hundreds of reptilian encounter testimonials that exist online. These are often homemade videos of ordinary people who share their stories of visitations by reptilian aliens. One such testimonial video is from a young man named Joseph Walsh, who describes his encounter with reptilian aliens during his otherwise unhappy time in the military as a low-ranking officer. Joseph describes his depression, anger, and hopelessness during service. He spends the first several minutes of his video talking about how mistreated he had felt at the hands of commanding officers. "They treated me like crap, just because I was a lower rank," he says softly into his computer camera. Throughout Joseph's story, we hear him talk about his time being treated for depression at the military facility.

As his story unfolds, Joseph says that he slowly discovered that many of the military personnel were actually "reptilians" who were purposefully putting him into a "fear state." In a shy, monotone voice, he tells us that this story is quite personal to him. "I haven't told my friends, my family," he says as his eyes shift down to the table. "If you're experiencing anything like this, you know, don't be scared. Because fear is what they . . . use to . . ." His voice starts and stops nervously as he tries to conclude. "I just want to share this little story," he says. "I just want to share this little story." He repeats the phrase in a way that sounds almost apologetic (Walsh). Another woman, who introduces herself as Natalie, also tells her story of reptilian encounters on her YouTube account. Natalie smiles peacefully and she tells her story in a soft and gentle voice. She tells us that she has spent time "working on herself" in order to become healthier both mentally and spiritually. And because she has done this work, she tells us that she wants to be a kind of ambassador between the human world and the alien world. "I communicate those bridges, those energies," she says quietly. She describes how aliens have been "harvesting" her sexual energy for a long time, yet she learned how to "release" and "merge" with the other entity. After this description, she struggles to help her audience understand. "You know what you guys? There has been a lot going on and I go into really deep, dark places. But I also go to very high. I go to different ends. . . . The reason I'm going in there is to clear stuff out." "This is why I'm here. . . . To explain to people what I'm experiencing so we can all work together on clearing a lot of this out" (AnahataOnline, "A Message").

Natalie's other videos share her experiences with New Age practices. But some of them also share her story of being arrested and placed in a mental hospital. She described the dark energy she felt while in prison. "I went through quite a lot this last year," she smiles and laughs softly. Other videos range from how to harvest astral energies to eating organic foods. Particular videos return to the dark energies of mental hospitals, which, she explains, are always laid out as an inverted cross. Mental health facilities are not designed for healing, therefore, but to harvest the energies of those who inhabit them. One of her earliest videos, titled "A message I sent out to my friends n family on fb," shows her standing outside, holding a phone, describing the new journey she is undertaking after moving to Utah: "Just know, there are reasons for me doing what I'm doing. I'm very clear minded. I'm healthy. Just know that I am of sound mind." She says she won't take offense if anyone wants to unfriend her: "If it's bothering you, some of the stuff that I reveal, I really will not take offense if you disfriend me on Facebook . . . whatever makes you comfortable. . . . And if I've done anything to hurt anybody, I am very sorry. . . . I'm not saying I know more than anyone else, but I'm just here to share my situation and my experience" (AnahataOnline).

These stories are merely two individual variations within the larger ecology that composes a political orientation we could dub "paranoia politics." The stories get us no closer to something like an objectivity, and by following them, that's not necessarily our purpose. Instead, I am more interested in retrieving other voices within a speaking ecology. Rather than thematizing the voices as part of an ecology, what happens if we follow these traces? In my experience of following these trajectories, I arrive at a few different places. I hear how depression and helplessness can sometimes sound. I hear how people describe how they see their own transformations. I hear how people tell a story to strangers. I hear how people reflect on belief and disbelief. I watch how people smile when talking—or do not smile at all. I hear two people describe their own ways of making sense of institutions where they feel powerless, as well as how they find ways to (re)gain a sense of empowerment within those spaces.

This moment of encountering the reptilian archive was a moment of disruption in my attempts to figure how these testimonies operated in relation to their claims. The encounters failed as hermeneutic endeavors. They fell apart as pieces of a larger rational process of argument building. If anything, they served as holes in the epistemic exchange that allows claims to be weighed on the basis of evidentiary fitness. They were unfitting, and my response as such was similarly unfitting. Far from qualitative parts of a larger whole, these narrative testimonies were more like single fragments that split apart from the larger whole that I had known as reptilian conspiracy theory. Without encountering anything more than those few minutes of narrative, I felt myself jutted into different trajectories altogether, ones that dipped into expressions of isolation and institutionalization. It's not that I understood any more about reptilian claims. I still don't. But I did experience a different type of encounter that I did not expect. What I had envisaged took me for a ride, interrupting the narrative figure I thought would appear.

RHETORICS OF ASSENT

Although I sometimes feel as if I have wandered far from the traditional boundaries of disciplinary rhetoric in my dalliances with reptilians and other anomalous discourse, I find some comfort in the fact that at least one rhetorical scholar has somewhat addressed the issue of how to respond to aliens. As far as I can tell, Wayne Booth is the first (and maybe only) rhetorical scholar who mentioned what to do with people who believe in things like UFOs or astral projection. His brief mention appears in his 1974 *Modern Dogma and the Rhetoric of Assent*. There Booth writes about the predicament of evidence and reasons as they are pitted against each other in dead-end arguments, where interlocutors think the other side is simply wrong, bad, evil, stupid, or misled. In these situations, Booth's answer is to look hard for good reasons.

"If neither of us has any chance of offering good reasons," writes Booth, "I can only trick you, or force you, or blackmail you, or shoot you—and thus change your mind permanently" (36–37). And with that bleak assessment, he argues that it is imperative that unlike-minded people must find a way to talk, or else we are all in for it.

In *Modern Dogma*, Booth laments the ways that public discourse in the 1960s and 1970s had overdosed on skepticism in many different forms. Some overdosed on a kind of hyperrational skepticism, giving no credence to any claim unless it can be demonstrated. Some overdosed on skepticism toward anything that is not personal, felt, lived, experiential. What counts as "good reasons," then, become limited to one's own tribalist form of skepticism. Everything else is not worth hearing. The original 1974 cover of *Modern Dogma* is like a visual shorthand for his whole argument. The cover features a photograph of three people huddled around a coffee shop table. Two women sit on either side of a man with a very artsy looking beard. One woman looks like she is speaking, and she is pointing at the woman across from her, who is almost smiling. Then man stares intensely at the woman speaking, his eyebrows dramatically furrowed, mouth agape like he cannot believe the shit he's hearing right now. I've stared at this picture so many times, wondering what they were talking about. I also imagine that the man—whose forehead is wrinkled in serious skepticism—is the poster boy for Booth's modern dogma.

If Booth had written the book today, maybe the cover would not be three people sitting around a coffee shop table, but a string of tweets back and forth between those three people. (Beard guy would eventually end the thread by telling the first woman to "delete your account.") The heavy doses of skepticism needed after the 2016 presidential election seem to be greater than in 1974, with a president who daily raises the stakes on publicly declaring invalid claims. In the social media age, we often get into tangles with friends and strangers over political and social issues. How many times have we posted long paragraphs, attempting to show how some person is wrong or misguided or misinformed or hateful? How many times does this exchange—almost always doomed from the start—end with unfriending that person, or blocking them, which is the only thing that is missing from Booth's list of alternatives to finding good reasons for talking. As an alterative to any of these literal or metaphorical deaths, Booth asks whether we can begin with assent rather than skepticism.

As much as I truly admire Booth's rhetoric of assent, it runs up against a roadblock when dealing with the truly strange or bizarre. He notes that in following a rhetoric of assent, "we are not suddenly flooded with every belief that anyone offers. We begin only with those beliefs that really recommend themselves to us, whoever we are and wherever we find ourselves. . . . [W]e needn't give ready credence to any report—of ghosts or astral projection or flying saucers—that does not in some degree fit our own experience" (*Modern* 107). To be fair, I feel pretty confident that I could offer compelling evidence to counter these extraordinary claims. Reports of flying saucers, for example, can often be coordinated with positions of satellites. Astral projection is not subject to the doctrine of falsifiability and has also failed to register in controlled experiments. There just aren't a lot of Booth's good reasons for assenting to these claims. And yet, there they are, persisting in the public sphere where we live, move, and have our being. If I have no good reasons to believe or engage the UFO believer, then it seems I am still locked within the violent alternatives of shutting them down. But that seems like a poor alternative for a fitting response.

Here is where I suggest that figuration and defiguration can help as useful concepts. I want to rethink a rhetoric of assent by decoupling it from what Booth calls good reasons. We can begin by making primary assent something of a tactical position, allowing for (and calling for) a different orientation to argument. At the risk of sounding like an etymology hack, I am tempted to draw something from the older senses of the word *argue,* which has its roots in the Latin *arg*—variously defined as "bright," "shining," "to make clear." Argument is an exchange of figurations, of the shining figures we all carry. If what we choose to hear in another person's claim is a figuration of desires, visions, and so on, then responding to that figuration can thus become a different form of argumentation as dialogic.

Saying yes—or beginning there—instead of starting with *no* is broad enough to mean all kinds of things. Yes to the belief that the "reasons" (or "evidence") someone gives you point to something real. That real thing is not another person's experience or knowledge or belief, but is simply the fact that they are: They exist, producing desires of all kinds. "For a rhetoric of assent," writes Booth, the Aristotelian logical and emotional proofs are secondary to "ethical proof—the art of taking in by contagion" (*Modern* 144). Contagion sounds fairly nasty, like the kind of thing we try to immunize against. Yet, as we also know, communal contagion is what immunizes us. Saying yes as a primary position, a rhetoric of assent, is to be infected by the basic fact of the encounter.

Reports of ghosts and astral projection and flying saucers are real. They are shining figurations. They shine so brightly that I get caught up in their glare sometimes. What I can say yes to is that glare. There it is, right before me. There I am, caught in its exposure. My choice as interlocutor is more than agreement or disagreement in that moment. I also have the opportunity to ask something else about that shiny figure: yes to a conversation, yes to a civic faith in the health of communal contagion, yes to a faith in encounter. Susan Lepselter provides a model of such engagement in her ethnographic work with people who claim to experience UFO abductions. In *The Resonance of Unseen Things: Poetics, Power, Captivity, and UFOs in the American Uncanny*, Lepselter describes how, when she hears accounts of alien abduction, she listens for "the real" as it has had "a chance to crystallize not as an outside referent, but inside the story itself" (16). For Lepselter—though not for Booth—there are always good reasons to "give ready credence" to alien abduction claims. Not because human bodies were actually beamed up to a spaceship, but because stories of captivity and invasion mark experiences that are all too real.

Listening in the way that Lepselter describes does not preclude the possibility that her interviewees were, in fact, abducted by aliens. *Who knows?* But her approach to the figurations is aimed at something beyond, or beside, epistemic judgment. Instead, she is practicing a tactical rhetoric of assent: the belief that claims always have good reasons for being made, even if the referent of those claims and evidence is something else altogether. As Lepselter writes, "Sometimes the phenomenology of power can only be told in how its effects reverberate" (54). The condition of living in the world pulls and pushes in ways that have no way to signal outwardly beyond the story.

If I could classify this rhetoric of assent, I'd call it a form of "weak argument theory." I stole this partly from geographer Sarah Wright (who takes it from Eve Sedgwick). Wright explains, "Weak theory promotes attention to affective assemblages, to the ways things [and] people with different trajectories may come together, albeit in often tentative, inconclusive or evolving ways" (393). In her comments on Sedgwick's "weak theory," Kathleen Stewart writes that weak theory "comes unstuck from its own line of thought to follow the objects it encounters, or becomes undone by its attention to things that just don't add up but take on a life of their own as problems for thought" ("Weak" 72). Weak argument theory does not aim for conclusions as much as it aims to listen for the new problems created by the encounter. This listening for new problems is precisely what a rhetoric of assent says yes to.

INCONCLUSIVE UNFITTING RESPONSES

Back to the question of the fitting response. Other scholars have framed response to conspiracy discourse in the context of an interlocutionary moment: one side responding to the claims and evidence of another side. E. G. Creps, for example, argues that conspiracy discourse is a "response to the problem of evil" (12). Creps sees conspiracy theories as emerging from some sense that evil lurks and must be addressed somehow. He writes, "If life is to have meaning, then, evil must have meaning. For it is in the interpretation of evil that one comes to grips with one's notions of the good and the nature of the world. Therefore, for the individual, the problem of evil must be understood in some meaningful way" (28–29). In this context, our response must emerge from a more fundamental understanding of how we address such anxiety of evil. And, of course, this kind of framework may position response as more empathetic to those who make anomalous claims. At the same time, by responding solely within the context of interlocution, we are caught up in the narrow world of claim/evidence and counterclaim/counter-evidence. As we have seen, the effectiveness of this strategy is quite limited.

If evidence has multiple registers, however, then it is just as possible that response also has multiple registers. Calvin O. Schrag, for one, has suggested that the fitting response is not simply a matter of responding to the discourse that is shouted in our face. "For a response to be fitting," according to Schrag, "it may require a radical revision of an established custom or convention, or indeed its overturn" (*Self* 99). Schrag puts response into a context that is much broader than the immediate situation between two (or more) interlocutors. "The self in community is a self . . . historically embedded, existing with others, inclusive of predecessors, contemporaries, and successors," he writes (*Self* 109). It is in this context that the "fitting response" must occur. When we respond, we are responding within a context that exceeds any given moment of debate or argument.

Seen in this way, the fitting response to a particular claim is like a dispatch sent out into the community. It is an offering in return for the invitation opened by whatever space cracked open by the claims that come our way. Schrag expands on this notion of a fitting response as one that looks toward the polis. "The fitting response preserves the ethos and the polis," he writes. "It is situated within them and always proceeds from them. The response is a response to the attitudes, behavior patterns, meaning-formations, and moral assessments that define the space shared by the rhetor and the interlocutor, the self and the other" (*Communicative* 207). In short, responding simply to another's claims is not the fullest possible extent of what should be imagined for a fitting response. Commenting on Schrag's concept of the fitting response, John Fritzman emphasizes that response is more than reaction. "The meaning of a situation is located in the future," writes Fritzman. For this reason, "the fitting response is an active—and not a reactive—force" (21). Intervention is on behalf of a future that never becomes present or past. Moreover, argues

Fritzman, "the judgment of an intervention is itself another intervention, and so the meaning of that judgment itself still remains in the future, waiting still another judgment" (23). In short, the fitting response is a continuation that will be further continued on and on.

If we enlarge our understanding of the fitting response to anomalous—and sometimes truly awful claims—then we might also begin to see response as a moment of invention. Of course, this shift also means that response is somewhat removed from the immediate context of interlocution. It is, as I said above, a weak argumentative strategy. This is not an argumentative strategy that aims to persuade the one who makes a claim. Rather, it is an attempt to contribute to an ongoing future of responses and discourse. The response is not to the one who speaks, but to the lifeworld of a public who can sometimes become stuck with given forms and ways of thinking.

While this enlarged concept of fitting response sounds quite lovely, what exactly is a fitting response to those who insist that Obama is a Kenyan pretender who lied about his true origins? What is a fitting response to birthers? For an example of how some people did indeed perform this different type of response, I look to writer Goldie Taylor, who comments quite frequently on both political and African American issues. In a 2011 essay for the online journal *The Grio,* Taylor begins by telling the story of Major Blackard, her great-great-grandfather. In 1899, when Blackard was nineteen years old, he was stopped by St. Louis police and ordered to show his papers. When Blackard explained that he had accidently left his wallet at home, he was arrested and beaten. After telling this story, Taylor then considers how the tradition of "showing your papers" is quite literally at play in the questions about Obama's birth certificate. "Some 112 years after my grandfather was snatched from a street corner in the central west end section of St. Louis, it seems we still need to prove our right to be here," writes Taylor. While Taylor addresses the claims made by Donald Trump and other birthers, the main focus of her essay looks to rearticulate a history that might otherwise be left unspoken.

Similarly, Latinx writer Victor Landa asked what "showing papers" means for others who are framed as Other. In considering the impact of birthers on Latinx communities, Landa asks: "What are we to expect for our own civil rights when the President has to show his papers?" For many Latinx, the prospect of having to "show papers" is not a historical phenomenon. Texas's Senate Bill 4 (2017) and Arizona's Senate Bill 1070 (2012) were both popularly known as the "show me your papers" laws, which would allow police to require anyone being detained to prove their citizenship. While these laws were challenged through multiple legal battles, the larger sense of "showing papers" remains an active part of the construction for nonwhites. Responses such as Landa's intervene in the many traces that coalesce in birther discourse. It is a response that grasps the opportunity to ask new questions.

By de-aggregating birther claims, we can also follow other traces in order to continue the work of (un)fitting responses. I also wish to deface the figure of Obama's birth certificate. The birther archive is not evidence of its own figuration (that which it claims to represent), but it is a spectacle of sensations and something real. The real in this archival encounter is the sickly panic of fear about legitimacy and legibility. Nietzsche was perhaps the first to put it in such blunt terms: We don't know our own bodies. Identity as a stable, fixed form is such a fragile story. How many times do we "fall apart" in a way to describe the experience of shattered subjectivity? Our attempts to keep it all together—the Self as a whole form—are sometimes a matter of documentary legitimacy. I read my own identity through the document. It is there that my legibility gathers some stability: my birth certificate, my social security number, my license, my marriage certificate, my divorce certificate, my contracts that guarantee my employment, my tax returns. These are the materials through which I can finally experience some kind of stability that does not fall apart.

These traces in birther discourse lead to broader questions of subjectivity and self-identity. We might attune to the presence of fear in other instances where legitimacy and legibility are disturbed, such as the public panics over identity theft and catfishing. Our confidence in the autonomous subject is cracked in these moments. Perhaps it is no wonder, then, that so much anxiety permeates the specter of illegible and illegitimate documents. If documents are some of our guarantees of Self, then the notion that even those have no stability serves as a threat to the smallest promises of stable identity. At the same time, there is no better way of delegitimizing a person than questioning their identity documents. By questioning one's identity papers, their entire being is put into question. No birth certificate, no social security number, no paper trail of a life? No identity. This move certainly seems to be undergirding birther discourse. Yet, the anxieties also show us something about the push and pull of subjectivity: When the form is defaced, we try our best to reface it.

In thinking about identity and paperwork and anxieties, my response to birther conspiracy claims drifts far from the (quite poor) evidence they offer. However, their discourse also provides evidence in a different register that should not be missed. Rather than responding to the immediate context of Obama-as-foreigner, the fitting response looks toward the lifeworld of a future public. The response may not pose answers, but may instead pose new questions. Persuasion as such is not the aim of this response; it seeks out new ways of engaging the pressure points that we collectively experience, even if we experience them unevenly.

Fitting responses are particularly unfitting, therefore, insofar as they do not (only) respond to the evidence offered in claims. Rather, responses are to the affects that congeal in thicknesses. They respond to the disruptions that happen when those figurations that were once solidified break apart. Admittedly, it is odd to think of response in this mode. Yet, as archival scholar Florence Bernault writes, we find "clusters of meaning" in "composite oddities." Encountering oddities, or seeking them out as unfitting responses are prone to do, "make[s] you confused and lost, so they make you think" (277).

Responses to such disfigurations can open up new spaces for what circulates through the polis, the public. Such response does not aim at persuasion as an end. In fact, this kind of response does not aim for an end at all. Instead, it aims for precisely the inverse: ongoing discourse that does not take certitude as a measure of success. It is a more like a wedge, holding open the door through which future conversations, questions, and ideas can pass before the matter is closed once and for all. The fitting response is not a conclusion. It is a tactic that forestalls conclusions.

CHAPTER 5

Writing Demon Archives

ON DECEMBER 4, 2016, a twenty-eight-year-old man named Edgar Welch drove 350 miles from North Carolina to Washington, DC, armed with a military-style assault rifle and revolver. When Welch arrived in Washington, he immediately headed to Comet Pizza, a popular pizza joint in the heart of the city. Upon entering Comet Pizza, he fired shots and declared his intention to rescue children who were being ritually and sexually tortured in the pizza parlor's basement. Welch was quickly apprehended, and the story of his attempted rescue made national headlines. In an interview with the *New York Times,* Welch explained that the idea for his mission came after "substantial evidence from a combination of sources had left him with the 'impression something nefarious was happening.' He said one article on the subject led to another and then another" (Goldman). To Welch's chagrin, however, there were no children being tortured in the basement of Comet Pizza.

Edgar Welch was one of many who believed in the conspiracy theory popularly called "Pizzagate." Pizzagate emerged in the final stages of the 2016 presidential elections after someone hacked the email account of John Podesta, Hillary Clinton's campaign manager, and dumped thousands of his emails into WikiLeaks for public consumption. It's not unreasonable to think that Podesta's emails might contain juicy political gossip, but that's not what stoked the ensuing conspiracy theory surrounding them. What stood out to the most dedicated of conspiracy theorists was pizza. More specifically, a very satanic pizza.

The various emails mentioning pizza read like ordinary messages between friends. James Alefantis, the owner of a hipster Washington, DC, pizza place called Comet Pizza sent Podesta a short email thanking him for helping with an Obama fundraiser event happening at Comet Pizza. "Raised over 40 grand," wrote Alefantis. "My only regret is I did not make you a nice pizza. When can I?" Another email from a Podesta friend discusses a dinner menu: "I will send you a list of dishes we can decide on, some of which we can make in the pizza oven. The shopping list will follow." In a similarly banal message, Tony Podesta, John's brother, wrote to ask if he'd like to have dinner at a nice restaurant or, if not, "I could bring a pizza home." To this, John replies: "I'm going to pass. I have too much to do before heading to Michigan tomorrow. No need for pizza." Aside from the voyeuristic thrill of reading through people's personal email exchanges, there is very little here that might set off alarms for many people. If nothing else, I suppose we know that the guy likes pizza.

As boring as these emails appear to be, they set off a frenzy of panic and hysteria in some corners of the internet. Through a complicated slew of messages on sites like 4Chan and Reddit, as well as numerous posts in social media, the hidden "codes" of these supposedly innocuous emails were exposed. One message declared, "'Cheese pizza' has long been known as code for child porn in pedophile communities comprising the deep web" ("DC Pizzagate"). Another widely circulated tweet from Jared Wyand, an ultra-right-wing social media figure and enthusiastic Trump supporter, encourages readers to "search all Podesta emails for these keywords. We are uncovering a child sex ring" (@JaredWyand). He then explains how a word like *cheese* is code for *little girl,* while *pasta* is code for *little boy.* The word *map* is code for *semen,* while the word *sauce* is code for *orgy.* Before long, narratives began circulating that accused the Clintons, the Obamas, and other Democratic insiders of running a demonic pedophilia ring, complete with human sacrifice, all in the basement of Comet Pizza. Infamous conspiracy theorist Texe Marrs went so far as to call Pizzagate the "greatest Satanic scandal of all time." In fact, for a mere $10 (plus shipping and handling), Marrs promised to reveal the depths of this scandal in his audio exposé.

What are we to do in the face of such troubling discourse? Writing against outrageous and false claims is one option, of course, and many have done that in the wake of conspiracies like Pizzagate. Yet, as Welch's story suggests, archives act even when they do not actually exist. In the last chapter, I explored disfigurement as a rhetorical strategy for responding to awful evidence. Extending that argument in search of (un)fitting responses, I want to go one step further in this chapter in order to explore how even the most flawed, faulty, and troubled archives can become the materials for a productive response to awful arguments. In what follows, I explore ways that we can write *with*, rather than merely *against*, evidence built from multiple registers. As a way out of seemingly hopeless dead-end discourse, this chapter introduces a strategic writing practice (which I call *demon archives*) in order to move beyond asking *What is this archive of?* to a more generative question: *What can this archive do?*

PAGES NOT FOUND

Welch's rescue operation was a bust. There was no evidence of satanic cults running a sex ring in the basement of a hipster pizza joint. No evidence of evil political figures orchestrating mass rituals. No evidence of anything at all except pizza. *404 error. Page not found.* But, as I argued in chapter 3, absent archives are not dead; their rhetorical impacts resonate strongly in the ways we come to distally dwell in them. Still, there are times when we do not feel ourselves dwelling there. Their absence is palpable. What do we do, then, if the archive is felt to be empty, but we are still called to act?

Historian Luise White addressed this conundrum in her scholarship on postcolonial African history. White points out that this area of study is particularly difficult due to the many "pages not found" in post-1960s Africa. She writes that while many of her colleagues lament the unavailability of these archival materials, she instead finds such archival absence as a good thing:

> For at least twenty-five years those of us who studied African social history and sought to rescue ordinary Africans from the condescension of the present (and even better, the condescension of our stodgy senior colleagues) boasted that we did not need the linguistic turn to interrogate archives: we'd been reading against the grain for years. . . . And because of our judicious reading, we prided ourselves on using the writings of the people who got it wrong to get it right. (308)

The archivist so possessed leads to a smug sense of correctness or salvation. White argues that if postcolonial African archives had been carefully maintained, they surely would have driven social historians like her toward such mania. Fortunately (or not), however, these archives were not carefully maintained. No orderly, neat documents exist in an accessible space for historians of post-1960s African history. They are absent. And, so, White finds herself asking different questions: "What do we do when archives aren't there? What do we do when material was . . . lost, or when it was mutilated or destroyed or filed under the wrong ministry or the wrong year or decade? How do we write the history of events that were never written down? What do we do when there's no archive?" (310).

What *do* we do? The stubborner among us can double down by pointing out the fact that documents and materials do actually exist. They have existed at some point: notes, photographs, registries, government papers, memos, letters, receipts, posters, pamphlets, whatever. Maybe they have been destroyed, or maybe they are scattered to the winds. They exist and we can hunt them down. But, even then, what we are left with in the absence of a well-maintained archive is a mess. Hunting for scattered materials that bear witness to a certain historical moment is just plain messy. This is the case for postcolonial African history scholars, who find themselves gathering disorderly bits and pieces that have ended up in bizarre places. Yet, White continues, mess is not necessarily a bad thing: "At the risk of sounding like someone from the 1990s who constantly reminded historians to listen to silences, I want to ask scholars of the postcolonial to take the mess as their starting point" (313). For White, the chaotic and haphazard state of historical documents tells its own story of life in postcolonial Africa. "Every misfiled document and missing five pages is not the key to political history, of course, but taken together they provide a lens, a way to enter into a world of disregarded protocols and slapdash paperwork, of policies made up as governance went along," she writes (313–14). Pages not found thus become a way in.

White's "hodgepodge historiography," as she calls it, offers one way of approaching absent archives by writing with absence. The same might be said about writing with any kind of messy archive or evidence that seems utterly hopeless. The *with* in *writing with* implies both use and parallel position: We are writing via the materialities of "mess," and we are also writing alongside it without necessarily engaging it directly. This kind of writing emphasizes potentiality over actuality. It also emphasizes speculative archival practices, which Dag Petersson describes as the invention of "an archive exclusively for events that can happen—regardless of whether or not they ever will or actually ever did happen" (39). Just like White's idea of hodgepodge histories, archives that emphasize potentiality and speculation look to juxtapose artifacts in ways that allow for unexpected, unthought, unseen disclosures: referents that exist in a different register.

I experienced something of this inventional capacity by chance one day, after stumbling across a reference to an art project called *The Speculative*

Archive. The name immediately caught my attention. I found it mentioned in a blog post by John Menick, an artist who was detailing his encounter with Julia Meltzer and David Thorne, two collaborating artists who created *The Speculative Archive*. As Menick described it, Meltzer and Thorne's video-based installation project uncovered secret government documents not in order to expose hidden state secrets, but to explore the intersections between memory and the ways that sociocultural life is embedded and directed through mountains of paperwork.

Menick's description was fascinating. I began searching for *The Speculative Archive* so that I could see it for myself. But, almost immediately, my search hit a wall. The link Menick provided to *The Speculative Archive*'s website was now nothing more than a spammy page filled with Japanese writing. The Google translator provided a rough translation for links to hair removal services across Japan. Thanks to a different site referencing *The Speculative Archive,* I learned that Meltzer and Thorne had collaborated on another project called *The Public Record*. When I clicked on the link for that site, however, I only found a notice saying, "Sorry! This site is not currently available."

A few more searches turned up descriptions of *The Speculative Archive*'s various short documentary pieces that centered around hidden documents, including a video called "It's Not My Memory of It: Three Recollected Documents." As I read one lengthy description of Meltzer and Thorne's project posted on a different blog, I saw a link to Menick's essay on "It's Not My Memory of It." When I clicked on this link, I was led back to Menick's website only to find a "page not found" notice. My search was beginning to feel like something from *Through the Looking Glass.*

More searches turned up so many nonexistent pages that I began to wonder if *The Speculative Archive* actually existed at all, or if it was a hoax. After enough "pages not found," I began to notice how these results were more than nothing. In one sense, I was encountering the daemon process designed to deliver me (or any other website user) the message that we are in a state of 404. In another sense, those pages not found formed their own kind of archival traces: an archive of present absences, haunting the "real" archive, echoing with an eerily doubled voice.

The online experience of "page not found" is a familiar one to most of us. Frustrating at times, and laughable at others, the encounter of missing pages is perhaps the digital era's version of Heidegger's hammer that suddenly brings us to awareness of being as enmeshed in world. As long as the hammer swings effortlessly into nails, the worldness of existence tends to recede into the background. I space out, somewhat oblivious. But then it happens—the hammer hits my thumb and I am immediately brought back to the realization that I have been working with this thing, this extension of my body that also is not my body, and we exist in a relation. (A terribly painful relation, as it happens to be in that moment.) Similarly, a "page not found" pops up in the course of my otherwise spaced-out clicking through web links. More than a disruption, the missing page draws me into a relation that is not of my choosing, nor is it of my own doing. Yet it involves me. "Page not found" serves as archival detritus that can be collected; it is the stuff from which something is invented.

It's tempting to see my search as a failed mission. I came up empty-handed. However, as White reminds us, coming up empty-handed is not meaningless. Archives tell multiple stories, she writes. Even in her own postcolonial African research, White reflects on the ways that, in "looking for and at all the things officials got wrong, I missed how the wrong itself told a story, a story about officials" (317). She notes that by only reading archives as records of certain events, "I had failed to see messy archives for what they are, fragmented records of shambolic events, of false starts" (317). Those shambolic events or false starts, in turn, are the stuff from which new narratives, insights, and curiosities can be invented. There are useful rhetorical strategies to be learned in this archival act. However, the goal of such practice is not truth or knowledge. The goal is *genius*.

DAIMONS AND GENIUSES

In 2016, the year Pizzagate broke, *post-truth* was the *Oxford English Dictionary*'s word of the year. The word's popularity reflected the sense that people like Donald Trump and his supporters were increasingly comfortable making unfalsifiable or unproven claims. Trump indignantly repeated "facts" about illegal voting, undocumented migrants, gang crime—all with very little data to support the claims' veracity. At the same time, President Trump was quite vocal about his displeasure of the mountain of "hoaxes" and "fake news" he saw taking over. It seemed as if even Trump himself was bemoaning the curse of living in a "post-truth" era. In January 2018, after the president made a slew of particularly manic social media posts about the "hoaxes" perpetrated by the "Fake News Mainstream Media," reporters began to openly question Trump's mental fitness. The president then took to his Twitter account to assure everyone that he qualifies as "not smart, but genius. . . . and a very stable genius at that!" (January 6, 2018). Within hours of this proclamation, the phrase "very stable genius" became the punch line to every joke imaginable. Late night talk show hosts mocked Trump without mercy. Mugs, shirts, magnets bearing the phrase "Very Stable Genius" immediately appeared online. And Congressman

Brendan Boyle of Pennsylvania introduced an act that would require presidential candidates to receive a medical exam before the general election. Boyle's act, the Standardizing Testing and Accountability Before Large Elections Giving Electors Necessary Information for Unobstructed Selection Act, was publicized more widely by its acronym: the STABLE GENIUS Act.

There is something truly laughable about a man (let alone a president) who declares himself to be a "very stable genius." But perhaps it is worth taking Trump at his word. While he might not be a genius in the intellectual sense, his genius has been working overtime ever since he took office. Then again, all of us have a genius. As Giorgio Agamben writes, the Latin god Genius, an entity closely linked to the Greek notion of daimon, is the god who is with each person at the point of their birth. In fact, Genius guides us before the moment of our birth, as his godly force swirls around *genialis lectus,* the bed that inevitably serves as the scene of birth-making activity. Genius is generative, birthing us into the world every moment. Agamben writes:

> To comprehend the concept of man which is implicit in Genius, means to understand that man is not only "I" and individual consciousness (coscienza), but that from the moment of his birth to that of his death he lives instead with an impersonal and pre-individual component. That is, man is a unique being in two phases, a being who is the result of the complicated dialectic between one side not (yet) singled out (individuata) and lived, and another side already marked by fate and by individual experience. (97)

Genius operates through a dialectic of care, or what Heidegger describes as a fundamental mode of absorption in the world. As Calvin O. Schrag summarizes Heidegger's sense of care: "To exist is to find oneself in a world to which one is related in one or several of the manifestations of care (Sorge)—in one's construction and use of tools, in one's undertaking and ordering of projects, or in one's encounter and dealings with other selves" ("Phenomenology" 123). Care is thus a kind of involvement with world. Involvement is different from acting as an autonomous agent who masters tools, but is rather an operative mutuality of working-with worlding encounters. Care is a structural entanglement, one that sustains the senses of "I" at the same time that an actual autonomous "I" is dissolved through constant enmeshment with world.

This structural entanglement is further theorized by Japanese philosopher Tetsuro Watsuji, who helps to expand upon Heidegger's sense of care (sorge). Although Watsuji certainly works in the same philosophical vein as Heidegger, he does not fall back on Heideggerian terminology. Instead of beginning with the concept of Dasein, Watsuji uses the Japanese term *sonzai* to describe the structure of being. As James Shields explains, "Watsuji suggests that the Japanese term sonzai (son = maintenance or subsistence against loss [time] + zai = remaining within relationships [space]) is a more appropriate term for describing 'the subjective, practical, and dynamic structure of human being' (21)" (Shields 269). That is, the practical structure of human being is a dialectic that alternates between maintenance against loss (which signals time) and the desire to remain in relationships (which signals space). The *son* of *sonzai* relates to a threat that a self always risks disappearance. Subsistence and maintenance works against this threat of loss. *Zai,* meanwhile, is a staying in place, which can only happen because there are other places we are related to. Watsuji's writes, "If it is tenable to hold that the son is self-sustenance of the self and zai means to remain within human relations, then son-zai is precisely the self-sustenance of the self as betweenness" (21).

The betweenness that Watsuji describes is caught specifically between the ongoing threat of losing self-sustenance and the places of human relations where we find ourselves. Between these are constant negotiation. Or, as Graham Mayeda puts it, "sonzai, the existence that characterizes human beings, is the temporal maintenance of the self in a particular location whose particularity is defined spatially by a web of relationships" (87–88). In short, sonzai marks the struggle of fighting a loss of self, trying to maintain the I one already is or has been, while also remaining enmeshed in the not-I world of relations and world. Care is thus a tugging between I and not-I. Genius is similarly care-full, existing within a tension or friction that marks human involvement. On one side, there is the self-sustenance of individual experience, and on the other side, there is the not-I of relations. This is the world of Genius.

It is also the world of the daimon, which is the Greek version of Genius. The daimon/genius plays a significant role in Hannah Arendt's account of the human condition, which is also informed by care. For Arendt, the human-making dialectic between I and not-I is made possible through disclosure. Specifically, she writes of disclosure as that which is most intimate to ourselves as individuals, though it can only happen before others. The daimon is that which is disclosed to others, but never to us. We disclose who we are to others in ways that surpass our self-concepts or best attempt at self-reflection. The daimon is thus more than "I," but it is also that which allows "I" to be human at all.

Arendt points to the example of Sophocles's Oedipus Rex and the terribly painful disclosure that is evident to the chorus though Oedipus is blind in more ways than one. "These others see," writes Arendt. "They 'have' Oedipus' daimon before their eyes as an example; the misery of the mortals is their blindness toward their own daimon" (*Human* 193n18). However, while Oedipus's daimon marks a tragedy, this is not to say that the daimon is a source of misery. As both Arendt and Agamben suggest, we have no place in the world without disclosure. The daimon is part of our enactment in the world, our disclosure to and with world.

The genius/daimon is a kind of para-archive, hovering over the top of our archival materials (in this case, our own life's materials), though it is not the selfsame as those archival contents. The genius or daimon's archive is a guiding spirit, leading the archivist toward disclosures. In a "post-truth" or "post-evidence" era, the daimon/genius does not aim at something like a return to whatever *truth* came before the *post*. Rather, this kind of archive repeatedly "birth[s] us into the world" through endless disclosures that toggle between the I and not-I.

Archives and evidence in this "post-truth" moment are thus very much guided by geniuses, though perhaps not stable ones. For simplicity's sake, or maybe for perversity's sake, I have come to call this para-archive a "demon archive," since demons themselves offer another way of thinking about what disclosure means. In certain evangelical Christian circles, demons must be cast out from those whose bodies have been possessed. Satan's evil spirits inhabit a human body and cause all kinds of turmoil that is out of the sufferer's control: not simply bad acts, such as rebellion, but all manner of sicknesses, disease, depression, lustful desires, money problems, and every other thing that falls short of what brings glory to God. These demons can be cast out in order to return the true self to her pure state, apart from the outside forces that attach to a single, individual body. Yet, casting out the demons imagined by Agamben and Arendt is an impossibility. It would mean a casting out of spatial involvement in the world altogether. We would be left with the temporality of "I" attempting to remain "I" apart from engagement with world. But no such deliverance is possible. The kind of care that involves us in the world leaves no temporal possibility of self-sustenance apart from the spatial relations with those to whom we disclose. Casting out the demon is the dream of every exorcist who falls back into the dream of an "I" whose identity is unaffected by space.

The ethos of creating a demon archive works against archivability as merely preserving memory against loss or as the maintenance of a given story. Indeed, rhetoricians and archival scholars have compellingly argued against viewing the archives as a fixed container from which the researcher draws meaning. As Barbara Biesecker writes, archives are more like a site of invention. We must take care not to approach the archives through what she calls "referential plentitude" (130), or the mistaken belief that archives are self-contained wombs. She writes, "The archive may best be understood as the scene of a doubled invention rather than as the site of a singular discovery" (124). The doubled invention is the invention of it and of us. A demon archive is thus inventional in its aim, as opposed to preservationist. Its ambition is not purification of narrative, in the sense of making the narrative clearer or better defined. Its aim is disclosure to others. Demon archives thus exist in a realm of potentiality, as they cannot determine in advance what will be found.

Demon archives do not resemble anything like a traditional archive, of course. I am not searching for something that mirrors useful information. Rather, the demon archive generates something in its tracings. What is recorded is the writing of the search itself: not the pages not found, but the traces of a search for those pages. In this way, it is akin to White's "hodge-podge historiography," which imagines a practice of writing with the absence of missing archives. It operates through the mode of narration. Yet, while it might appear to be a personal narrative, a demon archive is meant to disturb, tilt, and reorient the one who searches the archive for answers she already has in mind. Demons are strange in the way they are always both personal and universal. The demon of lust, for example, is universal enough to be a commonly named demon, but it also only inhabits a particular body. Similarly, a demon archive is not personal. It is not my testimony. Neither is it possible without me. It is both. I am writing with the absence in the way only I can. Public and individual, all at once.

In this sense, the demon archive resembles what Carlo Ginzburg describes a "microhistory." Ginzburg reflects on Giovanni Levi's declaration that micro-history is a "self-portrait" and not a "group portrait." Ginzburg writes:

> I had proposed doing the same, but did not succeed. Both the boundaries of the group to which I belonged and my own boundaries of self seemed retrospectively shifting and uncertain. To my surprise I discovered how important to me, unknowingly, were books I had never read, events and persons I did not know existed. If this is a self-portrait, then its model are the paintings of Umberto Boccioni in which the street enters into the house, the landscape into the face, the exterior invades the interior, the I is porous. (*Threads* 213)

Moreover, the telos of a demon archive is this experience of encountering the I's porousness. The street entering the house.

Whether we think of it as a para-archive, hodgepodge history, or micro-history, the demon archive is very much an unfitting response in action. Less a speculative archive than a de-speculative archive, this process is inventional. What conclusions can we draw from such a demon archive? Few. Many. But the conclusions are contingent and in flux. Neither speculative not factual, this kind of archival off-roading marks the traces and trajectories of what once seemed a solid figuration. It is also an anomaly in itself: an uneven and odd practice that will inevitably lead to some kind of reorientation to worlds.

Living in a post-truth era, as many of us seem to believe we are, does not limit our capacities for imagining different forms of public engagement with something truth-like—something that communicates. We can use the case of Pizzagate to see exactly how this inventional capacity can be tapped into. Although Pizzagate's archive contains many pages not found, that does not prevent us from writing *with* those (post-truth) artifacts. As a thought experiment, then, I'd like to offer one example of a what a demon archive might look like. What follows is a form of strategic writing, one attending to disclosure rather than truth. Following White, I want to discover how the wrong itself can tell stories. Even more, I want to also ask what we can do with these stories.

•

PIZZAGATE: A DEMON ARCHIVE

See also: Satan.

Writing in the *Washington Post,* anthropologist Richard Lancaster notes:

> Pizzagate shares much of its content with an outbreak of collective hysteria over imaginary occult pedophile rings three decades ago, which can now summed up in three words: satanic-ritual abuse. At the beginning of the 1980s, it seemed eminently plausible to many people that an extensive underground network of sadistic devil worshipers was sexually torturing large numbers of children in preschools and day-care centers across the country—and that these activities had somehow gone undetected for years, if not decades.

As Lancaster reveals, the discourse of this conspiracy theory is heavily coated by the sticky remnants of earlier public artifacts surrounding the "Satanic panic" of the 1980s and 1990s, which made satanic ritual abuse, occultic child sex rings, and human sacrifice so present in the public imaginary. As one writer put it, "The takeaway from the bizarre news" of Pizzagate is that "Satan sits at the edge of a continuum of crazy, and Donald Trump has moved us a lot closer to it" (Michaelson). Indeed, the details of sinister cults, led by the nation's most prominent governmental and public figures, changes very little from the 1980s' Satanic panic to the Pizzagate narrative that emerged three decades later.

Scroll back. Years before the internet became the source for all-things-conspiracy, frenzied news of satanic ritual abuse (SRA) became a staple for popular talk shows, magazines, radio programs, and newspapers. In tabloid style, television programs like *The Sally Jesse Raphael Show, Oprah, 20/20,* and *Geraldo* gave a platform to SRA "survivors," who were suddenly remembering the gruesome details of these large cult networks. There was the 1989 *Oprah* episode devoted to "child sacrifice" and the 1991 *Sally Jesse Raphael* episode on "Devil Babies." And, of course, Geraldo Rivera broke ratings records in 1988 with his ninety-minute special "Devil Worship: Exposing Satan's Underground." In their introduction to *The Satanism Scare,* James T. Richardson et al. argue that "while the prestige press virtually ignored satanism, the topic received plenty of coverage in the media, contributing to the perception that satanism must be increasing" (12). Adults across the country were driven by "the fear that covert Satanic machinations were at work everywhere around us—in our cartoons, commercials, music, movies, and, most tragically of all, our daycares," writes Kier-La Janisse (Janisse and Corupe 13). Thanks to Oprah, Sally, and Geraldo, this seemed to be the case.

I saw many of these shows as a preteen, frightened by the horrifying descriptions. "It's totally true," my friend told me. She showed me the book *Michelle Remembers,* which is (as the back cover says) "the true story of a woman who, as a child, was delivered into the hands of the Anti-Christ—the ancient and infamous Church of Satan. . . . Michelle relives the incredible and terrifying ordeal which she suffered at the hands of a group of Satanists." Survivor stories like *Michelle Remembers* told of unbelievably graphic occult abuse, including forced cannibalism, child rape, human sacrifice, and even more bizarre forms of satanic torture. My friend also showed me pamphlets made by evangelical cartoonist Jack Chick, who graphically illustrated how demonic powers were just waiting to enter our bodies through things like *Dungeons and Dragons* or rock music.

A man came to talk to our church about the dangerous world of these underground cults. His overhead projector showed drawings of certain "signs" we should watch for that might indicate cult presence in our communities. I was too frightened to draw them, so I tried to memorize as many as I could. Similar talks were happening in churches, schools, and police forces across the country, all led by the newly crowned "experts" on the dark world of ritualistic occult crime. Retired police officer Don Rimer, for example, built quite a career from leading training seminars for such governmental organizations as the Oklahoma Association of Chiefs of Police, Illinois Chiefs of Police Association, Virginia State Police, National Major Gang Task Force, and numerous others. Rimer's seminars began by introducing attendees to the worlds of "Satanism, Witchcraft, Goth Culture, [and] Vampirism" ("Ritual" iii). While Rimer notes that there are differences among these groups, "it is the common denominators of homicide, suicide, self mutilation, grave robbery, animal abuse, blood/death metal music and fantasy role playing games" that bind them together ("Ritual" iii).

Both local and federal law enforcement agencies took these threats seriously in the 1980s and 1990s. New task forces and police training manuals were devoted to tackling the satanic menace. One US Department of Justice training manual, titled *Satanic Cult Awareness*, began by describing "the occult explosion" as "a new police problem" faced by departments across the country. With a no-nonsense delivery, the forty-seven-page manual asserts that local police forces should be on the lookout for such ritualistic activities as human sacrifices, child sexual torture with religious objects, and other unimaginable scenes of horror. During these rituals, children are especially subjected to the most gruesome acts of satanic control: "the insertion of eyeballs into the [child's] vagina or rectum," "immersion in feces/blood buckets/ urine," "blood transfusions or skin grafts from sacrificial victims," and more (Hurst and Marsh 9). After describing similar ritualistic horrors, the manual goes on to provide law enforcement professionals with a list of decoded words and symbols that can help police navigate the hidden meanings used in satanic cults. The traditional "peace sign," for example, should now be seen as the "Cross of Nero," which represents "an 'upside down' cross with the cross member broken downward" (40). Even an ordinary triangle signals "the place where a demon would appear in a conjuration ritual" (41). The decoded symbols go on for many pages, providing an entire encyclopedia of satanic horror.

More prolifically, the Cult Crime Impact Network distributed a regular newsletter to law enforcement agencies throughout much of the late 1980s and early 1990s. The group, which described itself as "a network by and for law enforcement and qualified civilians who have entered the fight against cult crime," regularly instructed investigators on how to spot adults and children who were being controlled by satanic cults. For example, two or more of the following characteristics were said to suggest that someone was being ritualistically victimized: abdominal pain, collapsed rectal wall, nipples missing, right-side epilepsy, sexual or chemical dependency, God phobia, blackouts, seeming multiple personalities or dissociative dysfunction disorder, fixation with or references to Satan or demons (October 23, 1987). The newsletter also served as a place where local police departments could reach out for help in solving their own cult crimes. One such request read: "The phrase 'Yankee Rose' appears on the last page of LaVey's SATANIC BIBLE, it was the name of a song by David Lee Roth about a hooker, and it was recently written on the body of a male murder victim with lipstick. What is the significance of 'Yankee Rose?'" The network's newsletters were filled with graphic descriptions of gory ritual crimes that, while almost never documented or proven to be true, were framed as one of the country's biggest threats to children and adults alike.

Scroll forward. In 2018, a Twitter user posted images from a 1989 Chicago police manual titled *Identification, Investigation, and Understanding of Ritualistic Criminal Activity.* The manual's pages immediately became a viral sensation. The responses were again what you might call hysterical, though not in the same sense as the satanic panic hysteria. Social media erupted with collective laughter at the overblown and melodramatic warnings. Thousands of tweets shared the images, adding a heavy dose of mockery. Readers poked fun at the manual's "symptoms of increased involvement," which include such warning signs as tarot cards, black walls, drawings of magical symbols, candles, and the unexplained "Use of Alphabet (More advanced stages)." One commenter wryly responded: "So I was safe when I was just a bored lonely teen living precariously through my AD&D manual and listening to punk rock music. Never knew it'd be ALPHABETS that would push me over the edge" (@AnotherAspirin). A different commenter joked: "Tarot Cards, candles, AND oils?!?! Oh shit! Everyone I went to college with was a Satanist!!!" (@MarcMcD). The artifacts of a panic had now become the stuff of kitsch.

See also: laughter.

It's all good for a laugh. In fact, laughter has itself become a significant part of the satanic panic's archive. The influential Geraldo special that helped spark a decade of cultural terror now seems little more than a "sleazily overhyped fear-gumbo," as one writer recently put it (Raftery, "Satanic"). The cheesy hermeneutics of decoded "satanic" symbols appear now as a kind of freak show, something meant only to elicit embarrassed snickers and eye rolls. The alarmist cartoons produced by Jack Chick, once seen as a leading voice in the fight against satanism, now seem like amusing nostalgia. When Chick died in 2016, several cultural commenters noted that his cartoons continue to gain fans *because* of their incredible kitsch value. "Something about these comics made them lend themselves so easily to ironic recuperation," writes one fan (Kriss). Good for a laugh, indeed.

A strange assemblage emerges between satanism and laughter, creating a relationality out of disparate things. This satanism-laughter assemblage has become a commonplace, cueing our cultural responses to discourse like the Pizzagate conspiracy theories. This time, however, there's a sharp awareness among believers that their theories are being mocked by a wider public. The laughter is loud and clear. "It's important to understand the scope of this problem," writes one online Pizzagate promoter. "They are literally laughing at us, flaunting it" ("Full Text"). Another social media comment sums up the sentiments of many frustrated believers: "Libs are laughing at us they were able to make a big deal of 'grabbing pussy' while getting away with #pizzagate" (@gunnisonheath). And the conspiracy theorists are not necessarily wrong on this point. They were being laughed at everywhere from late night talk shows to a slew of comments via social media.

On *The Late Show,* host Stephen Colbert sardonically poked fun at the very premise of Pizzagate: "Apparently, some alt-right folks were combing through Clinton campaign emails hacked by Russia and published by WikiLeaks and noticed there seems to be more references to pizza and pizzerias than they had expected, which can only mean one thing: secret sex ring" (December 7, 2016). The audience erupted with laughter. *Saturday Night Live* jumped on board with their sketch featuring a "pizzagater" whose rambling, wacky diatribes made for easy chuckles (December 10, 2016). Even Hillary Clinton responded to a well-known Pizzagate believer by retweeting a link to a Domino's Pizza job. Pizzagate had become a national punch line.

It might seem strange to mark laughter as a meaningful archival artifact, yet the Pizzagate laughter just happened to unfold during a moment when laughter was taking on a new kind of political significance. During his 2016 presidential campaign, Donald Trump frequently identified laughter as a symptom of America's problems, and, at times, even suggested that laughter was the problem itself. "The world is laughing at us," Trump repeated like a mantra. His repetition was so noteworthy that the *Washington Post* went to the trouble of counting how many times Trump has publicly declared that the world is laughing at us. Their finding was that Trump made this declaration "in some form at least 103 times, going as far back as 1987" (Chokshi). It was in 1987, in fact, that Trump took out ad space in the *Washington Post, New York Times,* and *Boston Globe* to publish an open letter complaining about the US's military defense in foreign countries. It shouldn't be the US who pays to protect other countries, roars Trump. They should be able to pay their own way. After a lengthy list of complaints, Trump concludes his letter with: "Let's not let our great country be laughed at anymore" (September 2, 1987). As Michael A. Cohen puts it in an opinion piece for the *Boston Globe,* "The notion that other countries are laughing at America is perhaps the only consistent line of argument that Trump has made throughout his political career."

After the election, the troubling specter of laughter continued to haunt Trump. When Trump spoke at the United Nations (UN) in September 2018, he inadvertently caused an eruption of laughter in the audience after he declared, "In less than two years my administration has accomplished more than almost any administration in the history of our country." Loud guffaws overtook the UN crowd, as Trump looked a bit confused. Later, in a press conference, he appeared to have settled on a narrative that neutralized the laughter. "They weren't laughing at me, they were laughing with me," Trump told reporters. "We had fun. That was not laughing at me." Though Trump had long claimed that the world is laughing at us, it seems that he could not bring himself to believe they would dare to laugh at him.

The specter of laughter also haunts Trump's supporters who, like Trump, frequently repeat the claim that they are being laughed at. After the election, for example, one seventy-two-year-old woman told a reporter: "We were constantly being made to feel uneducated if we supported Trump. We felt like elitists were laughing at us" (Bradlee). President Trump seemed to hold the promise that the laughter will finally end. In fact, the day before the election, Trump shared a social media post with a quote (incorrectly) attributed to Gandhi: "First they ignore you, then they laugh at you, then they fight you, then you win" (figure 9). Putting aside the egregious misattribution, the narrative marks an important progression for Trumpian rhetoric: You must move past laughter in order to win.

Some commentators have speculated whether one particular scene of laughter is partly responsible for Trump's 2016 campaign in the first place. In Ta-Nehisi Coates's essay "The First White President," where he documents Trump's long public record of racism and antiblack sentiment, Coates speculates that President Obama's mockery of Trump at the 2011 White House Correspondents' Dinner pushed Trump over the edge. Trump was sitting in the audience, listening to President Obama poke fun at various political figures, when the spotlight suddenly turned to Trump's obsession with Obama's "fake" birth records:

Donald Trump is here tonight! (Laughter and applause.) Now, I know that he's taken some flak lately, but no one is happier, no one is prouder to put this birth certificate matter to rest than the Donald. (Laughter.) And that's because he can finally get back to focusing on the issues that matter—like, did we fake the moon landing? (Laughter.) What really happened in Roswell? (Laughter.) And where are Biggie and Tupac? (Laughter and applause.)

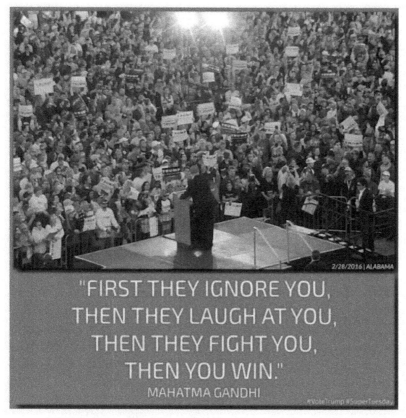

"FIRST THEY IGNORE YOU,
THEN THEY LAUGH AT YOU,
THEN THEY FIGHT YOU,
THEN YOU WIN."
MAHATMA GANDHI

FIGURE 9. Misattributed quote from Donald Trump's Instagram account

But all kidding aside, obviously, we all know about your credentials and breadth of experience. (Laughter.) For example—no, seriously, just recently, in an episode of Celebrity Apprentice—(laughter)—at the steakhouse, the men's cooking team cooking did not impress the judges from Omaha Steaks. And there was a lot of blame to go around. But you, Mr. Trump, recognized that the real problem was a lack of leadership. And so ultimately, you didn't blame Lil' Jon or Meatloaf. (Laughter.) You fired Gary Busey. (Laughter.) And these are the kind of decisions that would keep me up at night. (Laughter and applause.) Well handled, sir. (Laughter.)

Trump sat in the audience, never smiling once. "For Trump," writes Coates, "it almost seems that the fact of Obama, the fact of a black president, insulted him personally." Coates suggests that the experience of being mocked by a black president was the straw that broke everything. Reflecting on the event several years later, Adam Gopnik writes that the night "[took] on a potency that one might not have understood at the time. For the politics of populist nationalism are almost entirely the politics of felt humiliation—the politics of shame. And one can't help but suspect that, on that night, Trump's own sense of public humiliation became so overwhelming that he decided, perhaps at first unconsciously, that he would, somehow, get his own back—perhaps even pursue the Presidency after all." His presidency is built on the promise that (the) laughter will end.

Now might be a good time to pause and ask a perfectly reasonable question: *What is this archive evidence of?* It does not resemble an archive in any traditional sense. It doesn't even stick to the nominal subject that it claims to be archiving. Indeed, as a para-archive, it merely hovers around the edges of whatever a "real" Pizzagate archive might look like. It is a demon archive, neither fictional nor factual. It has little interest in objective assessments of historical moments. Rather, this archive is evidence of public life's disclosures. It is a scout report from a caught moment inside of a world.

Much like a typical scout report, this archival tracing looks to disclosures in their capacities for imagining possible futures. In this particular demon archive, laughter becomes disclosive. And, indeed, laughter itself can disclose a great deal. As Diane Davis argues in *Breaking up (at) Totality,* laughter often overtakes us like a sneeze, temporarily interrupting our sense of being fully in control of ourselves, our bodies, our agency (116). The laugh bursts through even in moments where we are doing our best to control it. But we cannot control it; laughter takes the reins. Maybe this is why being laughed at is so wounding. It shatters our own sense of who we are. A laugh that pops out at unintended moments discloses so many things, often to great embarrassment. Recently, as I was sitting with my friend and colleague Nathaniel Rivers in a particularly dry academic talk, he whispered a hilarious quip to me. Typical Nathaniel. Without time to stifle myself, I let out a loud laugh. Stares and scowls came at me like poisoned darts from the other audience members. My laughter said something about my entanglements and "where I was" in that moment.

Laughter in the Pizzagate archive similarly discloses quite a lot. It shows what was once whole (in seriousness) and has since been interrupted or shattered. More tellingly, complaints about being laughed at also disclose what certain publics do not want shattered. Laughter and its objection thus become a way to flush out those points of woundedness on the public body, the places where we tug between interruption and continuity. The archive I'm tracing here suggests that narratives of *purposeful darkness* and *transcendent evil* exist in a tension within public life. Laughter surrounding the stories of satanic crimes shatters these narratives, which must be reinforced and rebuilt in order to fix such interruption.

●

This particular demon archive I have traced here discloses laughter as a potentiality. This leads me to ask how laughter might serve as a basis for new forms of public engagement in this particular discursive scene. What do the laughter and anti-laughter gestures tell us about the tender spots on the public body? What do we make of those welcome interruptions to our sense of sovereign subjectivity? And what do we make of intense resistance to that interruption? Laughter as archival artifact pushes me to listen for the *real* inside the referent. When we hear laughter in such fraught moments of post-truth or conspiracy discourse, we might alternatively hear tension between feeling one's autonomous subjectivity and sensing its potential for shatteredness. Such disclosures offer different rhetorical frameworks within which to act, speak, and write. They are ways in.

But, make no mistake about it: This is merely one way to write Pizzagate's demon archive. The point I want to make here is not really about laughter. I am certainly not suggesting that we should (or shouldn't) laugh at troubling public discourse. After all, this is only one of many stories that can be told. One of many hodgepodge histories. Another archive will surely trace different searches and different entanglements. Not only is this the point of demon archives, but it is the very thing that makes this archival writing practice an inventional process. Evidence collected in demon archives aims at something beyond validity or fidelity. It is evidence of the multiple registers of evidence, some of which become buried beneath a myopic framework of validity, fidelity, and truth-value. As a rhetorical practice for invention, the demon archive writes *with* those artifacts that are absent, untrue, and singularly public. It see(k)s evidence in a poetic capacity, aimed above all else at inciting curiosity. It is a method for reclaiming evidence in a post-truth world.

Returning to the question I posed at the beginning of this chapter, it is only right to ask once again: *What can this archive do?* To answer both simply and complexly, I argue that this archive invents new theories of a given moment. Here I am thinking of theories in the sense of *theoria,* a vantage or way of seeing. In order to make inroads in public discourse—especially when facing recalcitrant rhetorics—we need new ways of seeing. We will inevitably fail by continuing to claim that *this* evidence outweighs *that* evidence, or *this* archive is superior to *that* archive. It's our challenge to invent new modes of responsible response, like the demons we are.

OUTRO

The What and the Where

AS I WAS writing this book, I tended to hear a handful of the same questions from friends and strangers alike: *How do you debate conspiracy theorists? How do you persuade people spewing toxic arguments that they're wrong? How do you argue with a person who is loaded down with bad evidence?* At a recent family gathering, after hearing me drone on about the nuances of evidence, my aunt got right to the point: "Can you just give me a user's guide or something on how to talk to these people?" I laughed at the time, but the idea of a user's guide did sound pretty appealing: a how-to manual for operating (or operationalizing) the theories I explored in previous chapters. While I reject the idea that there is only one way to effectively respond to awful evidence, I want to definitively answer the question *How do you debate conspiracy theorists?* My answer here is pretty simple. *You don't.*

Let me explain.

Throughout *Awful Archives,* I have attempted to toss out the basic premise that evidence is easy to grasp, let alone easy to disprove or effectively counter-argue. I have suggested that by broadening our concept of evidence to include evidentiary acts or evidentiary processes, we create a much richer toolbox for finding the fitting response in situations that seem like rhetorical dead ends. I argue that our (counter-)responses are actually stronger and more effective when they look to the *acts* of evidence, rather than the contents alone. Evidence is composed of actions that build and move in many different registers, both material and affective. They are structures in motion. Furthermore, while evidentiary processes or structures contain what is most commonly identified as "evidence," those structures are embedded within broader public scenes. Responses to evidentiary processes thus look much different from responses to static "evidence." Consequently, a different model of evidence calls for us to give up an overreliance on debate culture. While this phrase signals a range of meanings, I use *debate culture* here to refer to those rhetorical responses focused primarily on the veracity or legitimacy of an interlocutor's evidence.

Debate culture emerges in almost all aspects of public life, as well as academic worlds. It goes by many different names: *disproving, debunking, call-out culture, critique, calling bullshit,* and others. Don't get me wrong, I am all for public debate, yet I join other critics who have begun to note the civic injuries that come from overemphasizing the contents of another's evidence. For instance, in her blunt assessment of debate culture, author and journalist Laurie Penny writes, "There are some stupid mistakes that only very smart people make, and one of them is the notion that a sensible argument seriously presented can compete with a really good piece of theatre." Debate culture, Penny continues, is simply the "live-action roleplaying of a Classical fever-dream of a society where pedigreed intellectuals freely exchange ideas in front of a respectful audience." The stupid mistake, in Penny's estimation, is our willingness to buy the hype of what sensible argument seriously presented can actually do.

To borrow a phrase from political economist William Davies, we've put too much faith in a "bravado rationalism," or the smug insistence that rational counterargument is the only effective response to troubled, warrantless claims. We have probably all felt the thrill that comes from such bravado: pointing out factual inconsistency, identifying fallacious reasoning, delegitimizing shoddy sources, exposing logical flaws. While there are certainly times that such tactics are crucial, there are limitations to a rhetorical response that only seeks to (dis)prove the validity or legitimacy of another's evidence. Rather than drawing an artificially limited circle around the *contents* of a claim, we might instead ask a different question: *What and where are the acts of evidence?* Or, to put the question differently: *What and where are the structures in motion?* This question is meant to shift our rhetorical energies and resources in terms of *what* and *who* we respond to in those moments.

As an example of what this kind of shift looks like in practice, I want to trace the public discourse surrounding some of the most toxic conspiracy theories circulating during the time I was writing *Awful Archives*. Although I tried to avoid consuming media about conspiracy theory during the hours

I was "off the clock," it was nearly impossible to avoid hearing news and talk about Alex Jones and his Infowars empire. Jones is perhaps the most visible conspiracy theorist in popular culture today. At one point, Jones boasted over 2 million listeners to his radio program, 1.9 million subscribers to his YouTube channel, and nearly 7 million visitors to his Infowars website. The Southern Poverty Law Center goes so far as to call Jones's empire "the most far-reaching influence in the nation's history." Jones has helped to popularize conspiracy theories around everything from 9/11 to the Boston Marathon bombing to water fluoridization. Yet, none of Jones's theories has been more circulated, debated, criticized, and analyzed than his claims about the Sandy Hook shootings.

On December 14, 2012, a young man armed with a semiautomatic rifle walked into Sandy Hook Elementary School. The shooter, Adam Lanza, opened fire in the school, killing twenty children, all between the ages of six and seven years old. He also killed six adults who worked at the school. Before police arrived at the horrifying scene, Lanza took his own life. The details are overwhelmingly heartbreaking, and images of the murdered children gave news stories an emotional salience that (yet again) stopped many of us in our tracks (at least for a while). The usual conversations began immediately: Why do we continue to allow such violent weapons to be sold? Why do we not have better mental health care in the US? How can we make our schools safer? Why are we becoming more violent? What should we do?

But these were not the questions that Alex Jones was asking. Instead, over the span of several years, Jones passionately argued to his audiences that Sandy Hook had all been a big hoax. On one 2014 episode of *The Alex Jones Show,* he told listeners: "It took me about a year with Sandy Hook to come to grips with the fact that the whole thing was fake. I mean, I couldn't believe it. I knew they jumped on it, used the crisis, hyped it up. But then I did deep research and my gosh, it just pretty much didn't happen" (December 28, 2014). On his radio show, Infowars site, and online videos, Jones repeatedly claimed that Sandy Hook had been an elaborately staged ruse, complete with "crisis actors" who only pretended to be the parents of nonexistent dead kids. Even the so-called victims were simply hired actors pretending to be deceased children.

Following Jones, other Sandy Hook truthers began circulating images of these crisis actors—both adults and children—in order to expose "the hoax." Across the internet, popular memes compared images of Sandy Hook victims and images of living people who (truthers argued) are the actors "playing" victims for purposes of conspiratorial cover-up. According to Jones, the government had perpetrated this hoax in order to surreptitiously clamp down on gun rights and civil liberties, all in the name of public safety. Jones further argued that the government was lying to us in the worst way, causing a nation to mourn for children who had never even existed. As he told one caller on a 2015 episode of his radio show, "Sandy Hook is a synthetic completely fake with actors, in my view, manufactured. I couldn't believe it at first. I knew they had actors there, clearly, but I thought they killed some real kids. And it just shows how bold they are, that they clearly used actors" (January 13, 2015). As Jones's outrage seemed to build, his audience's anger likewise grew, sometimes with nightmarish results.

Sandy Hook truthers began taking it upon themselves to do the archival work necessary for exposing this hoax (see figure 10). Few people experienced more effects of conspiratorial archival work than Gene Rosen, who was a hero in the midst of the tragedy. On the day of the massacre, one classroom of Sandy Hook Elementary School children escaped Adam Lanza's deadly attacks by running to Rosen's neighboring house for help. After the children told him that their teacher had been shot dead, Rosen took them inside and called police. Rosen describes being barraged almost immediately by taunting emails and phone calls because the Sandy Hook truthers accused him of being an actor in a staged hoax. "I'm getting emails with . . . accusations that I'm lying, that I'm a crisis actor, 'how much am I being paid?,'" Rosen told one reporter (Seitz-Wald). Similarly, a number of families who lost children in the shooting also received death threats and unrelenting harassment from truthers who believe that the families are nothing more than government shills who are playing along in the big lie. In 2017, for example, a fifty-seven-year-old truther named Lucy Richards was convicted of making death threats to Lenny Pozner, whose six-year-old son Noah was killed in the massacre. In her voice-mail messages, Richards spewed horrifying words at Pozner:

> Did you hide your imaginary son in an attic? Are you still fucking him, you fucking Jew bastard? You're gonna die. You're gonna rot in hell. Death is coming to you real soon, and there's nothing you can do about it. So you're just gonna have to take it, OK? Jew bastard. Look behind you. Death is coming to you real soon. ("Beware")

In court, Richards explained that she got caught up in the crisis actor discourse and lashed out at Pozner for being what she considered to be an accomplice. This is one of those situations where that handful of questions seems particularly relevant: *How do you debate conspiracy theorists? How do you persuade people spewing toxic arguments that they're wrong? How do you argue with a person who is loaded down with bad evidence?*

FIGURE 10. Sandy Hook conspiracy meme

If we could create a user's guide for people dealing with Sandy Hook truthers, what would it look like? Actually, we might look to Lenny Pozner himself for an answer. Pozner, the father who experienced firsthand the violent fallout of truth actions, was one of the most eloquent and outspoken voices speaking against the truthers' awful archives. For years after the tragedy, Pozner attempted to disprove truthers' evidence by offering solid counterevidence that his six-year-old son had indeed been murdered. His actions were rooted in the premise that the way to fight back was through sensible argument seriously presented. Buying into the lofty idea that bad evidence can be debated away, his counterarguments aggressively debunked the validity, rationality, and legitimacy of Jones's evidence.

In 2014, for example, Pozner released Noah's death certificate and even his report card. As Pozner's estranged wife recalled, releasing Noah's death certificate "was a difficult decision that we made, but figured, after a while of providing this hard copy convincing evidence that reason would prevail, and they would say, 'oh, OK, yeah, you've made your point. I'm going to come around'" ("Beware"). Unfortunately, in response, Pozner only received even more vitriol and threats from those who doubted him. When this tactic did not slow down the truthers, Pozner then tried another sensible argument seriously presented. He created an online group called Conspiracy Theorists Anonymous, aimed at directly engaging and debating with conspiracy theorists in order to debunk their unwarranted claims. For over a year, Pozner debated the doubters, trying to prove that the massacre was not a hoax and he was very much a real, grieving father. Still, none of those counter-rhetorics seemed to make a dent in Sandy Hook truther discourse. He eventually gave up on the group after he found that he wasn't really changing minds.

Years after that painful day, Pozner found himself struggling to present the right evidence that would prove Noah was dead and that the Sandy Hook parents were not just government shills. Then, after years of frustratingly ineffective attempts, Pozner decided to shift the way he responded. Most notably, he stepped back from the contents of truther claims in order to focus on the *what* and *where* of the acts of evidence. He turned his attention to the material and structural processes of the claims' circulation, most notably the social media platforms that helped amplify truther discourse. Every time Pozner saw a conspiracy post that used Noah's image (or those of any other Sandy Hook families), he reported the posts for copyright violation. Instead of debating or debunking the (false) evidence offered by truthers, he instead threw his energy into reporting these copyright violations to YouTube and other social media platforms, forcing them to remove content about Noah and other families. It worked. In fact, Pozner was so successful that conspiracy theorists began to refer to the removals as "getting Poznered." Over time, people joined Pozner's fight, calling upon sites like Twitter, Facebook, YouTube, and iTunes to permanently remove content and content producers who were responsible for consistently circulating conspiracy theories. Their calls eventually led to Alex Jones's infamous ban from these platforms.

Pozner and his allies found that responding to evidence entails more than merely responding to evidentiary contents. What's more, they came to realize that debating evidence sometimes paradoxically produces even more toxic discourse. As writer Laura Hudson puts it in her analysis of harmful rhetoric, although some people claim that only "absolute, unfettered speech is the best and only way to cure it . . . if we have learned anything from history, research or even a cursory glance around the current political landscape, it is that trying to combat the disease of disinformation with *more* speech only makes the patient sicker." Perhaps one reason for this paradox is that, as we have seen, the telos of certain discourse (such as conspiracy theories) is to simply keep itself going. It is through ongoing accumulations that a sense of coherence and new orientations emerge. Rather than adding to the accumulation via competing facts and information, a structural approach responds procedurally. In Pozner's case, his response seeks to disrupt the structures that are part of truthers' figurations.

Pozner defigured these rhetorical acts by attending to the material structures that allow certain figurations to become thick evidence in the first place: websites, social media platforms, funding sources. While we may not typically think about disrupting material or technical structures of argument as a rhetorical response, let alone a counter-response to bad evidence, I argue that this conceptual shift is quite promising in an era of post-truth discourse. By purposefully rethinking the *what* and *where* of argument, I'm searching for new ways to find hope in and for public life. It is my way of fighting back against despair, thereby expanding my own toolbox of ethical, situated, and attuned rhetorical strategies.

Maybe the best way to encapsulate this strategic shift is to revisit this book's opening epigraph. T. H. Huxley was certain that the "foundation of morality is to have done, once and for all, with . . . pretending to believe that for which there is no evidence" (802). However, when we shift our concept of evidence as less of a *thing* and more of an *act,* then Huxley's formulation falls a bit flat. I might find certain claims and evidence misguided or even abhorrent, yet I inevitably miss opportunities for productive, engaged rhetorical response if I dismiss the claim as having *no* evidence. Tinkering with Huxley's phrasing just a bit, then, I suggest this as a more useful slogan: *The foundation of rhetorical responsibility is to have done, once and for all, with pretending to believe there is no evidence.*

To be sure, no single strategy is sufficient for every rhetorical situation. There are times when we are must respond directly to the veracity (or lack thereof) found in claims. Calling out a politician's false arguments about migrants, for example, is critically important to sustaining healthy democracy and even saving lives. At the same time, we should remember that different rhetorical strategies yield different results. Even as we call out problematic claims and evidence, we might simultaneously see this discourse as prospective material for writing-thinking new ways of seeing the world. This is a hopeful strategy, one that looks to invention as a resource for public life. When discourses appear to hit a dead end, we must find ways of engaging new rhetorical practices that are truly awe-full.

WORKS CITED

Aaronovitch, David. *Voodoo Histories: The Role of the Conspiracy Theory in Shaping Modern History.* Penguin, 2010.

Adamo, Thomas. *Conspiracy Rhetoric.* Woodbine Cottage, 2010.

Adorno, Theodor Wiesengrund, et al. *The Authoritarian Personality.* W. W. Norton, 1969.

Agamben, Giorgio. *"Genius."* Translated by Laurence Simmons. *Interstices: Journal of Architecture and Related Arts,* vol. 7, 2006, pp. 96–101.

AnahataOnline. "A Message I Sent out to My Friends n Family on Fb." *YouTube,* 6 Apr. 2014, www.youtube.com/watch?v=OKpUsfl_DrA.

———. "My Experience with a Reptilian and Grey Race." *YouTube,* 17 Mar. 2016, www.youtube.com/watch?v=40cVVrhfw9w.

@AnotherAspirin. "So I was safe . . . ." *Twitter,* 6 May 2018, 8:17 a.m., twitter.com/AnotherAspirin/status/993147853802524672.

Arendt, Hannah. *Eichmann in Jerusalem.* Viking Press, 1964.

———. *The Human Condition.* U of Chicago P, 2013.

Aristotle. *On Rhetoric: A Theory of Civic Discourse.* Translated by George Kennedy, Oxford UP, 2006.

———. *Poetics.* Translated by Stephen Halliwell, U of Chicago P, 1998.

Aurbach, Rachel. "This Is How It Started." *PoetryInHell,* poetryinhell.org/appendix-c-how-the-archives-were-collected-buried-unearthed-conserved-and-viewed/this-is-how-it-started/.

Auvray, Malika, et al. "There Is Something out There: Distal Attribution in Sensory Substitution, Twenty Years Later." *Journal of Integrative Neuroscience,* vol. 4, no. 4, Dec. 2005, pp. 505–21.

Ballif, Michelle. *Theorizing Histories of Rhetoric.* Southern Illinois UP, 2013.

Balzotti, Jonathan Mark, and Richard Benjamin Crosby. "Diocletian's Victory Column: Megethos and the Rhetoric of Spectacular Disruption." *Rhetoric Society Quarterly,* vol. 44, no. 4, 2014, pp. 323–42.

Barfield, Owen. *Saving the Appearances: A Study in Idolatry.* Wesleyan UP, 1988.

Barrett, Kevin. "US Military Ghouls Butchered JFK's Corpse!" *Veterans Today,* 31 Oct. 2013, www.veteranstoday.com/2013/10/31/jfk-ghouls/.

Bell, Andrew, et al. *Evidence.* Cambridge UP, 2008.

Benjamin, Walter. "Little History of Photography." *The Work of Art in the Age of Its Technological Reproducibility, and Other Writings on Media,* edited by Michael W. Jennings, Harvard UP, 2008.

———. *On Hashish.* Harvard UP, 2006.

———. *Selected Writings: 1931–1934.* Translated by Rodney Livingstone et al., edited by Michael W. Jennings, Harvard UP, 2004.

———. "Theses on the Philosophy of History." *Illuminations.* Translated by Henry Zohn. Shocken Books, 1968, pp. 253–67.

———. "Unpacking My Library." *Illuminations,* 1968, pp. 59–67.

Berlant, Lauren Gail. *The Queen of America Goes to Washington City: Essays on Sex and Citizenship.* Duke UP, 1997.

———. "Unworlding." *Supervalent Thought,* 13 May 2009, supervalentthought.com/2009/05/13/unworlding/.

Berlatsky, Noah. "Peter Thiel Wants America to Take Trump Seriously, but Not Literally. That's Dangerous." *Quartz,* 1 Nov. 2016, qz.com/824650/peter-thiel-wants-america-to-take-donald-trump-seriously-but-not-literally/.

Bernault, Florence. "Suitcases and the Poetics of Oddities: Writing History from Disorderly Archives." *History in Africa,* vol. 42, 2015, pp. 269–77.

"Beware the Jabberwock." *This American Life,* episode 670, 15 Mar. 2019.

Biesecker, Barbara A. "Of Historicity, Rhetoric: The Archive as Scene of Invention." *Rhetoric & Public Affairs,* vol. 9, no. 1, 2006, pp. 124–31.

Bitzer, Lloyd. "The Rhetorical Situation." *Philosophy and Rhetoric,* 1.1, 1968, pp.1–14.

Bizzell, Patricia, and Bruce Herzberg. *The Rhetorical Tradition: Readings from Classical Times to the Present.* Bedford/St. Martin's, 2001.

Booth, Wayne C. *Modern Dogma and the Rhetoric of Assent.* U of Chicago P, 1974.

———. *A Rhetoric of Irony.* Vol. 641, U of Chicago P, 1974.

Boyle, Casey. *Rhetoric as a Posthuman Practice.* The Ohio State UP, 2018.

Bradlee, Ben Jr. "I Found Trump's Biggest Fan." *Politico Magazine,* 3 Oct. 2018, www.politico.com/magazine/story/2018/10/03/trump-supporters-luzerne-county-ben-bradlee-jr-220841.

Brown, Richard Harvey, and Beth Davis-Brown. "The Making of Memory: The Politics of Archives, Libraries and Museums in the Construction of National Consciousness." *History of the Human Sciences,* vol. 11, no. 4, 1 Nov. 1998, pp. 17–32. doi.org/10.1177/095269519801100402.

Burke, Kenneth. *Permanence and Change: An Anatomy of Purpose.* U of California P, 1984.

———. "The Rhetoric of Hitler's 'Battle.'" *The Philosophy of Literary Form.* U of California P, 1974, 191–220.

Bytwerk, Randall L. "Believing in 'Inner Truth': The Protocols of the Elders of Zion in Nazi Propaganda, 1933–1945." *Holocaust and Genocide Studies,* vol. 29, no. 2, 2015, pp. 212–29.

CaptainDisillusion. "Reptilian Bieber-Mosh." *YouTube,* 17 Feb. 2015, www.youtube.com/watch?v=flBfxNTUIns&feature=youtu.be.

Carlosdanger. "Of course, the most upsetting and disturbing account . . . ." *BoingBoing,* 15 Nov. 2013, 2:48 p.m., bbs.boingboing.net/t/stabilized-interpolated-panoramic-footage-of-jfks -assassination/14343/30.

Central Intelligence Agency. "Remote Viewing Session XXXVI." CIA-RDP96–00788 R000900310001–9.

———. "Summary Analysis—Remote Viewing Session D-10." 28 Aug. 1980. CIA-RDP96–00788 R001000110001–9.

———. "Summary Analysis Remotive Viewing (RV) Session D-12." 28 Aug. 1980.

———. "Transcript Remote Viewing Session D-78." 10 Oct. 1980. CIA-RDP96–00788 R000500290001–6.

Chasmar, Jessica. "Louis Farrakhan: 'Israelis and Zionist Jews' Played Key Roles in 9/11 Attacks." *Washington Times,* 5 Mar. 2015, www.washingtontimes.com/news/2015/mar/5/louis -farrakhan-israelis-and-zionist-jews-played-k/.

Chellappan, Sriram, and Raghavendra Kotikalapudi. "How Depressives Surf the Web." *New York Times,* 15 June 2012, pp. 15.

Chokshi, Niraj. "The 100-Plus Times Donald Trump Assured Us That America Is a Laughing-stock." *The Washington Post,* 27 Jan. 2016, www.washingtonpost.com/news/the-fix/wp/2016/ 01/27/the-100-plus-times-donald-trump-has-assured-us-the-united-states-is-a-laughingstock/?utm_term=.f9b57e512d89.

Clark, Jerome. *The UFO Book: Encyclopedia of the Extraterrestrial.* Visible Ink, 1998.

Cluff, Rodney. *Our Hollow Earth Newsletter.* May 2012.

Coates, Ta-Nehisi. "The First White President." *The Atlantic,* vol. 320, no. 3, 2017, https://www. theatlantic.com/magazine/archive/2017/10/the-first-white-president-ta-nehisi-coates/537909/

Cohen, Michael A. "The Credo of Modern Conservatism: 'They're Laughing at Us.'" *The Boston Globe,* 5 June 2017, www.bostonglobe.com/opinion/2017/06/05/the-credo-modern -conservatism-they-laughing/E88zPaPFr7ZXMPbqEeouwJ/story.html.

Creps, E. G. "The Conspiracy Theory Argument as a Rhetorical Genre." Diss. Northwestern University, 1980. *Dissertation Abstracts International,* vol. 41. 1980.

Davies, William. *Nervous States: How Feeling Took Over the World.* Random House, 2018.

Davis, Diane. *Breaking up (at) Totality: A Rhetoric of Laughter.* Southern Illinois UP, 2000.

———. *Inessential Solidarity.* U of Pittsburgh P, 2010.

"DC Pizzagate: A Primer." Updated 13 July 19, dcpizzagate.wordpress.com/.

de Man, Paul. *The Rhetoric of Romanticism.* Columbia UP, 2000.

Dean, Jodi. *Aliens in America: Conspiracy Cultures from Outerspace to Cyberspace.* Cornell UP, 1998.

Deleuze, Gilles. *Francis Bacon: The Logic of Sensation.* U of Minnesota P, 2003.

Dice, Mark. *The Illuminati: Facts & Fiction.* Mark Dice, 2009.

"Discussion with Dr. Donald Schueck, Director of Research, Stanford Research Institute (SRI)." General CIA Collections. LSD File, SRI. 12 Feb. 1973. CIA-RDP76B00734R000200030009 –71.

Dubrow, Heather, et al. "The Status of Evidence: A Roundtable." *PMLA: Publications of the Modern Language Association of America,* vol. 111, no. 1, 1996, pp. 7–31.

Duke, David. "Help Us Publish This Incredible New Book! & Watch New Video: The Illustrated Protocols!" *DavidDuke.com*, 3 June 2014, daviddduke.com/illustrated-protocols-zion/.

Enoch, Jessica. "Releasing Hold: Feminist Historiography without the Tradition." *Theorizing Histories of Rhetoric*, edited by Michelle Baliff, Southern Illinois UP, 2013, pp. 58–73.

Ernst, Wolfgang. "Archival Action: The Archive as ROM and Its Political Instrumentalization under National Socialism." *History of the Human Sciences*, vol. 12, no. 2, 1999, pp. 13–34.

Farge, Arlette. *The Allure of the Archives.* Yale UP, 2013.

Farrell, Thomas B. "Sizing Things Up: Colloquial Reflection as Practical Wisdom." *Argumentation*, vol. 12, no. 1, 1 Feb. 1998, pp. 1–14. doi.org/10.1023/A:1007747321075.

———. "The Weight of Rhetoric: Studies in Cultural Delirium." *Philosophy & Rhetoric*, vol. 41, no. 4, 2008, pp. 467–87.

Finnegan, Cara A. "What Is This a Picture Of?: Some Thoughts on Images and Archives." *Rhetoric & Public Affairs*, vol. 9, no. 1, 2006, pp. 116–23.

Foote, Kenneth. "To Remember and Forget: Archives, Memory, and Culture." *The American Archivist*, vol. 53, no. 3, 1 July 1990, pp. 378–92. doi.org/10.17723/aarc.53.3.d87u013444j3g6r2.

Foss, Karen A., and Sonja K. Foss. "Personal Experience as Evidence in Feminist Scholarship." *Western Journal of Communication (includes Communication Reports)*, vol. 58, no. 1, 1994, pp. 39–43.

Fredal, James. "Rhetoric and Bullshit." *College English*, vol. 73, no. 3, 2011, pp. 243–59.

Fritzman, John M. "The Future of Nostalgia and the Time of the Sublime." *Clio*, vol. 23, no. 2, 1994, pp. 167–89.

Fritzsche, Peter. "The Archive." *History & Memory*, vol. 17, no. 1, 2005, pp. 15–44.

———. *Life and Death in the Third Reich.* Harvard UP, 2009.

Frohmann, Bernd. *Deflating Information: From Science Studies to Documentation.* U of Toronto P, 2004.

"Full Text of 'Pizzagate Pedophile Collection of Evidence.'" archive.org/stream/ PizzagateHow4ChanUncoveredTheSickWorldOfWashingtonsOccultEliteTheVigilantCitizen _201612/PizzagateForDummies-whatsAllTheFussAbout_-62_djvu.txt.

Gabielkov, Maksym, et al. "Social Clicks: What and Who Gets Read on Twitter?" ACM Sigmetrics / IFIP Performance 2016, June 2016, Antibes Juan-les-Pins, France, hal-01281190, hal. inria.fr/hal-01281190/document.

Gage, Richard, and Gregg Roberts. "AE911Truth Delivers the Evidence to the Media: Press Conference—National Press Club—Washington DC." *Architects & Engineers for 9/11 Truth*, 4 Oct. 2010, www1.ae911truth.org/en/news/41-articles/386-ae911truth-delivers-the-evidence -to-the-media-press-conference-national-press-club-wash-dc.

Ganeri, Anita. *The Smart Girl's Guide to Growing Up.* Scholastic Non-Fiction, 2015.

Gardner, Martin. *Fads and Fallacies in the Name of Science.* Courier Corporation, 1957.

Garrett, Gregory. *The Scientism Delusion Techno Mysticism And Techno Spiritual Warfare Exploring the Connections Between Scientism and Luciferianism.* Lulu P, 2018.

Gillis, John R. *Commemorations: The Politics of National Identity.* Princeton UP, 1996.

Ginzburg, Carlo. "Representing the Enemy: Historical Evidence and Its Ambiguities." *Evidence*, edited by Andrew Bell et al., Cambridge UP, 2008, pp. 19–29.

———. *Threads and Traces: True False Fictive.* U of California P, 2012.

Girgus, Joel J., et al. "The Effect of Knowledge of Reversibility on the Reversibility of Ambiguous Figures." *Perception & Psychophysics,* vol. 22, no. 6, 1977, pp. 550–56.

Goldberg, Jonah. "Take Trump Seriously but Not Literally? How, Exactly?" *Los Angeles Times,* 6 Dec. 2016, www.latimes.com/opinion/op-ed/la-oe-goldberg-trump-seriously-literally -20161206-story.html.

Goldman, Adam. "The Comet Ping Pong Gunman Answers Our Reporter's Questions." *The New York Times,* 7 Dec. 2016, www.nytimes.com/2016/12/07/us/edgar-welch-comet-pizza-fake -news.html.

Good, I. J. *Good Thinking: The Foundations of Probability and its Applications.* U of Minnesota P, 1983.

———. "Weight of Evidence, Corroboration, Explanatory Power, Information and the Utility of Experiments." *Journal of the Royal Statistical Society: Series B (Methodological),* vol. 22, no. 2, 1960, pp. 319–31.

Goodnight, G. Thomas, and John Poulakos. "Conspiracy Rhetoric: From Pragmatism to Fantasy in Public Discourse." *Western Journal of Speech Communication,* vol. 45, no. 4, 1981, pp. 299–316.

Gopnik, Adam. "Trump and Obama: A Night to Remember." *The New Yorker,* 19 June 2017, www.newyorker.com/news/daily-comment/trump-and-obama-a-night-to-remember.

Gosa, Travis L., and Danielle Porter Sanchez. "Fear of a Black President." *Race Still Matters: The Reality of African American Lives and the Myth of Postracial Society,* edited by Yuya Kiuchi, State U of New York, 2016, pp. 101–32.

Gregg, Melissa, and Gregory J. Seigworth. *The Affect Theory Reader.* Duke UP, 2010.

Gregg, Richard B. "The Rhetoric of Evidence." *Western Speech,* vol. 31, 1967, pp. 180–89.

Griffin, Edward G. "Report from Iron Mountain." *FreedomForce,* www.freedom-force.org/pdf/ Report_from_Iron_Mountain.pdf.

@gunnisonheath "Libs are laughing at us." *Twitter,* 21 November 2015, 12:04 p.m., https://twitter. com/gunnisonheath/status/800746639740702720.

Hagemeister, Michael. "The Protocols of the Elders of Zion: Between History and Fiction." *New German Critique* 103 (2008): 83–95.

Halberstam, Judith. "What's That Smell? Queer Temporalities and Subcultural Lives." *The Scholar and Feminist Online,* vol. 2, no. 1, 2003, http://sfonline.barnard.edu/ps/printjha.htm.

Hamilton, Carolyn, et al. *Refiguring the Archive.* Springer Science & Business Media, 2012.

Hansen, Miriam Bratu. "Benjamin's Aura." *Critical Inquiry,* vol. 34, no. 2, 2008, pp. 336–75. doi.org/10.1086/529060.

Hartcher-O'Brien, Jess, and Malika Auvray. "The Process of Distal Attribution Illuminated through Studies of Sensory Substitution." *Multisensory Research,* vol. 27, no. 5–6, 2014, pp. 421–41.

Hasian, Marouf Jr. "Understanding the Power of Conspiratorial Rhetoric: A Case Study of the Protocols of the Elders of Zion." *Communication Studies,* vol. 48, no. 3, 1997, pp. 195–214.

Hastings, Robert. "MJ-12: The Hoax That Quickly Became a Disinformation Operation." *The UFO Chronicles,* 11 Oct. 2014, www.theufochronicles.com/2014/10/mj-12-hoax-that-quickly -became.html.

Hawhee, Debra. "Looking into Aristotle's Eyes: Toward a Theory of Rhetorical Vision." *Advances in the History of Rhetoric,* vol. 14, no. 2, 2011, pp. 139–65.

———. *Rhetoric in Tooth and Claw: Animals, Language, Sensation.* U of Chicago P, 2016.

Hawkins, John. "Five Big Problems with Christine Blasey Ford's Testimony at the Kavanaugh Hearings." *PJ Media,* 27 Sept. 2018, pjmedia.com/trending/5-big-problems-with-christine -blasey-fords-testimony-at-the-kavanaugh-hearings/.

Heidegger, Martin. "The Age of the World Picture." *Science and the Quest for Reality,* edited by Alfred I. Tauber, Palgrave Macmillan, 1977, pp. 70–88. doi.org/10.1007/978-1-349-25249-7_3.

———. *Contributions to Philosophy (From Enowning).* Indiana UP, 1999.

———. *Pathmarks.* Cambridge UP, 1998.

Henig, Jess. "Born in the U.S.A.: The Truth about Obama's Birth Certificate." *FactCheck.org,* 21 Aug. 2008, www.factcheck.org/2008/08/born-in-the-usa/.

Hill, Roscoe R. "Archival Terminology." *The American Archivist,* vol. 6, no. 4, 1943, pp. 206–11.

Hitler, Adolph. *Mein Kampf.* Translated by Marco Roberto, independently published, 2017.

Hofstadter, Richard. *The Paranoid Style in American Politics.* Knopf Doubleday Publishing Group, 2012.

"Holocaust Denial and the Next 9/11 Conference?" *TruthMove Forum,* www.truthmove.org/ forum/topic/272.

Houck, Davis W. "On or about June 1988." *Rhetoric & Public Affairs,* vol. 9, no. 1, 5 June 2006, pp. 132–37. doi.org/10.1353/rap.2006.0025.

Hudson, Laura. "Twitter Is Wrong: Facts Are Not Enough to Combat Alex Jones." *The Verge,* 10 Aug. 2018, www.theverge.com/2018/8/10/17675232/twitter-alex-jones-jack-dorsey-free -speech.

Hume, David. *Selected Essays,* edited by Stephen Copley and Andrew Edgar, Oxford UP, 2008.

Hurst, G.W., and R.L. Marsh. *Satanic Cult Awareness.* Date unknown, https://www.ncjrs.gov/ pdffiles1/Photocopy/140554NCJRS.pdf.

Huxley, Aldous. "A Case for ESP, PK and PSI." *Life Magazine,* 11 Jan. 1954, pp. 96–108.

Huxley, Thomas Henry. "Science and Morals." *Fortnightly,* vol. 40, no. 240, 1886, pp. 788–802.

Jacobsen, Annie. *Phenomena: The Secret History of the US Government's Investigations into Extra- sensory Perception and Psychokinesis.* Little, Brown, 2017.

James, Clive. "Aldous Huxley, Short of Sight." *New Yorker,* 17 Mar. 2003, https://www.newyorker. com/magazine/2003/03/17/aldous-huxley-short-of-sight.

Jameson, Fredric. *Postmodernism, or, the Cultural Logic of Late Capitalism.* Duke UP, 1991.

Janisse, Kier-La, and Paul Corupe, editors. *Satanic Panic: Pop-Cultural Paranoia in the 1980s.* Spectacular Optical, 2015.

@JaredWyand. "Search All Podesta Emails," *Twitter,* 3 Nov. 2016, 5:00 p.m.

Jasinski, James. *Sourcebook on Rhetoric.* Sage, 2001.

"Julian Assange and WikiLeaks." *AllCreatures.org,* www.all-creatures.org/cre/art-julian.shtml.

Kahneman, Daniel, et al. *Judgment under Uncertainty: Heuristics and Biases.* Cambridge UP, 1982.

Kant, Immanuel, and Werner S. Pluhar. *Critique of Judgment.* Hackett Publishing, 1987.

Katz, Steven B. "The Ethic of Expediency: Classical Rhetoric, Technology, and the Holocaust." *College English,* vol. 54, no. 3, 1992, pp. 255–75.

Kelty, Christopher M., and Boris Jardine. "Preface: The Total Archive." *Limn,* 4 Mar. 2016, limn. it/articles/preface-the-total-archive/.

Keynes, John Maynard. *A Treatise on Probability.* Courier Corporation, 2013.

Krassner, Paul. *Confessions of a Raving, Unconfined Nut: Misadventures in the Counterculture.* Soft Skull Press, 2012.

Kriss, Sam. "Jack Chick Is Dead but His Horrible, Ridiculous Cartoons Will Never Die." *Vice,* 27 Oct. 2016, www.vice.com/en_us/article/avakej/obituary-for-jack-chick-evangelical -cartoonist.

Lancaster, Roger. "What the Pizzagate Conspiracy Theory Borrows from a Bogus Satanic Sex Panic of the 1980s." *The Washington Post,* 8 Dec. 2016, www.washingtonpost.com/ posteverything/wp/2016/12/08/the-satanic-roots-of-pizzagate-how-a-30-year-old-sex-panic -explains-today/?utm_term=.41b9714e51ff.

Landa, Victor. "Birthers to Obama: Show Us Your Papers." *News Taco,* 2 May 2011, newstaco. com/2011/05/02/birthers-to-obama-show-us-your-papers/.

Larouche, Lyndon. "From MK-Ultra Brainwashing to the American Family Foundation." *Executive Intelligence Review,* vol. 40, no. 16, 1989, pp. 34–35.

Latour, Bruno. *Reassembling the Social: An Introduction to Actor-Network-Theory.* Oxford UP, 2005.

———. "Tarde's Idea of Quantification." *The Social after Gabriel Tarde: Debates and Assessments,* edited by Matei Candea, Routledge, 2010, pp. 145–62.

Lee, Harper. *To Kill a Mockingbird, 50th Anniversary Edition.* Harper, 1960, rpt. 2010.

Lepselter, Susan. *The Resonance of Unseen Things: Poetics, Power, Captivity, and UFOs in the American Uncanny.* U of Michigan P, 2016.

Longinus. *Longinus on the Sublime.* Translated by Rhys W. Roberts, Cambridge UP, 2011.

Lynch, Michael. "Archives in Formation: Privileged Spaces, Popular Archives and Paper Trails." *History of the Human Sciences,* vol. 12, no. 2, 1 May 1999, pp. 65–87. doi.org/10.1177/ 09526959922120252.

Manjoo, Farhad. "You Won't Finish This Article: Why People Online Don't Read to the End." *Slate,* 6 June 2013, https://slate.com/technology/2013/06/how-people-read-online-why-you -wont-finish-this-article.html.

@MarcMcD. "Tarot Cards, candles, AND oils?!?!" *Twitter,* 6 May 2018, 12:40 p.m., twitter.com/ MarcMcD/status/993213820129562624.

Merewether, Charles. *The Archive.* Whitechapel London, 2006.

Mayeda, Graham. *Time, Space and Ethics in the Philosophy of Watsuji Tetsurō, Kuki Shūzō, and Martin Heidegger.* Routledge, 2015.

Michaelson, Jay. "#Pizzagate Is the 'Satanic Panic' of Our Age—But This Time, the President's Men Believe It." *The Daily Beast,* 6 Dec. 2016, www.thedailybeast.com/pizzagate-is-the -satanic-panic-of-our-agebut-this-time-the-presidents-men-believe-it.

Miller, Shane. "Conspiracy Theories: Public Arguments as Coded Social Critiques: A Rhetorical Analysis of the TWA Flight 800 Conspiracy Theories." *Argumentation and Advocacy,* vol. 39, no. 1, 2002, pp. 40–56.

"The MK-ULTRA Milieu Surrounding the 'Scribing' of A Course In Miracles." *ce399 | Research Archive (Esoterica),* 26 Jan. 2011, ce399esoterica.wordpress.com/2011/01/26/the-mkultra -milieu-surrounding-the-scribing-of-a-course-in-miracles/.

Morris, Charles E. "The Archival Turn in Rhetorical Studies; Or, the Archive's Rhetorical (Re) Turn." *Rhetoric & Public Affairs,* vol. 9, no. 1, 5 June 2006, pp. 113–15.

Muñoz, José Esteban. "Ephemera as Evidence: Introductory Notes to Queer Acts." *Women & Performance: A Journal of Feminist Theory*, vol. 8, no. 2, 1996, pp. 5–16.

Nietzsche, Friedrich. *Friedrich Nietzsche on Rhetoric and Language.* Translated by Carole Blair et al., Oxford UP, 1989.

Nyhan, Brendan, and Jason Reifler. "When Corrections Fail: The Persistence of Political Misperceptions." *Political Behavior,* vol. 32, no. 2, 2010, pp. 303–30.

O'Gorman, Ned. "Aristotle's Phantasia in the Rhetoric: Lexis, Appearance, and the Epideictic Function of Discourse." *Philosophy and Rhetoric,* vol. 38, no. 1, 2005, pp. 16–40.

Osborne, Thomas. "The Ordinariness of the Archive." *History of the Human Sciences,* vol. 12, no. 2, 1 May 1999, pp. 51–64.

"The Parts That Were Left out of the Kennedy Book." *The Realist,* vol. 74, 1967.

Peacham, Henry. *The Garden of Eloquence: A Facsimile Reproduction.* Scholars' Facsimiles & Reprint, 1593, rpt. 1954.

Penny, Laurie. "No, I Will Not Debate You." *LongReads,* 18 Sept. 2018, longreads.com/2018/09/18/no-i-will-not-debate-you/.

Perelman, Chaim. *The New Rhetoric and the Humanities: Essays on Rhetoric and Its Applications.* Springer, 2012.

Perelman, Chaim, and Lucie Olbrechts-Tyteca. *The New Rhetoric: A Treatise on Argumentation.* U of Notre Dame P, 1973.

Petersson, Dag. "Archiving the Potentialities of Events." *ESC: English Studies in Canada,* vol. 30, no. 1, 2007, pp. 39–50.

Petit, Angela. "The Stylistic Semicolon: Teaching Punctuation as Rhetorical Choice." *English Journal,* vol. 92, no. 3, pp. 66–72.

Petty, Richard E., and John T. Cacioppo. "The Effects of Involvement on Responses to Argument Quantity and Quality: Central and Peripheral Routes to Persuasion." *Journal of Personality and Social Psychology,* vol. 46, no. 1, 1984, p. 68–81.

Plato. *Phaedrus.* Translated by Harold North Fowler, Loeb Classical Library 36, Harvard UP, 1914.

"Poland's New Defense Minister Defended 'Protocols of the Elders of Zion' as True." *Haaretz,* 12 Nov. 2015, www.haaretz.com/jewish/poland-s-new-defense-minister-defended-protocols -1.5421246.

Polanyi, Michael. *Personal Knowledge: Towards a Post-Critical Philosophy.* U of Chicago P, 2015.

"Preserver of Literary Derelicts." *Kansas City Star.* 17 October 1894.

Prouty, L. Fletcher. *JFK: The CIA, Vietnam, and the Plot to Assassinate John F. Kennedy.* Skyhorse Publishing, 2011.

Raferty, Brian. "The Satanic Panic of the '80s is Back." *Wired,* 3 June 2017, https://www.wired.com /2016/05/satanic-panic-summer-reads/.

Reyes, Ian, and Jason K. Smith. "What They Don't Want You to Know about Planet X: Surviving 2012 and the Aesthetics of Conspiracy Rhetoric." *Communication Quarterly,* vol. 62, no. 4, 2014, pp. 399–415.

Rhetorica ad Herennium. Translated by Harry Caplan. *The Rhetorical Tradition: Readings from Classical Times to the Present,* 2nd ed., edited by Patricia Bizzell and Bruce Herzberg, Bedford/St. Martin's, 2001, pp. 243–82.

Rhine, Joseph B., and J. G. Pratt. *Parapsychology: Frontier Science of the Mind.* Kessinger Publishing, 2006.

Richardson, James T., et al. *The Satanism Scare.* Transaction Publishers, 1991.

Ricoeur, Paul. *Memory, History, Forgetting.* Translated by Kathleen Blamey and David Pellauer, U of Chicago P, 2004.

Rimer, Don. "Ritual Crime and the Occult." Date unknown, https://info.publicintelligence.net/OccultCrime.pdf.

Robertson, David G. "David Icke's Reptilian Thesis and the Development of New Age Theodicy." *International Journal for the Study of New Religions,* vol. 4, no. 1, 2013, pp. 27–47.

Rogers, Lee. "Evil Jews Transformed the Kavanaugh Confirmation Hearing into a Disgusting Circus." *Daily Stormer,* 30 Sept. 2018, dailystormer.name/evil-jews-transformed-the-kavanaugh-confirmation-hearing-into-a-disgusting-circus/.

Rushkoff, Douglas. *Media Virus!: Hidden Agendas in Popular Culture.* Ballantine Books, 2010.

Sagan, Carl, and Ann Druyan. *The Demon-Haunted World: Science as a Candle in the Dark.* Ballantine Books, 1997.

Schiappa, Edward. *Warranting Assent: Case Studies in Argument Evaluation.* SUNY Press, 1995.

Schrag, Calvin O. *Communicative Praxis and the Space of Subjectivity.* Indiana UP, 1986.

———. "Phenomenology, Ontology, and History in the Philosophy of Heidegger." *Revue Internationale de Philosophie,* 1958, pp. 117–32.

———. *The Self after Postmodernity.* Yale UP, 1999.

Sedgwick, Eve Kosofsky. "Against Epistemology." *Questions of Evidence: Proof, Practice, and Persuasion across Disciplines,* edited by James Chandler et al., U of Chicago P, 1994, pp. 132–36.

Seitz-Wald, Alex. "This Man Helped Save Six Children, Is Now Getting Harassed for It." *Salon,* 15 Jan. 2013, www.salon.com/2013/01/15/this_man_helped_save_six_children_is_now_getting_harassed_for_it/.

Shields, James M. "The Art of Aidagara: Ethics, Aesthetics, and the Quest for an Ontology of Social Existence in Watsuji Tetsurō's Rinrigaku." *Asian Philosophy,* vol. 19, no. 3, 2009, pp. 265–83.

Siegle, Joshua H., and William H. Warren. "Distal Attribution and Distance Perception in Sensory Substitution." *Perception,* vol. 39, no. 2, 2010, pp. 208–23.

Simril, Cat. "Cat Simril Interviews Paul Krassner." *Adbusters Quarterly,* vol. 3, no., 3, Winter 1995, pp. 85–86.

Smith, Gary. *Standard Deviations: Flawed Assumptions, Tortured Date and Other Ways to Lie With Statistics.* Gerald Duckworth, 2016.

"Some of the Best Evidences of Reptilian Hybrids." *DavidIcke.com,* 15 Jan. 2010, forum.davidicke.com/showthread.php?t=99493.

Steedman, Carolyn. *Dust: The Archive and Cultural History.* Rutgers UP, 2002.

Stewart, Kathleen. "Atmospheric Attunements." *Rubric,* issue 1, 2010, pp. 1–14.

———. "Cultural Poesis." *Handbook of Qualitative Research.* Sage, 1994, pp. 1015–30.

———. *Ordinary Affects.* Duke UP, 2007.

———. "Weak Theory in an Unfinished World." *Journal of Folklore Research,* 2008, pp. 71–82.

———. "Worlding Refrains." *The Affect Theory Reader,* edited by Melissa Gregg and Gregory J. Seigworth, Duke UP, 2010, pp. 339–54.

Stewart, Susan. *On Longing: Narratives of the Miniature, the Gigantic, the Souvenir, the Collection.* Duke UP, 1984.

Stormer, Nathan, and Bridie McGreavy. "Thinking Ecologically about Rhetoric's Ontology: Capacity, Vulnerability, and Resilience." *Philosophy and Rhetoric,* vol. 50, no. 1, 2017, pp. 1–25.

Sunstein, Cass R., and Adrian Vermeule. "Conspiracy Theories: Causes and Cures." *Journal of Political Philosophy,* vol. 17, no. 2, 2009, pp. 202–22.

Syal, Rajeev. "Polish Defence Minister Condemned over Jewish Conspiracy Theory." *The Guardian,* 10 Nov. 2015, www.theguardian.com/world/2015/nov/10/polish-defence-minister-condemned-over-jewish-conspiracy-theory.

Taylor, Goldie. "Why Obama Shouldn't Have Had to 'Show His Papers.'" *TheGrio,* 28 Apr. 2011, thegrio.com/2011/04/28/why-obama-shouldnt-have-had-to-show-his-papers/.

Thiel, Peter. Speech to National Press Club. 31 Oct. 2016, https://www.press.org/events/peter-Thiel.

Trace, Ciaran B. "What Is Recorded Is Never Simply 'What Happened': Record Keeping in Modern Organizational Culture." *Archival Science,* vol. 2, no. 1–2, 1 Mar. 2002, pp. 137–59.

Travis, Shannon. "CNN Poll: Quarter Doubt Obama Was Born in U. S." *CNN,* 4 Aug. 2010, politicalticker.blogs.cnn.com/2010/08/04/cnn-poll-quarter-doubt-president-was-born-in-u-s/.

Tucker, Susan, et al. *The Scrapbook in American Life.* Temple UP, 2006.

Turing, A. M. "The Applications of Probability to Cryptography." *Report, GCHQ, Cheltenham, UK,* 1941.

Tversky, Amos, and Daniel Kahneman. "Extensional versus Intuitive Reasoning: The Conjunction Fallacy in Probability Judgment." *Psychological Review,* vol. 90, no. 4, 1983, p. 293.

Van Alphen, Ernst. "Visual Archives as Preposterous History." *Art History,* vol. 30, no. 3, 2007, pp. 364–82.

Voss, Paul J., and Marta L. Werner. "Toward a Poetics of the Archive: Introduction." *Studies in the Literary Imagination,* vol. 32, no. 1, 1999, pp. i–viii.

Waldman, Scott. "Climate Web Pages Erased and Obscured under Trump." *Scientific American,* 10 Jan. 2018, www.scientificamerican.com/article/climate-web-pages-erased-and-obscured-under-trump/.

Walker, Jeffrey. *Rhetoric and Poetics in Antiquity.* Oxford UP on Demand, 2000.

Walsh, Joseph. "My Reptilian Experience." *YouTube,* 4 Sept. 2013, www.youtube.com/watch?v=JOtoKgbQZUo.

Walton, Bruce A. *A Guide to the Inner Earth.* Health Research Books, 1983.

Watsuji, Tetsuro. *Watsuji Tetsuro's Rinrigaku: Ethics in Japan.* SUNY Press, 1996.

White, Luise. "Hodgepodge Historiography: Documents, Itineraries, and the Absence of Archives." *History in Africa,* vol. 42, 2015, pp. 308–18.

Whitson, Steve, and John Poulakos. "Nietzsche and the Aesthetics of Rhetoric." *Quarterly Journal of Speech,* vol. 79, no. 2, 1993, pp. 131–45.

Willard, Charles Arthur. "Some Speculations about Evidence." *Proceedings of the [First] Summer Conference on Argumentation,* 1980, pp. 267–68.

Wood, Bob. "Research Question." Message to Jenny Rice. 20 June 2017. Email.

Wood, Michael J., et al. "Dead and Alive: Beliefs in Contradictory Conspiracy Theories." *Social Psychological and Personality Science,* vol. 3, no. 6, 1 Nov. 2012, pp. 1–7.

Wright, Sarah. "More-Than-Human, Emergent Belongings: A Weak Theory Approach." *Progress in Human Geography,* vol. 39, no. 4, 2015, pp. 391–411.

Yad Vashem Holocaust Resource. "Reply from Yad Vashem ref. no. 29871." Message to Jenny Rice. 13 July 2015. Email.

Young, Marilyn J., and Michael K. Launer. "The Need for Evaluative Criteria: Conspiracy Argument Revisited." *Warranting Assent: Case Studies in Argument Evaluation,* edited by Edward Schiappa, SUNY Press, 1995, pp. 3–32.

Zito, Salena. "Taking Trump Seriously, Not Literally." *The Atlantic,* 23 Sept. 2016, www.theatlantic .com/politics/archive/2016/09/trump-makes-his-case-in-pittsburgh/501335/.

INDEX

Printed in the USA
CPSIA information can be obtained
at www.ICGtesting.com
JSHW080315280823
47288JS00005B/34